Answering the New Atheists: How Science Points to God and to the Benefits of Christianity

Anthony Walsh

Boise State University

Series in Philosophy of Religion

VERNON PRESS

www.vernonpress.com

In the Americas:
Vernon Press
1000 N West Street,
Suite 1200, Wilmington,
Delaware 19801
United States

In the rest of the world:
Vernon Press
C/Sancti Espiritu 17,
Malaga, 29006
Spain

Series in Philosophy of Religion

Library of Congress Control Number: 2018904925

ISBN: 978-1-62273-411-5

Cover design by Vernon Press using elements by Kjpargeter - Kotkoa - Freepik.com,
geralt – pixabay.com

Table of Contents

Acknowledgements   *v*

Preface   *vii*

Chapter 1   Science Points the Way to God   1

Chapter 2   Christianity, Rationality, and Militant New
             Atheism   15

Chapter 3   Christianity, Atheism, and Morality   29

Chapter 4   Christianity, Western Democracy, and Cultural
             Marxism   43

Chapter 5   The Big Bang and Fine Tuning of the Universe   59

Chapter 6   Earth: The Privileged Planet   75

Chapter 7   Cosmological Fine-Tuning and the Multiverse   91

Chapter 8   Abiogenesis: The Search for the Origin of Life   107

Chapter 9   Cracks in Neo-Darwinism: Micro is not Macro   125

Chapter 10   Answering the Tough Questions: God of the
             Gaps, Free Will, and the Problem of Evil   141

Chapter Footnotes   *157*

References   *171*

Index   *187*

Acknowledgements

I would first of all like to thank commissioning editor, Dr. Carolina Sanchez, for her faith in this project. Thanks also to the very able, very efficient, and very cheerful editorial manager Argiris Legatos, for his guidance, and to Rosario Batana director. They are all very pleasant people with whom to work.

I want to acknowledge those people who read all or parts of the manuscript. First is prominent physicist/astrobiologist Dr. Guillermo Gonzalez, co-author (with Dr. Jay Richards) of the best-selling *The Privileged Planet*. My brother, Robert J. Walsh, a retired English professor and active theologian, read the manuscript for theological errors and/or provided suggestions for improvement. Last but not least, my drop-dead gorgeous wife, Grace, used her uncanny eagle eye for spotting dangling participles and other such grammatical peculiarities in the manuscript. I also acknowledge anonymous reviewers and the physicists and chemists I have bugged without mercy during the writing of this book about areas in which I needed clarification. Needless to say, any errors remaining are mine.

Preface

This book is about answering atheistic arguments against God's existence with solid evidence from physics, chemistry, biology, psychology, sociology, philosophy, history, and theology to highlight the signposts to God and the many benefits of Christianity to society. Its major focus is to provide Christians with the scientific "ammunition" to battle the claims against God made by militant "new atheists." Arguments from revealed theology will not cut it in a debate with atheists who insist that science is on their side. The only theology that an atheist may afford a hearing is natural theology. Natural theology offers proof of God's existence and divine purpose through scientific observation of nature and the use of human reason.

My own field is biosocial science and statistics, and my research involves looking at the genetic and neurobiological bases of behavior, particularly criminal behavior. Outside of these areas, I claim no expertise. No one can claim to be an expert, even in the science in which they earned their PhD, because scientific knowledge increases exponentially. One can only claim to be an expert in very specific areas of one's discipline. As science expands the pressure for specialization in one tiny area of a discipline grows stronger. Every science spawns subfields that then may become separate disciplines, which in turn spawn further specialized areas of research. There are many advantages to this which include the efficiency and speed with which new knowledge is produced, but it carries with it the danger of intellectual isolation as fewer and fewer scientists are able to critically evaluate work done outside of their own narrow area of specialization. In the areas in which I work there are subfields with which I am only dimly acquainted and must "hit the books" when asked to peer review articles pertaining to those subfields. Geneticists and neurobiologists continue to make discovery after discovery as new technology arrives on the scene to enable them to do so, and statisticians continually develop better ways of analyzing the data that spring from these discoveries.

Nor am I a theologian with an intimate acquaintance with the Bible. But I do know enough about science and religion to know that science points the way to understanding God's creation and to how Christianity is of immense benefit to a free, moral, and prosperous society, and even to science itself. This runs against the grain of radical atheist claims that science and religion are incompatible and in constant conflict. The great Albert Einstein disagrees, stating that "Science without religion is lame, religion without science is blind." As we shall see, science itself (particularly physics) has forced many scientists who have thought deeply about the philosophical meaning of their work, some kicking and screaming, to accept Almighty God as the Grand Creator of everything.

This book also exposes and rebuts the destructive agenda of the so-called "new atheists" who want God banned entirely from the public square. It is my belief, formed from years of debating atheists, that Christians should acquaint themselves with a basic understanding of science since atheists claim that it is science that has buried God. Of course, God needs no defending by me or anyone else, but Christianity is retreating in the Western world in the face of secular attacks. It is Christianity that requires robust arguments from science when confronted by vocal atheists who view science as "God's undertaker," to steal a phrase from the brilliant and inspirational Oxford mathematician and theologian Dr. John Lennox.

I have previously published 38 books and over 150 articles, but none have presented the challenge that this one has. To write this book, I have set aside my own research agenda (the privilege of a tenured full professor) and delved into this topic for more time than I spent on any five previous books combined. I have reviewed high stacks of peer-reviewed articles and books written by top-notch scientists and philosophers and talked with scientists from a variety of fields. Some of the scientific writings are highly technical, so when I use them I make every effort to explain their content in terms understandable to all who might read this book without scientific training, making no assumptions about prior knowledge.

I have also written with the strong conviction that anyone espousing a position on any matter be it scientific, political, or religious, should be able to stoutly defend it. I do not say that this stout defense is for the conceited purpose of one-upmanship, but rather in the hope that such a defense will convince an atheist to examine his or her position with an open mind and come to know God. Most atheists have never given much thought to their position and simply believe that it is a reasonable position that puts them on the side of science. If a believer can show how reasoning to the best explanation *from science* leads to theism and not atheism, as countless scientists have found, perhaps they will also abandon their empty, hopeless, and nihilistic atheism for the love of God.

The first chapter shows how scientific insights that emerged it the 20th-century point the way to God and the reasoning used by theistic scientists to make their claim. The alternative offered by materialist scientists is that the universe created itself from nothing for no reason. Or even more bizarrely, the universe was created from the mathematical equations of so-called M-theory of the multiverse, as the late Stephen Hawking claimed. The subsequent three chapters examine the bounty that Christianity has provided for individuals and society in the Western world and how the "new atheists" are attempting with almost evangelical zeal to drive God out of our lives. The new atheists are strongly leftist who subscribe to Karl Marx's assertion that "Communism begins where atheism begins."

The next chapter examines the profound theistic implications of the Big Bang of creation and the exquisite fine-tuning of the laws of nature that allows for intelligent life to exist on Earth. The Big Bang was stoutly resisted by many scientists at first because of the "spooky" resemblance to Genesis, but it was eventually established as settled science and drove many former atheist scientists into the theistic camp. The following chapter looks how everything from our solar system's location in the galaxy to plate tectonics is "just right" to permit life. The probabilities associated most of these circumstances and things occurring by chance far exceed the probability boundaries established by statisticians. In the following chapter we see that atheists don't want God, so they have given us a multiverse of trillions of other universes with laws of nature different from ours to overcome the probability boundary. If you posit enough universes, they believe that at least one (ours) is likely to contain all the right parameters for life. The multiverse hypothesis is highly speculative and has been heavily criticized by physicists as metaphysical because even multiverse proponents admit they these other universes can never be observed—even in principle.

The following chapter leaves physics and takes us into chemistry and biology and the largely clueless search for abiogenesis—the search for the process by which dead matter supposedly gave birth to living things. Over 150 theories of abiogenesis have been offered, but all have faded away when put to the test. They all face the infamous chicken-or-egg problem since all components of the protein-making machinery must be online at once. The probability of obtaining only a short chain of amino acids required to make a protein by chance are astronomical. As we shall see, one team of physicists calculated that the probability of obtaining the right sugar backbone for DNA/RNA and all the required enzymes is $10^{40,000}$. This is an impossibly large number and one that rules chance entirely out of court.

I then examine Darwinist evolution by natural selection. No one rejects observable microevolution, which simply means small-scale changes in within a species. What is strongly challenged is macroevolution—large-scale innovations in bodily structures and qualitatively new genetic material. Darwin himself viewed this as a major problem, and contrary to atheistic claims, Darwin was not an atheist. He stated this on many occasions, and in his book *Origin of Species*, he wrote that evolution was ultimately due to "the laws impressed on matter by the Creator." The biggest problem encounter in macroevolution is the time problem. It has been estimated by a number of biochemists that to create a new gene that would contribute to a new function would take far more times than all the seconds that have ticked away since the Big Bang.

The tenth and final chapter looks at the big philosophical questions that Christians must be able to answer to counter atheistic arguments against God's existence—God of the gaps, free will, and the problem of evil. Christians are often accused of using God to fill in the gaps in current scientific knowledge. If we use such arguments we push God further out if or when science fills the gap. God does not reside in gaps and we must base our arguments on what we know, not what we do not. In order to accept the Creator and to enjoy a personal relationship with him, we must freely choose to do so. Atheists deny free will and insist that our behavior and our choices are determined by our genes and environment. Everything is determined by these things to some extent, but I argue that this 'soft' determinism is entirely compatible with free will. The problem of evil is often described as the "rock of atheism;" how can a loving and omnipotent God allow all the suffering his creatures must bear? After I examine various answers to this question I conclude that ultimately the best answer is in the promise of Revelation 21:4: And God shall wipe away all tears from their eyes; and there shall be no more death, neither sorrow of crying, neither shall there be any more pain; for the former things are passed away."

Chapter 1

Science Points the Way to God

"Everyone who is seriously involved in the pursuit of science becomes convinced that a spirit is manifest in the laws of the Universe–a spirit vastly superior to that of man, and one in the face of which we with our modest powers must feel humble."
Nobel Prize winning physicist Albert Einstein

The God Hypothesis

In 1798, the French mathematician and physicist Pierre-Simon Laplace published the first of his five-volume work *Treatise on Celestial Mechanics*. He gave a copy to his friend, the Emperor Napoleon Bonaparte, who asked him why in a book explaining the mechanics of the universe that he had not mentioned its Creator. Laplace is reported to have replied, "Sir, I had no need of that hypothesis."[1] When Napoleon told mathematician and astronomer Joseph-Louis Lagrange of Laplace's response, Lagrange exclaimed: "Ah, it [the God hypothesis] is a fine hypothesis; it explains many things." Laplace's reply to this, although this is disputed as apocryphal, was: "This hypothesis, Sir, explains, in fact, everything, but does not permit to predict anything. As a scholar, I must provide you with works permitting predictions."[2]

Laplace's remark was not made with atheistic intent since he was a practicing Roman Catholic, but technically speaking, he was absolutely correct. A physicist does not need to insert a "God term" in an equation to figure out, for instance, the frequency of an average yellow light wave. But what if Napoleon had asked Laplace the origin of that light, why we are here, what is the purpose of life, or one of the deepest philosophical questions of all time, asked by one of the greatest thinkers of all time, Gottfried Leibniz: "Why is there something rather than nothing?" These are questions that science cannot answer, so God is hardly irrelevant if we wish answers to these profound questions.

This is not a "God of the gaps" position whereby God is invoked to explain what science cannot explain naturalistically. God's existence is not contingent on science's current inability to explain something or other in the natural world. Theists who invoke God of the gaps arguments do theism a disservice because if and/or when science does explain the phenomenon they get egg on their faces, and it plays into the notion that religion and science are in conflict. Scientists readily acknowledge that the big questions of meaning are outside of their purview, so rather than lazily arguing from what we don't know to God (of the gaps) I want to argue from what we *do* know from science to show how it logically leads to the transcendent Creator of the universe who is the foundation of all explanation. I also show from historical, sociological, and psychological studies that, contrary to the claims of militant atheists that it negatively impacts everything, Christianity has led to multiple benefits on Western civilization and leads to healthier, happier, and more fulfilled lives for those who live by its principles.

To interpret Laplace's answer as implying that God is as unnecessary to explain the most meaningful "why" questions as he is to explain the more mundane "how" questions of the workings of creation is to make the category mistake of confusing impersonal principles with personal agency. Oxford mathematician and philosopher John Lennox uses the example of a Ford automobile to make this point. An engineer, he says, could fully explain *how* the car worked using the principles of internal combustion. However, if he wanted to know *why* the car existed, he would have to invoke agency. That is, why Henry Ford chose to manufacture automobiles in the first place. Ford's agency would have no place whatsoever in the description of how the car works, but he is necessary to explain its existence. In other words, one needs both explanations to have a necessary and sufficient explanation of the car. Likewise, to have a necessary and sufficient explanation of all that exists in the cosmos we need both science and the Creator.

John Lennox's evaluation of Laplace's remark to Napoleon is revealing: "Considered as a serious observation, his remark could scarcely have been more misleading. Laplace and his colleagues had not learned to do without theology; they had merely learned to mind their own business."[3] "Their own business" is the business of natural science; a business that can be pursued by even the most devout scientists without the God hypothesis entering their work. But affirming the utility of science does not imply disclaiming God, as countless first-rate scientists can attest. However, there are scientists who refuse to let God into their world at all and place all their faith in materialism/naturalism. Atheist and Marxist (two sides of the same coin) geneticist Richard Lewontin honestly reported his commitment to the materialist position despite some of the issues he points out:

> Our willingness to accept scientific claims that are against common sense is the key to an understanding of the real struggle between science and the supernatural. We take the side of science *in spite* of the patent absurdity of some of its constructs, *in spite* of its failure to fulfill

many of its extravagant promises of health and life, *in spite* of the tolerance of the scientific community for unsubstantiated just-so stories, because we have a prior commitment, a commitment to materialism. It is not that the methods and institutions of science somehow compel us to accept a material explanation of the phenomenal world, but, on the contrary, that we are forced by our *a priori* adherence to material causes to create an apparatus of investigation and a set of concepts that produce material explanations, no matter how counter-intuitive, no matter how mystifying to the uninitiated. Moreover, that materialism is absolute, for we cannot allow a Divine Foot in the door. [4]

If scientists believe they cannot allow a Divine Foot in the door, they have to struggle with explaining the origin of the universe and of life on Earth. To avoid a creation event for the universe, scientists have posited everything from a static and eternal universe to countless trillions of other universes beyond our ability to ever perceive. It is interesting to note the words of physics Nobel laureate George P. Thomson as to why this situation exists. He observed that based on modern evidence, "Probably every physicist would believe in a creation if the Bible had not, unfortunately, said something about it many years ago and made it seem old-fashioned."[5] As for the origin of life from non-life, some of the best chemists and biologists working on the problem have simply thrown up their hands; others keep proposing new theories because that's their job. It has been noted that there were 150 naturalistic theories of the origin of life in the literature between 1950 and 2000, and the list is still growing.[6] These theories invoke everything from space aliens to superhot thermal sea vents as possible naturalistic mechanisms for kick-starting life. The creation of the universe and the origin of life are the big—very BIG—questions of existence that theology has answered for centuries, and with which science is slowing coming into agreement. But first, what of the atheist claim of antipathy between Christianity and science?

Christianity and Science: Conflict or Concord?

Unlike Laplace who simply ignored the Creator in his work while retaining Him in his life, Lewontin takes for granted that science is in a struggle with the supernatural. He makes it plain that even in areas where the big questions are, scientists must stick to their naturalist/materialistic guns no matter how absurd, as he said, their explanations might be. Lewontin admits that it is not the demands of the scientific method that compel scientists to accept only materialist explanations, but rather their faith in materialism that forces them. It is obvious that Lewontin sees science and religion as oil and water.

From where does the idea that science and religion are in conflict come? Atheists like to push the notion that they believe only in science and reason, and that Christians reject reason in favor of blind faith in the same way that Lewontin says scientists *must* accept materialism on blind faith. It is true that science only seeks tentative truths based on empirical evidence while religion claims absolute truth based on faith *and* on the very evidence science provides. It is also true that faith can be subjective and emotional, but subjectivism and emotion are not incompatible with reason. Albert Einstein, the greatest reasoner of all, and who revolutionized science with pure thought, had the following to say about the sensation of the mystical basis of faith in a Supreme Being: "The most beautiful and most profound emotion we can experience is the sensation of the mystical. It is the sower of all true science. He to whom this emotion is a stranger, who can no longer stand rapt in awe, is as good as dead. That deeply emotional conviction of the presence of a superior Reasoning Power, which is revealed in the incomprehensible Universe, forms my idea of God."[7] Far from being "blind," faith can be evidence-based as well as subjective. We do see conflicts from time to time, such as when biblical literalists claim such things as a young Earth created in six 24-hour days, but this is a minority view in Christianity. Faith is a good thing, but believers should be able to justify their faith *through science*, not by ignoring it or casting aspersions on it.

There are two classical incidents used by atheists to argue that science is at war with religion: Galileo and the Catholic Church, and the Huxley-Wilberforce debate on Darwinism. There can be no excuse for the Church for muzzling Galileo, but Galileo considered philosophers and scientist to be the chief opponents of the heliocentric (Sun-centered) theory advanced by Nicolaus Copernicus 90 years earlier. He wrote to his friend, the great German mathematician and astronomer, Johann Kepler, asking him: "What do you have to say about the principal philosophers of this academy who are filled with the stubbornness of an asp and do not want to look at either the planets, the moon or the telescope, even though I have freely and deliberately offered them the opportunity a thousand times?"[8]

In Galileo's time almost all philosophers and scientists subscribed to the geocentric model of the solar system; that is, the Earth was at its center and all else revolved around it. They believed that Aristotle, taken at that time by most scientists to be the ultimate authority on science, had refuted the heliocentric model of the solar system. It was the Jesuits, a religious order with a very solid scientific reputation, who questioned Aristotle's geocentric view.[9] (Parenthetically, the Vatican has an observatory which employs a dozen PhD astronomers today). A colleague of Galileo, Cesare Cremonini, took up Galileo's challenge and looked through the telescope. After he did, he complained that it gave him a headache and that he did not want to hear anything more about it. For Cremonini to have endorsed the evidence that Galileo presented would have called into question his life's work. In Cremonini' defense, the heliocentric model not only defied common sense, but it produced ridicule from fellow scientists. We can understand that ridicule because we would all subscribe to the geocentric model if all we had to go on were our unaided sensory observations. The geocentric theory comports with our immediate sense experiences in a way that the heliocentric theory does not. After all, we don't feel the Earth moving as it spins on its axis at just over 1,000 miles per hour while hurtling through space in orbit around the Sun at about 67,000 miles per hour, and we see the Sun rise in the east, move across the sky, and then set in the west.

The famous 1860 debate between Thomas Henry Huxley ("Darwin's bull-dog;" and an agnostic) and Bishop Samuel Wilberforce on evolution is the second instance. Atheistic accounts of the debate to paint Wilberforce as an ignoramus, but he had degrees in mathematics and the classics, and Darwin himself regarded Wilberforce's 50-page review of his work "uncommonly clever... It quizzes me most splendidly."[10] The debate was not science versus religion, as many have claimed, but at Wilberforce's insistence it was science against science. As was the case with Galileo, a number of scientists, including the leading anatomist of the day, Richard Owen, and the eminent physicist Lord Kelvin, were among those who opposed Darwin. Thus, the two events that people hostile to religion use as props for their view that science and religion have been forever at loggerheads has been kicked out from under them. Historian of science, Colin Russell, comments on the atheistic notion of conflict and hostility between science and religion: "The common belief that the actual relations between religion and science over the last few centuries have been marked by deep and enduring hostility...is not only historically inaccurate, but actually a caricature so grotesque that what needs to be explained is how it could possibly have achieved any degree of respectability."[11]

The Christian Origin of the Science

Far from being in conflict, Christianity and science are intimately linked. While it is certainly true that some *scientists* are at war with God, this is not the same as saying that *science* itself is at war with God. The deep study of science offers a clearer path to God for the skeptic than any argument from theology. The greatest scientist of them all, Albert Einstein, has said, "The more I study science the more I believe in God."[12] He also said, "Everyone who is seriously involved in the pursuit of science becomes convinced that a spirit is manifest in the laws of the Universe–a spirit vastly superior to that of man, and one in the face of which we with our modest powers must feel humble."[13] It is surprising to atheists to find out that so many of the advances in early science were made by men of God. Roger Bacon, a friar, is the father of the scientific method; Jesuit priest Roger Boscovich, a mathematician and philosopher, produced the precursor of atomic theory, and perhaps the greatest example is Georges Lamaitre. Lamaitre, a Jesuit priest and physicist who found holes in Einstein's famous cosmological constant, and who predicted the Big Bang theory of the expanding universe when almost all physicists believed the universe to be static and eternal.

It is thus hard to take seriously that science and Christian theism are in conflict, indeed, many historians, philosophers, and scientists have claimed that the spirit of science grew out of the Christian belief in a rational and orderly God who created us in His image. Nobel Prize-winner in biochemistry Melvin Calvin comments on his understanding of the origin of the scientific conviction that the universe is orderly and knowable:

> As I try to discern the origin of that conviction, I seem to find it in a basic notion discovered 2,000 or 3,000 years ago, and enunciated first in the Western world by the ancient Hebrews: namely that the universe is governed by a single God and is not the product of the whims of many gods, each governing his own province according to his own laws. This monotheistic view seems to be the historical foundation for modern science.[14]

This God of order and reason designed a predictable universe intelligible to the human mind so that we can to know Him by understanding His creation. We see the spirit reason articulated in Solomon's prayer in Wisdom 7:17-22 (in the Catholic and Eastern Orthodox Bibles) in which he praises God for giving him the ability to do what he could to discover what God has hidden for us to find:

> For He gave me sound knowledge of what exists, that I might know the structure of the universe and the force of its elements, The beginning and the end and the midpoint of times, the changes in the sun's course and the variations of the seasons, Cycles of years, positions of stars, natures of living things, tempers of beasts, Powers of the winds and thoughts of human beings, uses of plants and virtues of roots— Whatever is hidden or plain I learned, for Wisdom, the artisan of all, taught me.

From the very earliest days of Christianity, the Church taught that reason is a unique gift of God, and that we must use this gift to come to know Him through incrementally coming to understand His creation. As early as the second century AD, Quintus Tertullian of Carthage, gifted with the title of the founder of Western theology, informed us that, "Reason is a thing of God, inasmuch as there is nothing which God the Maker of all has not provided, disposed, ordained by reason—nothing which He has not willed should be handled and understood by reason."[15] The Catholic Church founded the first university—the University of Bologna—in 1088 and made mathematics and science compulsory parts of the education of anyone wanting to study theology.[16]

Ultimately, the great contribution of Christian theology lay in its conviction that there are laws of nature front-loaded by God at the beginning of time and await discovery. The 13th-century patron saint of science, St. Albertus Magnus, wrote: "It is the task of natural science not simply to accept what we are told but to inquire into the causes of things."[17] In another work, Magnus stated that: "In studying nature we have not to inquire how God the Creator may, as He freely wills, use His creatures to work miracles and thereby show forth His power; we have rather to inquire what Nature with its immanent causes can naturally bring to pass."[18] This hardly sounds like "blind" unreasoned faith. Physicist Paul Davies writes of the influence of this belief in order and reason on Isaac Newton: "Isaac Newton first got the idea of absolute, universal, perfect, immutable laws from the Christian doctrine that God created the world and ordered it in a rational way." [19] Other scientists have found their work to be a form of revelation and worship. Geneticist and physician Francis Collins, former head of the Human Genome Project, and former atheist was one who found God in his science: "I have found there is a wonderful harmony in the complementary truths of science and faith. The God of the Bible is also the God of the genome. God can be found in the cathedral or in the laboratory. By investigating God's majestic and awesome creation, science can actually be a means of worship."[20]

The Judeo-Christian exhortation to explore the fingerprints of God in the natural world is absent in the theology of other religions. Although Islam accepts that God is the all-powerful, all knowing, Creator of the universe, it asserts that humans exist solely to surrender (this is what "Islam" means) to God and worship him and that we cannot come to know Him through his creation. According to Rodney Stark, "Allah is not presented as a lawful creator but has been conceived of as an extremely active God who intrudes on the world as he deems it appropriate. Consequently, there soon arose a major theological bloc within Islam that condemned all efforts to formulate natural laws as blasphemy insofar as they denied Allah's freedom to act."[21] Accordingly, Islamic theology does not provide the fundamental assumptions necessary for the emergence of empirical science devoted to discovering God's natural laws. This may be the reason why, despite all the excellent scholarship of many medieval Muslims in philosophy, mathematics, and medicine, the Islamic world never produced anything like the science of the Western world.

Materialism and Naturalism

Recall that Lewontin noted that the supposed struggle between science and the supernatural as one involving science's commitment to naturalism/materialism. There is no conflict between science and theism, but there is conflict between theism and naturalism. The atheistic scientist is committed to the metaphysics of ultimate existential meaninglessness; viewing everything that exists as either being due to a "random process" (a placeholder for "We don't know.") or a product of "necessity;" that is, of the predictable law of physics and chemistry. They rule out design by fiat: "we cannot allow a Divine Foot in the door." However, scientists can be thoroughgoing naturalists in their daily work, but still reject the notion that the matter of nature that they work with is not all that is. These are the scientists who agree with Nobel Prize winning physicist Max Plank's words delivered in a lecture titled *Religion and Natural Science*: "Both Religion and science require a belief in God. For believers, God is in the beginning, and for physicists He is at the end of all considerations... To the former He is the foundation, to the latter, the crown of the edifice of every generalized world view."[22]

I take materialism and naturalism to be synonymous, although if we want to split fine philosophical hairs we can see minor differences. Materialism makes an argument about the ontology of the universe; that is, all existence is matter, only matter (stuff you can see, touch, measure, and manipulate) is real, the world is just physical, and that there is no metaphysical reality. Naturalism takes the materialist premise that nature is matter and it self-sufficient and the whole of reality. It, therefore, denies any causal mechanisms outside of the natural, which means that it denies the supernatural, just like materialism. Theism, of course, affirms that there is a supernatural reality outside of nature, and calls that reality God.

For the materialist, mental phenomena are illusionary and are merely electrical energy moving stuff around in the brain. Francis Crick, one of the discoverers of the genetic code, has infamously written that, " 'You,' your joys and your sorrows, your memories and your ambitions, your sense of personal identity and free will, are in fact no more than the behavior of a vast assembly of nerve cells and their associated molecules. Who you are is nothing but a pack of neurons."[23] If Crick is going to travel that route he might have gone a little further because neurons are made of atoms, and atoms are made of even smaller particles, so he might have said that we are nothing but a pack of quarks. Mental phenomena cannot exist without their physical substrates, but surely the mind cannot be reduced to them without remainder. Crick's reductionist quote comes from his book, *The Astonishing Hypothesis.* It is indeed astonishing, and one wonders why he didn't subtitle it "The Zombie Within."

Take the phenomenon we call love as an example of Crick's folly. Neuroscientists have looked at the neurochemical correlates of romantic love in a soup of neurotransmitters lighting up the brain's major pleasure centers.[24] However, we cannot reduce the intoxication of romantic love to soup and sparks of brain activity. These physical things do not come remotely close to explaining why Romeo fell in love with Juliet; they merely tell us what happened in his brain when he did. This is very much an example of "top-down" causation (because love came before and generated the soup and sparks). To be sure, the product of the process (the soup and sparks) is necessary for the process (falling in love) to exist, but the physical product is a consequence of the mental process and not the other way around.

I have no problem with materialistic/naturalistic science as a working assumption. As a working assumption, it has been enormously successful in our understanding, prediction, and control of natural phenomenon precisely because nature is susceptible to these things. My problem with it is when its adherents jump from a working assumption to a comprehensive philosophy of absolutely everything; that is, the assumption that there is nothing beyond the materialist/naturalistic realm of being. The inherent atheism of materialism/naturalism as an ontological philosophy is made transparent in a speech made by the infamous Madalyn Murray O' Hair, founder of the American Atheists, and who was instrumental in removing the Bible from American schoolrooms. In a 1962 speech, she said, "Atheism is based upon a materialist philosophy which holds that nothing exists but natural phenomena. There are no supernatural forces or entities, nor can there be any. Nature simply exists."[25] A chain of rational reasoning explaining human existence that ends abruptly when the materialist arrives at the beginning of creation with "Well, that's just the way it is," is expecting us to accept the notion that the whole of existence is ultimately reasonless; not a very satisfactory "explanation" at all.

Those who hold a materialist worldview rarely address how the concept of matter was affected by new scientific discoveries such as quantum mechanics and Einstein's famous $E = MC^2$ in which matter and energy are equated. No longer is matter simply lumps of "stuff." Max Planck, the father of quantum mechanics, had the following to say about matter:

> As a man who has devoted his whole life to the most clear headed science, to the study of matter, I can tell you as a result of my research about atoms this much: There is no matter as such. All matter originates and exists only by virtue of a force which brings the particle of an atom to vibration and holds this most minute solar system of the atom

together. We must assume behind this force the existence of a conscious and intelligent Mind. This Mind is the matrix of all matter.[26]

Some naturalists argue that there are emergent properties not reducible to
matter, which is one way that it is different from materialism. Planck's mentalism—the belief that at the most fundamental level that the universe is
made of "mind stuff"—is shared by a number of other physicists. The great
astrophysicist Sir James Jeans famously wrote that: "The stream of knowledge
is heading towards a non-mechanical reality; the Universe begins to look
more like a great thought [can you read God here?] than like a great machine.
Mind no longer appears to be an accidental intruder into the realm of matter... we ought rather hail it as the creator and governor of the realm of matter."[27] Another great British astrophysicist, Arthur Eddington, wrote: "The
universe is of the nature of a thought or sensation in a universal Mind."[28]
When we think about the apparently infinite divisibility of matter we have to
wonder what it "ultimately" is; is matter really only the gathering of the four
non-material fundamental forces of the universe (gravity, electromagnetism,
and the weak and strong nuclear force), or does it point to John 1:1 "In the
beginning was the Word, and the Word was with God, and the Word was God"?

Explanation in Science

Christianity-inspired science is humankind's greatest intellectual achieve-
ment, enabling humans to perceive, understand, and manipulate the natural
world. It has lifted humanity to a level of health, prosperity, freedom, and
comfort beyond the wildest imagination of people living in pre-scientific
days. It has so richly transformed our material lives that it is reasonable to
argue that the average Westerner enjoys far better health, comfort, and diver-
sity of experience than any ancient monarch. Science can do this because the
scientific way of knowing yields justified beliefs verifiable across all cultures.
If it gets things wrong, and it often does, scientists know that their work is
tentative and self-correcting. Science is a process by which the answers lead
to more questions; it feeds on ignorance for what is already known is boring,
but it does not claim to answer the big questions of existence. Christian theism has always done that without science, but we are in an age when science's
evidential force supports it. It is for this reason that the Christian must know
how science points to God so that he or she can bear witness in the only way
an atheist will accept.

Science relies on three methods of reasoning to arrive at explanations: deduction, induction, and abduction. Deduction, the most reliable of the three,
is a "top-down" method that reasons from a premise that is self-evidently true
("All men are mortal.") to a minor premise ("Plato is a man."), and on to a

conclusion ("Therefore Plato is mortal."). There are people belonging to a school of thought called rationalism who contend that the world can only be understood as *it is* through the intellect because the senses allow us only to see it as *it appears*. They say that world comes to us through the buzzing confusion of sense perceptions and must be filtered and organized by the intellect. While it is true that our senses may deceive us, they appear to be saying that our intellect cannot; which is a serious error because it deceives even the greatest of minds.

Rationalists idealize mathematics as the only true paradigm of truth because mathematical thinking is analytic; that is, it rests on a priori knowledge that is true by definition. If x = 2 and y = 3, then (x) (y) = 6 is absolute in all possible instances. Deductive "top-down" reasoning from truths considered self-evident had been taken as the ideal path to knowledge ever since Plato because it guarantees the truth of the conclusion given that it is already present in the premise ("All crimes are against the law."), and any denial of it is self-contradictory.

Once we leave the certainty of mathematics, we run into trouble with deductive reasoning because except in the most trivial sense ("All mothers are females") we have precious few major premises that are self-evidently true. We cannot simply "rationalize" ourselves into knowing; it must be established by observation and experiment. This is "bottom-up" reasoning from the specific to the general is called induction. To conduct experiments or to make observations, scientists are guided by theories from which hypotheses are logically deduced. However, theories are not true by definition as mathematical axioms are, so our deductions from theory must predispose broad inductions to validate their major premises. All real knowledge of the world can only achieve with some degree of confidence when we test our concepts in the world outside our own minds. Empirical science cannot produce the absolutely knowledge demanded by those who identify all true knowledge with mathematics, but the experimental/observational inductive method is the bedrock of science. Mathematical models of reality may be internally consistent, but if they cannot be empirically verified they do not reflect reality.

The third method of reasoning is abduction. Abductive reasoning starts with all available relevant observations and proceeds to the most reasonable possible explanation for them but leaves open other possible explanations. Peter Lipton offers an example of abductive reasoning:

> When a detective infers that it was Moriarty who committed the crime, he does so because this hypothesis would best explain the fingerprints, blood stains and other forensic evidence. Sherlock Holmes to the contrary, this is not a matter of deduction. The evidence will not entail that

Moriarty is to blame, since it always remains possible that someone else was the perpetrator. Nevertheless, Holmes is right to make his inference, since Moriarty's guilt would provide a better explanation of the evidence than would anyone else's.[29]

Given all the evidence that Lipton presents, any jury would conclude that Moriarty is guilty "beyond a reasonable doubt," but not beyond all doubt. Abduction is the process of linking multiple lines of converging, complementary, and corroborative evidence in a logical way to arrive at a rational conclusion. Unlike deductive reasoning whereby the conclusion is guaranteed by the axiom, the jury is reaching what it considers the simplest and most logical conclusion it could draw from converging lines of evidence. In other words, abductive reasoning is the result of testing of multiple competing hypotheses (ruling out other possible suspects) and making an "inference to the best explanation." Reasoning from multiple observations to the best explanation is a method graced with simplicity and elegance and is in accord with Occam's razor ("Entities are not to be multiplied without necessity"), which basically means that among competing hypotheses the one with the fewest assumptions should be chosen. My aim is to use the abductive method to reason about God and the many benefits of Christianity. The eminent philosopher of science Stephen Meyer illustrates how abduction is used in science and how science is pointing to the existence of the Creator "beyond a reasonable doubt."

As one surveys several classes of evidence from the natural sciences cosmology, physics, biochemistry, and molecular biology theism emerges as a worldview with extraordinary explanatory scope and power. Theism explains a wide ensemble of metaphysically-significant scientific evidences and theoretical results more simply, adequately, and comprehensively than other major competing worldviews or metaphysical systems. This does not, of course, prove God's existence, since superior explanatory power does not constitute deductive certainty. It does suggest, however, that the natural sciences now provide strong epistemological support for the existence of God as affirmed by both a theistic and Judeo-Christian worldview.[30]

Do we need an Explanation of the Explanation?

We will see later that prior to the early 1930s the standard position of science was that the universe is past eternal, static, and uncaused. This was a convenient position because it relieved scientists of having to explain its origin. Science now knows otherwise but is in a quandary regarding how it began and its theistic implications. Christianity has always asserted a beginning of everything as revealed in Genesis, and that everything that exists has a cause. If we assert that the inference to the best explanation is that God is the cause of the existence of the universe, a standard atheist "checkmate" response is "If everything requires a cause, what caused God?" This kind of response asks for an explanation of the explanation and demonstrates a faulty understanding of God as Christians know Him. "Who made God" is a meaningless question because God is not bound by naturalistic parameters of time, space, and causality—He is the Uncaused Cause. When atheists argue that Christian claims that everything has a cause but that God has no cause is contradictory, they miss this point entirely. When we assert that everything is caused; we mean that everything *contingent*, everything in the *material universe;* everything in *time*, and everything *imperfect* requires a cause. God, who is unconditional, immaterial, timeless, and perfect, does not. God is God precisely because He does not have a creator.

Another reason why asking Christians to explain the explanation is simply not logical, is that all explanations must arrive at a stopping point beyond which it is impossible to go. I completely agree with philosopher of science and theology William Craig, who says that "one needn't have an explanation of the explanation. This is an elementary point concerning inference to the best explanation as practiced in the philosophy of science."[31] Craig tells us that an attempt to explain the explanation (God) would lead to an infinite regress: If X created God; who created X? Y created X. Who then created Y? And so on ad infinitum. All explanations must have an ultimate terminus; an uncaused First Cause.

One of the greatest mathematicians of the 20th century, David Hilbert, provided a mathematical proof of the impossibility of such an infinite regress, concluding his famous paper on the subject saying: "Our principal result is that the infinite is nowhere to be found in reality. It neither exists in nature nor provides a legitimate basis for rational thought. ...The role that remains for the infinite is solely that of an idea."[32] Because there is no "before" the Big Bang (the moment of creation), an infinite regress in the large causal chain that produced the universe is impossible because there is a stopping point. Even is this the universe was created by something else in a different timeline, say from the highly speculative notion of a "multiverse" (the notion that there are countless other universes beyond our perception), the logic still holds; the regress must ultimately arrive at the First Cause who exists outside of all possible timelines. Something caused the Big Bang, so that "something" must be outside of time and be itself infinite.

If the atheist wants to stop the infinite regress with the universe as a brute fact, he would make an argument similar to the one above. He would have to assert that while it is true that everything manifest in the universe has a cause, the universe itself requires no explanation because it is the final uncaused cause. That is, nothing existed before the universe, and yet the universe exists, so for the atheist the universe pulled itself up by its own bootstraps and did it so astoundingly well that it would eventually produce sentient beings capable of probing its secrets. On that argument alone, which is the most logical inference to the best explanation: God or nothing? If taken as fact, an "omnipotent" but mindless universe takes us back to the pre-1930s world in which the universe is simply a brute fact with which we need not bother ourselves. Such an argument would hobble the entire enterprise of cosmology, which exists precisely to discover how the universe came into existence.

A moment's reflection will reveal that atheism's "creation" is more miraculous than theism's because it posits that all energy/matter came from nothing, was designed by no agent, and for no reason. This not only defies logic; it defies the first law of thermodynamics that decrees that under *natural* conditions matter/energy can neither be created or destroyed but, once it is in existence, it can be transformed. What was this Godless naturalistic "nothing" that circumvented its own law and created matter/energy from nothing? The atheist has neither a natural nor a supernatural explanation for creation, which underlines the hollowness (literally) of his arguments—nothing created something from nothing for no reason!

Chapter 2

Christianity, Rationality, and Militant New Atheism

"The first gulp from the glass of natural sciences will turn you into an atheist, but at the bottom of the glass God is waiting for you."
Werner Heisenberg, Nobel Laureate in physicist

Creeping Atheism

The Christian foundations of American morality and freedom are under attack by a loose confederation of public intellectuals dubbed the "new atheists." Ironically, they couch their message in terms of freedom, but their "freedom" is freedom from God and morality. These new atheists are militantly pushing their Godless agenda on America and other Western societies. Their "in your face" propaganda is having an effect. According to the Pew Research Center's Religious Landscape Study, the number of self-identified atheists in the United States almost doubled from 1.6 percent in 2007 to 3.1% in 2016.[1] This number may be greater, since some people who nominally identify with a religion may not believe in God. On the other hand, some self-identified atheists are really deists, since they claim to believe in a universal spirit. Whatever the case may be, atheism is creeping upwards in America, and this upward creep, driven by aggressive atheist propaganda in best-selling books, is having a negative effect on America's cultural landscape and on its foundational Christian values.

Indicative of this effect, in 2016 the International Christian Concern (ICC) *Hall of Shame Report* included the United States for the first time among the nations that are persecuting Christians, citing events that occurred from 2012 to 2015. The report stated that the "ICC sees these worrying trends as an alarming indication of the decline in religious liberty in the United States."[2] Another 2016 report from the First Liberty Institute highlighted a relentlessly growing pattern of hostility. The report lists more than 600 incidents over the previous 10 years in all areas of public life from public schools, to the workplace, to the military.[3] Persecution in the United States is typically aimed at using legal means to crush small business people and others who refuse to cave into government mandates that violate their faith. The major victims of these attacks have been wedding vendors who, while gladly serving gays in any other way, refuse to lend their services facilitate same-sex weddings since to do so would be both participating in the wedding and signaling their approval of it.

To counter the huge increase in government anti-Christian activity during the Obama administration, President Trump signed the *First Amendment Defense Act* barring the federal government from discriminating against individuals and organizations based upon their religious convictions. Not surprisingly, Democratic politicians and various anti-Christian groups have mounted a campaign against the Act, calling it "anti-gay." What is surprising (and shocking) is that an act to protect a First Amendment right would be necessary in 21st century America. When a constitutional right held sacred by previous generations of Americans needs a congressional act to back it up, you know religious freedom is on the line.

The new atheist agenda is given support by the ultra-liberal organization Southern Poverty Law Center (SPLC) who has designated numerous religious and family-oriented groups as "hate groups." The SPLC's reason for being, or so it seems, consists of finding new groups to call hate groups and "Keeping an eye on the radical right," as their official website puts it. As of 2017, the SPLC website lists 917 groups designated as hate groups in the United States. Groups such as the KKK and the American Nazi Party justly deserve to be on the list, but the SPLC includes organizations defending religious freedom and the family such as the Alliance Defending Religious Freedom, First Liberty Institute, and the American Family Association in their ever-growing list. The SPLC even put The American College of Pediatricians on their list as an anti-gay hate group because it published an article warning adolescents of the possible medical consequences of a gay lifestyle. It seems that every group in the United States except those who share the SPLC's anti-Christian and anti-family agenda is a hate group. Putting religious and family values groups in the same box as Klansmen and Nazis serves the purpose of demonizing them and making attacks on them more acceptable to more people.[4]

Clearly, new atheism not only rejects God, but also wants to make the rest of us reject Him also. We are America's "deplorables" who cling to our "guns and religion," as Hillary Clinton and Barack Obama, respective, called mainstream Americans. Atheists are even attacking the Constitutional basis of religious liberty, which makes it easier for the state to justify attacks on Christians. In his book *Why Tolerate Religion?*, law professor Brian Leiter argues that the religious liberty clause of the First Amendment protecting the free exercise of religion is no longer tenable. He claims that religion is insulated from "reason and evidence" which he defines as "believing in something notwithstanding the evidence and reasons that fail to support it or even contradict it."[5] This atheist "freethinker" is of the opinion that God has been given his walking papers by reason. The Founders of this country were hardly irrational; they believed that religion was vastly important as a moral foundation of society that the very first words in the Bill of Rights are: "Congress shall make no law respecting an establishment of religion or prohibiting the free exercise thereof." For the Founding Fathers, the government should not just "tolerate" Christianity, but respect it, revere it, accommodate it, and promote it.

The "Four Horsemen" of New Atheism

New atheism is a social movement led by the intellectually gifted and articulate "Four Horsemen" of atheism: Richard Dawkins, Daniel Dennett, Christopher Hitchens, and Sam Harris. In the hands of these wordsmiths, atheism has repackaged the old philosophical arguments as doctrinal commitment and delivered in an aggressive and dogmatic way, so people sit up and take notice (and buy their books). The basic tenet of the movement is that religion is irrational, should not be tolerated, and must be robustly attacked by "rational" folk who take science as their guide.

Not all atheists, of course, are militantly anti-Christian. Many—perhaps most—simply asset that they don't believe in God and leave it at that and may even wish those well who do. A good number of them may well believe that Christianity is a good thing for society and would never attack it, but they just do not buy into it themselves. Many of them do not bother to examine either theistic or atheistic evidence, and simply dismiss God in the same way they dismiss Santa Clause. They are indifferent to all arguments for or against God's existence, and thus we can define this weak form of atheism as simply an unexamined absence of belief in God. These people harm only themselves by depriving themselves of God's love and spiritual sustenance but do not seek to harm Christianity. People who attack Christianity are better described as anti-theists rather than atheists, and it is these people pose a real danger to society. When I use the terms "atheist" and "atheism" from now on it is to the strong anti-theist to which I am referring.

There is very little "new" in new atheism except for its political activism and confrontational tone. Political scientist Marcus Schulzke maintains that new atheists view the traditional atheist as too willing to let their contrasting worldviews coexist as separate discourses and keep their non-belief a private thing. New atheists don't want to accommodate such a notion and urge atheists to "come out of the closet" and let the world know what they think.[6] Schulzke is a supporter of new atheism and views it as a political movement designed to spread the liberal/progressive worldview. Well before the emergence of the new atheists, there were atheist missionaries for the values of the

hard left fighting an aggressive war against traditional American values under-
lain by the Christian beliefs, but this is a subject for chapter four.

The major "horseman" pushing the overtly political/social side (as opposed
to limited to an anti-religious agenda) of new atheism was the recently deceased British-American journalist and fiercely combative public intellectual
Christopher Hitchens. This is evidenced by the disingenuous subtitle of his
2007 book, *God is not Great: Religion Poisons Everything.* Hitchens forecloses
on any possibility of a constructive dialog between secularism and theism
with such abusive and incendiary words, but they do sell books! Hitchens
called himself a "conservative Marxist" (whatever that means) and was an
admirer of bloodthirsty communist revolutionaries such as Lenin and Che
Guevara—no wonder he hated God. As a public intellectual, he often debated
theists from a position announced in the online magazine *Slate:* "Extraordinary claims [regarding the existence of God] require extraordinary evidence
and that what can be asserted without evidence can also be dismissed without evidence."[7] In other words, he didn't really need to present any contrary
evidence since theism offers no credible evidence for him to refute. This is the
kind of hubris that Ian Markham, President of Episcopal Virginia Theological
Seminary, describes as "fundamentalist atheism" in its claim that God does
not exist, and for whom "there is no room for ambiguity or humility or nu-
ance."[8]

Understanding and Confronting Militant Atheism

Marcus Schulzke is quite right in his assertion that that militant atheism is an
attempt to foist a left-wing agenda on Western civilization. The new atheists
are leftist to the core and have declared Christians to be their enemy, and in
the spirit of the ancient Chinese sage Sun Tzu, to effectively engage the enemy
one must know him. There are many atheist websites featuring major atheist
figures that Christians should not be afraid of visiting in the spirit of "know
thy enemy." If you do, you will not be stepping into Satan's lair, but you will
encounter arguments you will not like. This is good because criticism of our
faith makes us more intellectually muscular as we wrestle with it. If there is no
enemy at the gates we grow fat and complacent in our certainty of safety. To
find these websites you may visit the *Born Atheist* website, which lists 11 well-
funded atheist organizations. The largest of these organizations appears to be
the *American Atheist*, with 70 national and international affiliates.

Rather than using the term "atheist," some atheists groups identify their
groups as "Brights" or "Freethinkers," which makes their members feel that
they have the intellectual high ground looking down on irrational theists, who
are evidently seen in contrast as "Dulls" or "Enslaved Thinkers." The irrationality of Christianity (or any other religion) and the rationality of atheism is

taken for granted, as is in evidence by the American Atheist website definition of atheism as "the mental attitude which unreservedly accepts the supremacy of reason," which in effect means that the mental attitude of its opposite, theism, rejects reason in favor of blind faith.

The atheist/Marxist biologist Richard Lewontin emphasizes the atheist's view of theists' supposed blindness in his *New York Times* review of famous astronomer Carl Sagan's book *The Demon-Haunted World: Science as a Candle in the Dark*. In this 1995 book, Sagan equated belief in God with the belief in little green men from Mars, UFOs, Santa Claus, and many other fictions. Sagan decries such beliefs and offers the lack of science education as the root of it all. Of course, equating belief in God with belief in fictions such as Santa Clause is a massive non-sequitur. No great scientist has ever been forced to accept "Santa Clausism" by his or her science the way those mentioned throughout this book have been forced to accept the Creator. Nevertheless, Lewontin writes, "The only explanation that he [Sagan] offers for the dogged resistance of the masses to the obvious virtues of the scientific way of knowing is that "through indifference, inattention, incompetence, or fear of skepticism, we discourage children from science."[9] I hope this is not the case with committed Christians since the wonders that science has revealed point more convincingly to the Creator today than ever before.

It is doubtless true that few of us become believers through long philosophical conversations with ourselves about the pros and cons of theism. Most people "inherit" their faith from their parents and either they grow in it or it withers. Many among the lapsed may return to their religious roots after their youthful years of rebellion and doubt. Others become committed Christians through deeply emotional experience that takes root. Once it has taken root, we need to be able to defend it on objective, rational grounds and not on subjective emotions. We need to learn the best Christian apologetics, which is perhaps an unfortunate word which has nothing to do with apologizing. It comes from a Greek meaning "to make a defense," and if we cannot make a robust defense for our faith, atheists may be forgiven for not taking us seriously.

Atheists need not necessarily defend their position since it is an entirely negative one. Atheism is like the prisoner in the dock; he need say nothing at all. It is we who are prosecuting the prisoner and who are making an affirmative claim about the existence of the Creator who must speak. We must offer sufficient probative evidence for our case for the jury to reject the assumption "beyond a reasonable doubt" that atheism is innocent. They say you should never argue about politics or religion, but the more I discuss religion with non-believers the more convinced I am of a creator God. But to discuss reasonably, we have to have a solid defense of our own position and an equally solid offense against the position of our opponents.

It may be commendable to accept God on faith alone and have a purely emotional attachment to it, but such an appeal to emotion is hardly useful when answering the points made by an aggressive atheist. A person holding any position, religious or otherwise, should be able to defend it intellectually. As Paul put it in Romans 10:2: "For I bear them record [I hear them] that they have a zeal of God, but not according to knowledge." Although intellectual knowledge of God is necessary for the Christian to answer atheists on their own terms, justifying one's faith through science is not sufficient for one's self. A saving faith requires more than intellectual assent; it requires a commitment to God at the intellectual, emotional, and spiritual levels. As the philosopher and theologian Martin Buber observed, viewing God only intellectually as the Creator is to place Him in an I-It (subject and object) relationship with you in which He is wholly "other," cold, distant and inaccessible. A spiritual Christian accepts God as both the Creator and the Father with whom we can enter an I-Thou subject-subject relationship.[10]

Emotional attachment to a position is certainly not confined to theists; it is also true of many strong atheists as well. Although philosopher Thomas Nagel is quite able to defend his atheistic beliefs with reasoned arguments, he also admitted his emotional attachment to it: "I want atheism to be true and am made uneasy by the fact that some of the most intelligent and well-informed people I know are religious believers. It is just that I don't believe in God and, naturally, hope that I am right in that belief. It's that I hope there is no God! I don't want there to be a God; I don't want the universe to be like that."[11] It is sad to see someone locate his hope in a negative. I am reminded by this of a statement made by the genial genius John Lennox in one of his debates. He relates that an atheist at a scientific conference told him that: "You Christians believe in God because you are afraid of the dark;" to which Lennox replied: "You atheists don't believe in God because you are afraid of the light."

If the atheist takes the stand to protest his innocence by an affirmative stance proclaiming that there is no God, his position requires justification and you, the Christian "prosecutor," must be able to vigorously interrogate him. Just as we do not know with absolute certainty whether Moriarty is guilty as charged, even though all the available evidence points in that directions when arguing with a committed atheist we can only reason to the best explanation given the evidence science presents to us. Science can tell us *how* the universe came into existence which, incidentally, coincides with *Genesis,* but it cannot tell us *why*. Of course, if we are here simply by the blind random chance, as atheists claim, there is no purpose and no meaning in life, so asking "why" makes no sense to them. Science may not be the best reason for the committed Christian's faith, but it is the only way of knowing that a committed atheist will listen to, which is why we need to embrace it. Philosopher Beatrice Bruteau is of the opinion, which I share, that contemplative Christians should be excited and knowledgeable about science because it "is part of our religious life, our practice, the way we live divine life."[12]

There are Christians who find apologetics based on natural theology to be unbiblical and that revealed theology and preaching the gospel is enough, but Ephesians 4:15 tells us to "speak the truth in love" with Christians and unbelievers alike. And 1 Peter 3:15 commands "Always be prepared to give an answer to everyone who asks you to give the reason for the hope that you have. But do this with gentleness and respect." The new atheist's case, they say, rests on science, so if we are to effectively engage them or those whom they have convinced, it is necessary to enter their territory and speak the truths of science in love, and then perhaps we can begin to speak the truths of the Gospel.

The Benefits of Christianity: The Success of Western Civilization

Although each of the Four Horsemen claims that Christianity is in conflict with science and we would be better off without God, there is abundant evidence in the historical, political, and economic literature that the freedoms and prosperity of the Western world owes its success to the belief in a God of order and reason. Sociologist and historian Rodney Stark's book *The Victory of Reason: How Christianity Led to Freedom, Capitalism, and Western Success,* and physicist and philosopher James Hannam's book *God's Philosophers: How the Medieval World Laid the Foundations of Modern Science,* give lie to atheist claims that Christianity is in conflict with science. They and many other historians and philosophers over the years have argued that the reasoned mindset instilled by Christianity led to the embrace of science, economic freedom, and prosperity, and finally to the political freedoms of democracy. The famous German sociologist, historian, and economist Max Weber's studies of the world's religions explored the reasons why Western civilization became the center of science and economic progress in his 1905 masterpiece *The Protestant Ethic and the Spirit of Capitalism.* In his own words: "Only in the West does science exist at a stage of development which we recognize today as valid. Empirical knowledge, reflection on problems of the cosmos and of life, philosophical and theological wisdom of the most profound sort, are not confined to it, though in the case of the last the full development of a systematic theology must be credited to Christianity."[13]

It is not just Western scholars that hold Christianity to be the bedrock of Western success. *Time Magazine* correspondent to China David Aikman quotes a leading Chinese scholar from the Chinese Academy of Social Science who led a research team charged by the Chinese government to discover reasons why the West is preeminent in almost all spheres of human endeavor. As this scholar describes the findings of his team:

> One of the things we were asked to look into was what accounted for the success, in fact, the preeminence of the West all over the world. We studied everything we could from the historical, political, economic, and cultural perspective. At first, we thought it was because you had more powerful guns than we had. Then we thought it was because you had the best political system. Next we focused on your economic system. But in the past twenty years, we have realized that the heart of your culture is your religion: Christianity. That is why the West is so powerful. The Christian moral foundation of social and cultural life was what made possible the emergence of capitalism and then the successful transition to democratic politics. We don't have any doubt about this.[14]

No one claims that Christianity is a necessary and sufficient cause of Western success, only that it provided a highly decisive foundation. It is hardly a coincidence that of the 88 countries designated "free" in the 2015 Freedom in the World Index, 80 (90.9%) are Christian.[15] Non-Christian countries that have successfully transitioned to free status have done so through either by colonization (e.g., Singapore), occupation (e.g., Japan), or long-term influence (e.g., South Korea). "Could modern science have arisen outside the theological matrix of Western Christendom?" asks Peter Harrison, professor of science and religion. He answers: "It is difficult to say. What can be said for certain is that it did arise in that environment and that theological ideas underpinned some of its central assumptions. Those who argue for the incompatibility of science and religion will draw little comfort from history"[16]

Compatibility of Science and Christianity Revisited

Those who argue for the incompatibility of science and religion may not draw comfort from history as Harrison states, but can they draw it from the opinions of modern scientists? Elaine Ecklund and Jerry Park surveyed 1,646 scientists at 21 elite universities and asked them if they see a conflict between science and religion. Of those who saw a conflict, 17.1 percent "strongly agreed" and 19.5 "agreed somewhat." Among those who disagreed that there is a conflict, 33.1 percent "strongly disagreed" and 23.8 percent "disagreed somewhat" (6.4% had no opinion). Thus, the plurality of elite scientists (56.9%) did not believe that there is a conflict between science and religion. Sixty-eight percent said that they were "spiritual" to some degree, and 46.6 percent said they attended a place of worship at least a few times a year.[17]

Atheists also take great delight in claiming that most scientists are atheists, like them, which they perhaps imagine puts them in the same intellectual ballpark. Unfortunately for them, this is not true. A national study of 1,400 scientists found that a mere 9.8 percent described themselves as atheists. Of the remainder, 34.9 percent believed in God without doubts, 16.6 percent believed in God but had doubts, 19.2 percent believed in a higher power (deism), 4.4 percent believed in God "some of the time," and 13.1 percent were agnostics.[18] While it is true that the rate of religious belief among scientists is below that of the general American public, the rate is higher among physicians, with 76 percent of a national sample of physicians affirming their belief in God.[19] Ninety percent of these physicians attend religious services at least occasionally. With almost two-thirds of scientists and just over three-quarters of physicians reporting some degree of belief in a divine Creator, it is plainly false that science and reason are on the side of atheism—science and reason are on the side of God. As prize-winning mathematical physicist Robert Griffiths has said: "If we need an atheist for a debate, we go to the philosophy department. The physics department isn't much use."[20] It seems that the borders between science and religion are more permeable than atheists believe.

The light grows ever dimmer for atheists when we examine the number of Nobel Laureates who were/are atheists, agnostic, or "freethinkers." Geneticist Baruch Shalev wrote a book documenting various aspects of the lives of all 719 Nobel Prize winners from 1901 to 2000. It was found that only about 10.5 percent of these brilliant men and women fell into atheists, agnostic, or freethinker category, with winners in literature, not science, making up by far the biggest category of non-believers (see Figure 2.1). Christians and Jews made up 86.5 percent of Nobel winners (92% in science).[21] We cannot know how devout those who were not atheists, agnostics, or freethinkers, but it is enough to say that they were not in the Godless category. Here's what Christian Anfinsen, a Nobel Laureate in chemistry, had to say about atheists: "I think only an idiot can be an atheist. We must admit that there exists an incomprehensible power or force with limitless foresight and knowledge that started the whole universe going in the first place."[22]

Defending your faith does not mean that you should go around calling your atheist friends and colleagues idiots because they do not share our views. We can defend our faith without becoming defensive and present arguments without becoming emotional and cantankerous. When you resort to name calling the battle is lost, and you have lost it. You will find the more good arguments in support of your faith the less defensive and quarrelsome you will become and the more effective you will be. You can learn by watching great defenders of the faith such as William Craig, John Lennox, and Stephen Meyer debate atheists on YouTube without becoming defensive and quarrelsome; which is more than I can say about some of their opponents. People tend to lose their composure and resort to name-calling only when they run out of good arguments or deliberately want to be insulting.

Einstein's Music of the Spheres

Albert Einstein, the greatest mind of the 20th century, has given grist for much thought to many regarding the relationship of science and religion. In a 1941 symposium on science, philosophy and religion and their relationship to American democracy, he had the following to say about the compatibility of science and Judeo-Christian religion:

> Though religion may be that which determines the goal, it has, never-theless, learned from science, in the broadest sense, what means will contribute to the attainment of the goals it has set up. But science can only be created by those who are thoroughly imbued with the aspiration toward truth and understanding. This source of feeling, however, springs from the sphere of religion. To this there also belongs the faith in the possibility that the regulations valid for the world of existence are rational, that is, comprehensible to reason. I cannot conceive of a genuine scientist without that profound faith. The situation may be expressed by an image: *science without religion is lame, religion without science is blind.*[23]

Exactly what Einstein meant in the italicized quote has long been a source of contention. I believe that he meant that religion attempts to explain the ultimate questions of meaning, but without science, it won't find any answers that may satisfy religious seekers (as distinct from committed theists), and thus it will be blind. By "science without religion is lame," perhaps he meant that many of our deepest questions and concerns seem beyond the boundaries of science, and for that we require a transcendental God whose cosmic design encourages scientific growth. Perhaps his words were in agreement with Joseph Taylor, who won the Nobel Prize in 1993 for physics: "A scientific discovery is also a religious discovery. There is no conflict between science and religion. Our knowledge of God is made larger with every discovery we make about the world." [24]

Einstein had harsh words for atheists who quote him or science in general in support of atheistic claims. He wrote: "The fanatical atheists are like slaves who are still feeling the weight of their chains which they have thrown off after hard struggle. They are creatures who – in their grudge against tradition-al religion as the 'opium of the masses' – cannot hear the music of the spheres."[25] If only atheists would open up their minds to the data surrounding the "music of the spheres" they may come to see that they have been in error.

Figure 2.1 Percentage of Nobel Prizes won by Atheists, Agnostics, and "Freethinkers" Between 1901 and 2000 (Jobas / CC BY-SA 4.0)
https://commons.wikimedia.org/wiki/File:Distribution_of_Atheists,_agnostics,_and_Freethinkers_in_Nobel_Prizes_between_1901-2000.png

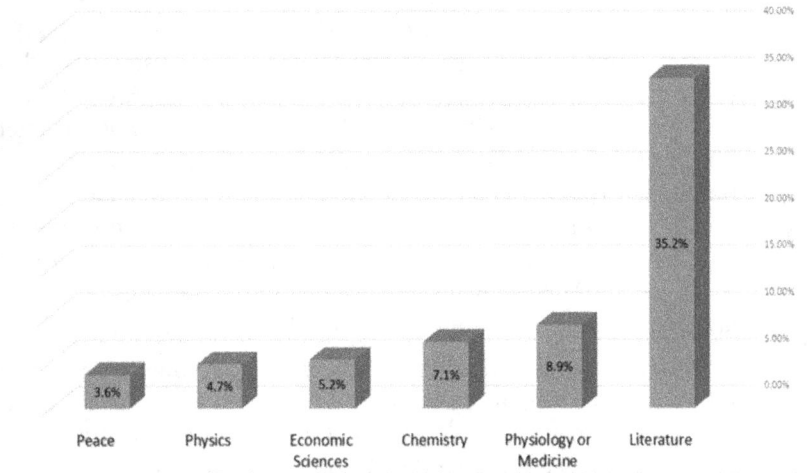

Philosopher Antony Flew is one famous atheist who was led to reconsider his beliefs after reflecting on the data, particularly on the mind-boggling complexity of DNA and the mystery of its origins. In 2004, Flew shocked the atheist world by announcing he had come to believe in God. It was as if Pope Francis announced that he had become a Muslim because Flew was atheism's pope; a man who had written many books and articles peddling it for 50 or so years. When asked in an interview with Benjamin Wiker if he had "heard a voice" leading him to God, Flew replied that basically there were two decisive factors. One was the increasing number of noted scientists who affirm that there has to be a super-Intelligence behind the complexity of the universe, and the other was the amazing complexity of DNA and the utter impossibility of a non-intelligent source of the origin of life. He goes on to say:

I believe that the origin of life and reproduction simply cannot be explained from a biological standpoint despite numerous efforts to do so. With every passing year, the more that was discovered about the richness and inherent intelligence of life, the less it seemed likely that a chemical soup could magically generate the genetic code. The difference between life and non-life, it became apparent to me, was onto-logical and not chemical. The best confirmation of this radical gulf is Richard Dawkins' comical effort to argue in *The God Delusion* that the origin of life can be attributed to a "lucky chance." If that's the best ar-gument you have, then the game is over. No, I did not hear a Voice. It was the evidence itself that led me to this conclusion.[26]

In Flew's 2007 book, *There is a God*, he traces his intellectual journey from atheism to deism by following the evidence wherever it may lead him. As if to vindicate French Premier Georges Clemenceau's trenchant statement that, "Not to be a socialist at twenty is proof of want of heart; to be one at thirty is proof of want of head," Flew tells us that in his youth he was a "hotly energet-ic left-wing socialist" (an affliction that that may young men, including my-self, suffer in their youth), but abandoned it in his thirties.[27] Abandoning this Godless creed is the first step toward abandoning atheism, and after Flew did he became a vigorous defender of free market capitalism, and much later, came to accept God. Unfortunately, Flew came to know God only as the im-personal Creator, but he never quite got to know Him as the personal Father.

Alister McGrath is another world-famous former atheist who fell to the early allure of Marxism, although he wasn't as tardy as Flew in rejecting it. He saw the bottom of Heisenberg's science glass (see chapter epigraph) fairly quickly when at Oxford University studying molecular biophysics, in which he re-ceived a PhD. It was during this time, he wrote, "I was discovering that Chris-tianity was far more intellectually robust than I had ever imagined. I had some major rethinking to do, and by the end of November [1971], my decision was made: I turned my back on one faith [Marxism] and embraced another."[28] The wondrous ordered complexity he saw in the structure of the cell (akin to Flew's wonder of the complexity of DNA) was a major part of the reason he became a committed Christian.

Who's Irrational Now?

Let us return to the atheists' weapon that they wield with glee against theism; believers in God are irrational clods (just like all those Nobel Laureates) who accept their faith blindly and will believe anything. Commenting on Gallop Poll study commissioned by Baylor University titled *What Americans Really Believe*, Mollie Ziegler Hemingway wrote a telling piece about rationality among Christians and atheists (actually, about weekly church attenders and non-or seldom attenders; the latter not necessarily consisting entirely of athe-ists) in a *Wall Street Journal* piece aptly titled "Look who's irrational now." She writes:

"What Americans Really Believe," a comprehensive new study released by Baylor University yesterday, shows that traditional Christian religion greatly decreases belief in everything from the efficacy of palm readers to the usefulness of astrology. It also shows that the irreligious and the members of more liberal Protestant denominations, far from being resistant to superstition, tend to be much more likely to believe in the paranormal and in pseudoscience than evangelical Christians.[29]

The Gallop Poll asked a number of questions about people's belief in such things as Bigfoot, the Loch Ness Monster, Atlantis, haunted houses, dreams foretelling the future, and so forth. These beliefs were placed in a cumulative index of "belief in the paranormal." Much to the chagrin of liberals and atheists, almost four times (31%) as many people who never attend church expressed strong belief in the paranormal than did weekly church attenders (8%). In fact, the more traditional and evangelical the respondent, the less likely he or she was to believe in fortune telling or the "possibility of communicating with people who are dead."

In an attempt to explain these findings, Ziegler Hemingway referenced a 1980 study that "cited the decline of traditional religious belief among the better educated as one of the causes for an increase in pseudoscience, cults and superstition...and that irreligious college students to be by far the most likely to embrace paranormal beliefs, while born-again Christian college students were the least likely."[30] Francis Bacon's observation is apropos here: "A little philosophy inclineth man's mind to atheism, but depth in philosophy bringeth men's minds about to religion."[31] Because irreligious college students have had a "little philosophy," or perhaps Heisenberg's "first gulp of natural science," they probably feel that it was more intellectually respectable to drop religion and embrace some other form of belief.

A later poll taken by the Pew Research Center rubbed more salt into atheist arrogance. It showed that Christians who attend church weekly, conservatives, and Republicans express much lower levels of belief in ghosts, fortune tellers, astrology, the "evil eye" (some people can cast spells and curses on others) yoga (as a spiritual practice), and spiritual energy located in physical things (mountains, trees, and so on) than liberals, Democrats, and non-church attenders. Among those who attend church weekly or more, 11 percent believe in ghosts and the same percentage believed in fortune tellers, whereas 23 percent and 15 percent of non-attenders believe in ghosts and fortune tellers, respectively. Yoga as a spiritual practice was believed by 25 percent of non-or infrequent attenders, versus 8 percent of weekly church attenders. Statistics bore, so I will just say that practicing Christians, as well as conservatives and Republicans, have far less belief in all "New Age" beliefs than non-attenders, liberals, and Democrats. 2009. [32]

Despite contrary evidence, atheists and liberals still like to think that Christian beliefs are irrational. The goal of this book is to lay out the evidence for God's existence from the works of science itself, as well as the many benefits of Christianity. It is indisputable that bizarre New Age beliefs have grown stronger among atheists the more science has progressed, and that they do not take hold nearly as strongly among practicing Christians, conservatives, and Republicans.

Having forsaken God, atheists, and hard leftists in general, attach themselves with religious fervor not only to relatively harmless "New Age" beliefs but to more harmful moonshine such as socialism, multiculturalism, radical feminism, and moral relativism. They do so because they have to believe in something greater than themselves to which they can pledge allegiance. None other than Richard Dawkins (a hard leftist) expressed this inner need in a debated with John Lennox: "I think that when you consider the beauty of the world and you wonder how it came to be what it is, you are naturally overwhelmed with a feeling of awe, a feeling of admiration ... and you almost feel a desire to worship something."[33] Perhaps Dawkins has found his belief in fundamentalist atheism. Practicing Christians are almost always conservatives because they already have a religion that has stood the test of time and have no need of destructive alternatives. G. K. Chesterton said it best in one of his *Father Brown* books. He had his famous fictional detective say: "It's the first effect of not believing in God that you lose your common sense. It's drowning all your old rationalism and scepticism, it's coming in like a sea; and the name of it is superstition. The first effect of not believing in God is to believe in anything. And a dog is an omen and a cat is a mystery" [34]

Chapter 3

Christianity, Atheism, and Morality

"In view of such harmony in the cosmos which I, with my limited human mind, am able to recognize, there are yet people who say here is no God. But what really makes me angry is that they quote me for the support of such views."
Albert Einstein Nobel Prize winning physicist

Christianity and a Moral Society

We all want to live next to good neighbors and to live in a good society, but rarely ask what makes people and societies good rather than bad. We call people and societies good when they seek to help us rather than exploit us; value us and have an active concern our well-being, and generally seek to do the "right thing." Behaving in such a way is called moral behavior. Moral people obviously act in more virtuous and principled ways than immoral people, which benefits both themselves and society, and whatever benefits society benefits everyone, including atheists. Even the 18th century French philosopher and skeptic Voltaire knew the value of religion to himself: "I want my attorney, my tailor, my servants, even my wife to believe in God...because then I shall be robbed and cuckolded less often."[1]

A free society is held together by the voluntary obedience of its citizens to moral rules. We get these moral rules from parents, teachers, and others with our best interests in mind, but ultimately, they come from God and His commandments ("Thou shalt not steal," "Love thy neighbor as thyself," "Do unto others as you would have them do onto you," and so forth). It was this sense of morality that moved the great British public intellectual and medieval historian, C.S. Lewis, to abandon his atheism for Christianity. Lewis wrote that "human beings, all over the earth, have this curious idea that they ought to behave in a certain way, and cannot really get rid of it."[2] He argued that because there is this pressing moral law there must be a moral law giver and that God as reasons for imbuing humans with moral awareness. True morality stems from the nature of God because only He can provide a coherent foundation for objective moral values and duties. Without God, we do not have an objective basis by which to make moral judgments and are left with a moral relativism that asserts "good" and "bad" depend on culture or on whom you ask.

Neuroscientist Sam Harris (one of the Four Horsemen of atheism) says that God does not exist, and that the foundation for objective moral values and duties lies in science, which he evidently conflates with atheism. Albert Einstein would say Harris got it backwards: "You are right in speaking of the moral foundations of science, but you cannot turn round and speak of the scientific foundations of morality...every attempt to reduce ethics to scientific formulae must fail."[3] While many atheists probably subscribe to the universality of human rights and are good and moral people who care about others, care about justice, value the good and denounce evil, they cannot provide the ultimate justification necessary for a universal objective morality by which good and evil are clearly understood and delineated. When atheists prove to be of excellent moral character, they unknowingly are obeying C. S. Lewis' pressing moral law that we call conscience. Romans 2:14-15 probably put it best many centuries before Lewis: "For when Gentiles, who do not have the law, by nature do the things in the law, these, although not having the law, are a law to themselves, who show the work of the law written in their hearts, their conscience also bearing witness, and between themselves their thoughts accusing or else excusing them." This essentially means that unbelievers cannot do whatever they please because there is something that reveals God in themselves. God has placed a *capacity* within them called a conscience to identify what is right or wrong which they must obey.

Atheism as a worldview is nihilistic and provides no basis for affirming objective moral values. It is a cynical, pessimistic view that views human beings as mere byproducts of pitiless nature that have evolved on an insignificant rocky planet located in one of the billions of galaxies swirling around in a hostile, mindless, and accidental universe. Why in this view should we think that human beings have any more moral worth than cockroaches? Richard Dawkins put the atheistic view of human worth honestly when he says, "there is at bottom no design, no purpose, no evil, no good, nothing but pointless indifference...We are machines for propagating DNA. . . It is every living object's sole reason for being."[4] If these depressing words are a reality, then all is permissible.

To my knowledge, the first person to proclaim that if God is dead all is permissible was the 19th century arch-atheist German philosopher Friedrich Wilhelm Nietzsche. Nietzsche was a strange creature who considered love "the greatest danger" and morality as humanity's greatest weakness. He taught that humanity can only become free if it rejects the idea of the divine, arguing like Dawkins that good and evil are simply social constructs that the weak have imposed on the moral neutrality of nature to control the strong.

Good and evil do not exist in reality and are inventions that lead to the development of a conscience, which he abhorred because it inhibits the greatness of the strong. Nietzsche believed that we must get rid of our false morality, and to do this we have to abandon Christianity. Nietzsche's *ubermensch* ("supermen") will evolve their own morality to fill the vacuum. He wrote: "All superior men who were irresistibly drawn to throw off the yoke of any kind of morality and to frame new laws."[5] If God is dead, meaning, morality, and reason die with him, and all that is left are the relentless drives and desires of the *ubermensch*, as Nietzsche candidly acknowledged:

> When one gives up Christian belief one thereby deprives oneself of the right to Christian morality... Christianity is a system, a consistently thought out and complete view of things. If one breaks out of it a fundamental idea, the belief in God, one thereby breaks the whole thing to pieces: one has nothing of any consequence left in one's hand... Christian morality is a command: its origin is transcendental... it possesses truth only if God is truth – *it stands or falls with the belief in God* (my emphasis).[6]

Unlike Nietzsche, Sam Harris values morality and argues that the purpose of morality is to advance human well-being, a position with which I wholeheartedly agree. He defines well-being in terms of being in a state of happiness and satisfaction with one's life. I can agree with this too, but he trashed religion as inimical to these goals and doesn't want to acknowledge any underlying purpose of our search for these things. He thus believes that a secular/atheist morality is not only possible, but superior to that supplied by Christianity. Along with Christopher Hitchens, Harris believes "that "religion poisons everything," and its practice leads to poorer health and impedes social progress. We will interrogate these absurd claims in the historical, psychological, medical, and sociological literature. If atheistic morality is superior to Christian morality, we should expect atheism to lead to good societies and happy individuals, families, and societies, and Christianity to produce the opposite.

Atheist Morality: The Soviet Union, China, and Nazi Germany

The utter destructiveness of atheism was made as plain as day in the 20th century by the practices of former Soviet Union, China, and Hitler's Germany. Atheism splattered the 20th century with the blood and tears of millions. Militant atheists turn a blind eye to the historical record and the cruel legacy of atheist morality because it is a black hole in the center of their worldview that they know will suck in their arguments if they dare approach it. The legacy of atheism has left an indelible blotch on the soul of humanity, resulting in the death of over 100 million people around the globe, and with many millions more plodding through a life of meaninglessness and degradation as Dawkinsian "survival machines" waiting for death and oblivion.

Karl Marx knew that if the socialist revolution is to be successful anywhere, the people must be spiritually disarmed by ridding a country of its two epicenters of morality—religion and the family. Marx wrote: "Once the earthly family is discovered to be the secret of the heavenly family, the former must be destroyed in theory and in practice."[7] After the Russian Revolution the Soviet Union destroyed thousands of churches and declared the state to be officially atheist, and then went after Marx's "earthly family." The Soviets passed legislation legitimizing the offspring of the unmarried, made divorce available on demand, and encouraged "free love" as the "essence of communist living."[8] This atheistic agenda threw morality out of the window and Ivan's abandoned their Natasha's from Riga to Vladivostok. This led to millions of father-absent children roaming the streets who formed criminal gangs and ran rampant across the country.[9] After 10 years of chaos, the government turned 180 degrees and began praising marriage and the family, condemning divorce, and restored the legal concepts of legitimacy and illegitimacy.

But this about-turn did not stop the rot because atheism remained the official state religion. Peter Hitchens has harrowing tales to tell of his time as a journalist in Moscow before the fall of the Soviet Union in his book *The rage against God*. He wrote of bribes to receive good treatment at hospitals, riots over cancelled vodka rations, abortion as a means of birth control, mistrust of neighbors as possible informants, two families living in squalid apartments meant for one, theft of everything not nailed down, and a level of incivility that made a New Yorker sound like an English gentleman. The experience Hitchens had of an atheist society helped to convert this former socialist and atheist (and brother of Christopher Hitchens) to Christianity.[10]

Nobel Prize winner for literature, Aleksandr Solzhenitsyn, told us why Russia became a dystopian nightmare in his 1983 Templeton Lecture:

> More than half a century ago, while I was still a child, I recall hearing a number of older people offer the following explanation for the great disasters that had befallen Russia: Men have forgotten God; that's why all this has happened...I have read hundreds of books, collected hundreds of personal testimonies, and have already contributed eight volumes of my own toward the effort of clearing away the rubble left by that upheaval. But if I were asked today to formulate as concisely as possible the main cause of the ruinous Revolution that swallowed up some sixty million of our people, I could not put it more accurately

than to repeat: Men have forgotten God; that's why all this has happened.[11]

The current president of Russia, Vladimir Putin, agrees with Solzhenitsyn. In his 2014 state of the nation address to the Russian people, Putin said: "Many Euro-Atlantic countries have moved away from their roots, including Christian values...Policies are being pursued that place on the same level a multi-child family and a same-sex partnership, a faith in God and a belief in Satan. This is the path to degradation." He further said that social and religious conservatism is the only key to preventing the world from slipping into "chaotic darkness." The head of the Russian Orthodox Church, Patriarch Kirill I, also noted the spiritual disarmament of the people in Western countries: "The general political direction of the elite bears, without doubt, an anti-Christian and anti-religious character...We have been through an epoch of atheism, and we know what it is to live without God...We want to shout to the whole world, 'Stop!'" [12] Putin and Kirill know better than most how important Christianity is because both lived most of their lives in Godless Russia and experienced its social and spiritual malaise.

Qingbo Xu documents similar efforts to kill the Christianity and the family during the Chinese Cultural Revolution. The communists destroyed hundreds of churches and imprisoned or killed thousands of priests, ministers, and practicing Christians. Atheism was proclaimed the official religion, and the family was to be destroyed as far as possible:

> Nepotism or kindness to blood relatives was forcibly disrupted in this decade, especially in the families who were not from the proletariat. They had no right to love their children, parents, and other family members. The function of individual-level interactions of these people was not to develop and maintain long-term relationships with kin and friends. Kin and friend networks had to be dismantled since [according to the party line] they ruined one's subsistence and well-being.[13]

The Russian government is now rebuilding hundreds of destroyed churches and actively promoting Christianity in all levels of society. The Chinese government is still officially atheist but is having to tolerate Christianity given its widespread popularity since Mao Zedong's death as people seek meaning in their lives. Fenggang Yang, a leading scholar of Chinese religion, estimates that if the current rate of growth continues, by 2030 China will have the largest Christian congregation in the world at about 247 million.[14] However, Chinese politician Zhu Weiqun has stated that the Communist Party should "unambiguously promote Marxist atheism to society," describing it as "the nations' mainstream ideology," and the party should seek to "strengthen propaganda education about a scientific worldview, including atheism." [15]

Although never "officially" atheist, Nazi Germany is yet another example of the evil of atheism running amok. The anti-Jewish holocaust is known to everyone, but little is known about Nazi attacks on Christianity. Much of the evidence of the Nazi's plans for religion comes from the historical record of the Nuremberg war-crimes trials of 1945 compiled by General William Donovan of the OSS, the precursor of today's CIA. There is also much evidence from other sources that Hitler hated Christianity and was a staunch believer in Nietzsche's concept of the *ubermensch*. But Hitler was anything but ignorant of politics or mass psychology. When he was struggling for power in Weimar Germany in the 1920s, his arch enemies were communists and avowed atheists, so it was politically expedient to paint himself as a "defender of the faith" and traditional Western values against the Godless communists. When Hitler became chancellor of German in 1933, however, he began to do whatever he could to de-Christianize Germany and move it toward a pagan world of "religion of race and blood" and worship of the state. During Hitler's dictatorship, more than 6,000 pastors, priests, monks, and nuns were imprisoned or executed in Germany, and the same measures were taken in all occupied countries.[16]

The Nazis could not overly antagonize religious Germans during the war, but Nazi documents show that after their expected victory, they would attack Christianity the way they attacked Judaism: The Nuremberg war crimes indictment reads in part: "The Nazi's persecution of Catholic and Protestant churches was a classic power struggle. At first, the Party followed Hitler's politically pragmatic policy of placating the Churches while undermining their political power. Once political dominance had been achieved, the churches were no longer needed, and the Party turned to a more radical and aggressive policy spearheaded by Himmler."[17] According to other Nuremberg war-crimes documents: "The Nazi conspirators, by promoting beliefs and practices incompatible with Christian teaching, sought to subvert the influence of the Churches over the people and in particular over the youth of Germany. They avowed their aim to eliminate the Christian Churches in Germany and sought to substitute Nazi institutions and Nazi beliefs and pursued a programme of persecution of priests, clergy and members of monastic orders whom they deemed opposed to their purposes and confiscated Church property." [18]

I don't think anyone who lived in any of these three countries during these time periods believes that atheism builds better moral foundations for better societies. A story told by philosopher of science and great Christian apologist William Lane Craig is instructive. He tells of meeting an eminent Russian cosmologist, Andrei Grib, in St, Petersburg and asking him why there was a great upsurge of Christianity following the collapse of communism. Grib replied, "Well, in mathematics we have something called 'proof by the opposite.' You can prove something is true by showing its opposite to be false. For seventy years we have tried Marxist atheism in this country, and it didn't work. So, everyone figured the opposite must be true."[19]

Individual Happiness: Atheism v. Christianity

Although he doesn't acknowledge it, Richard Dawkins is surely aware of the pain, misery, and squalor in counties that embrace an atheistic worldview, yet he wants to turn his own country in the same direction. He was instrumental in a £100,000 (about $145,000 at the time) atheist campaign to litter London's buses with the slogan "There probably is no God, so relax and enjoy life," Commenting on the campaign, Mary Kenny wrote: "Far from relaxing and enjoying life, most atheists I have encountered are gloomy blighters with a depressing and nihilistic message that there is no purpose to life so where's the point of anything?"[20] The bus campaign doesn't seem to have had much impact on people who use them because 2016 figures published by Britain's Office for National Statistics Well-Being research program found that atheists report lower levels of happiness, life satisfaction, and feeling of self-worth than religious people, with practicing Christians and Jews topping the list on all indicators of well-being.[21] Another U.K. study comparing evangelical Christians with national norms of a number of health and well-being indicators found that the evangelicals score higher on all of them. The study's author concluded "In general, the faith and values and the disciplined lifestyles reported by evangelicals appear to be beneficial to health and well-being. This could well be enhanced by their strong sense of purpose and belonging to God, stable families, and caring faith communities"[22]

In the United States, the Pew Research Center conducted more than 35,000 telephone interviews and found that highly religious people—defined as those who say they pray every day and attend religious services each week—"are more engaged with their extended families, more likely to volunteer, more involved in their communities and generally happier with the way things are going in their lives." The study also finds that almost half of highly religious people visit extended family at least once or twice a month compared with only three-in-ten who are less religious. Furthermore, 65 percent of the highly religious donated money, time or goods to help the poor in the past week compared with 41 percent of the less religious, and 40 percent of the highly religious said they were "very happy" compared to 29 percent of the less religious.[23]

Extreme unhappiness can mean clinical-level depression. In a book about depression and suicide, psychiatrist Julia Kristeva agreed with Mary Kenny that atheists are "gloomy blighters;" writing that: "The depressed person is a radical, sullen atheist."[24] Being depressed may lead to suicidal thoughts and then suicide itself. Kristeva was on the money; a 2004 study reported in the *American Journal of Psychiatry* concluded that:

> Religiously unaffiliated subjects had significantly more lifetime suicide attempts and more first-degree relatives who committed suicide than subjects who endorsed a religious affiliation...Furthermore, subjects with no religious affiliation perceived fewer reasons for living, particularly fewer moral objections to suicide. In terms of clinical characteristics, religiously unaffiliated subjects had more lifetime impulsivity, aggression, and past substance use disorder.[25]

Another such study examining the relationship between spiritual values and church attendance with suicidal thoughts in the nationwide Canadian Community Health Survey found similar results. The research team concluded: "Results suggest that religious attendance is associated with decreased suicide attempts in the general population and in those with a mental illness independent of the effects of social supports." [26]

It is understandable that anyone who actively reflects on their atheism (which very few probably do) has a very good chance at being depressed at the meaninglessness of it all; a "gloomy blighter" is not a pleasant person to be around. Blaise Pascal, the brilliant 17th century French mathematician and physicist, wrote in his insightful book *Pensees* ("thoughts") that, "There are only three types of people; those who have found God and serve him; those who have not found God and seek him, and those who live not seeking, or finding him. The first are rational and happy; the second unhappy and rational, and the third foolish and unhappy." [27] This is indicated by the above mentioned Pew Research Forum comparing atheist and Christian relations with extended families, as is the finding that 37 percent of atheists never marry as opposed to 17 percent of Protestants and Catholics. Whichever comes first—atheist or "gloomy blighter"—it is undeniable that people who wish others a Merry Christmas in the true spirit of that day are far happier eating their Christmas plum pudding than atheists just going through the motions.

Christianity and Loving Families

We have all heard the old saying that "The family that prays together, stays together" and wondered how true it is. It is very true and has been established by numerous studies. Marriages in which both spouses attend church regularly are 2.4 times less likely to end in divorce than marriages in neither spouse attends a place of worship.[28] In fact, more than 6 decades of studies show that religious commitment is the most important predictor of stability and happiness in marriage.[29] Not only are religious families more likely to stay together, they do so happier and healthier than non-religious families. A stable marriage—religious or otherwise—is positively associated with better physical, mental, and emotional health of parents and children. A strong and stable marriage is related to religious practices such as church attendance and living one's faith. A study of the marital well-being of 354 couples found that religiousness is related to marital well-being through what the authors call "relational virtues" (commitment, forgiveness, emotional closeness, and sacrifice).[30] Another study found that the more married couples practiced their religious faith, the more satisfied they were with their marriages. Sixty percent of those couples who attended a place of worship at least once a month rated their marriages "very satisfactory" compared with 43 percent who attended less often or not at all.[31]

Drawing on studies composed of over 30,000 respondents, Bradford Wilcox found that the more husbands attended religious services, the happier their wives were with the level of affection, understanding, and quality time spent with them.[32] Another national study of over 9,000 respondents showed that adults who frequently attend religious services as children were significantly more likely to provide assistance to parents in their old age. Religious attenders also reported higher quality relationships and more frequent contact with parents. The researchers concluded, "It appears that the influence of religion in fostering early parent–child ties noted in prior research extends throughout the life course, influencing ties between adult children and their parents."[33] These results are in line with the Pew Center study finding that religious people are much more likely that the non-religious to maintain strong ties with extended family. This recalls the wisdom of Proverbs 22:6: "Train up a child in the way he should go; even when he is old he will not depart from it."

The Family, Religion, and Antisocial Behavior

In the Broadway musical *West Side Story*, a group of delinquents informed Officer Krupke that their mothers all are junkies and their fathers all are drunks, so "natcherly we're punks." The moral and spiritual values of Christian parents preclude the kinds of behavior, such as alcohol and drug abuse, divorce, and out-of-wedlock births that lead many children to engage in antisocial behaviors. In an examination of 113 studies linking attendance at religious services to criminal offending and illegal drug use, the authors concluded that: "attending religious services is the best documented correlate of [the prevention of] crime."[34]

Religious families monitor their children's educational and extra-curricular behavior, providing them with moral guidance in the context of warmth and caring in God, and parents and children in religious households rate the quality of their relationships with one another significantly higher than do parents and children in non-religious households. A review of relevant research noted that: "The tendency of religious beliefs to place great value on children increases parental motivation to spend time and energy on their children. Not only are religious parents less likely to abuse or yell at their children but they are also more likely to hug and praise them often and to display better parent functioning."[35]

On the other hand, growing up in a fatherless home, as an ever-increasing number of children are, increases the probability on being reared in amoral circumstances in unstable families by single, poor, and often isolated mothers. Religious belief reduces the probability of an unmarried woman bearing children. A Fragile Families Research Brief found that "Mothers who attend religious services frequently are 73 percent more likely to be married at childbirth than mothers who attend services infrequently or not at all." [36] The sad legacy of growing up in a fatherless home is reported vividly:

Eighty-five percent of youth in prison have an absent father, 71% of high school dropouts are fatherless, 90% of homeless and runaway children have an absent father and fatherless children and youth exhibit higher levels of depression and suicide, delinquency, promiscuity and teen pregnancy, behavioral problems and illicit and licit substance abuse, diminished self-concepts, and are more likely to be victims of exploitation and abuse.[37]

The U.S. Department of Health and Human Services reports rates of out-of-wedlock births of 73.5 percent for African Americans, 53.3 percent for Hispanics, 29 percent for whites, and 17 percent for Asian Americans.[38] It is thus no surprise that poor minority children are vastly overrepresented in American prisons due to the tragically high rate of single-parent households in which they are raised. A survey of the benefits of family stability prepared for the U.S. Department of Health and Human Services noted that " children from two-parent families live longer and enjoy overall better health than children from single-parent families or whose parents divorced in childhood."[39]A huge Swedish study of 986,342 children likewise found that children living in a single-parent household showed greatly elevated risks of psychiatric disease, suicide or attempted suicide, injury, and drug and alcohol addiction. [40]

Religion and Physical and Mental Health

A survey of physicians in the *Journal of Family Practice* found that 96 percent of them agreed that spiritual well-being is important for physical and mental health.[41] Karl Marx, on the other hand, believed that religion is the opiate of the masses; a childish fairy tale with a hope of an afterlife whose soothing comfort prevented believers from embracing his vision of a communist paradise on earth. Sigmund Freud likewise saw religion as superstition and a sign of psychological immaturity, but for Freud we are all at least a little neurotic and psychologically immature. There may be some religious believers that fit the description of Marx and Freud but reasoned Christianity leads to personal and social enlightenment, psychological maturity, and greater happiness and physical and mental health.

Take longevity for instance. Robert Hummer and his colleagues looked at the National Health Interview Survey data on cause of death to examine look at the role of religious involvement and concluded: "We showed that religious involvement is strongly associated with adult mortality in a graded fashion. Those who never attend services exhibit the highest risk of death, and those who attend more than once a week exhibit the lowest risk."[42] The risk of death is 1.87 times greater for those who never attend services compared with those who attend more than once a week, which translates to a seven-year difference in life expectancy at age 20. Another study followed an initial group of 5,286 adults for 28 years and found that individuals who attended church one or more times a week were 23 percent less likely to die in follow-up periods than non-attenders.[43]

Hypertension and associated cardiovascular problems are the number-one health scourge of modern America, and religion is a spiritual anti-body. Physician Daniel Hall conducted a review of a number of studies involving more than 21,000 subjects comparing various mechanisms such as exercise, diet, and medication that lower the risk of heart disease. His conclusion is startling: "The real-world, practical significance of regular religious attendance is comparable to commonly recommended therapies, and rough estimates even suggest that religious attendance may be more cost-effective than statins [cholesterol lowering medication]."[44] A study of 36,000 Norwegians found that people who regularly attended religious services had significantly lower blood pressure. This study found a gradient such that churchgoers with increasing attendance had decreasing blood pressure.[45] One of my own studies of hypertension found that after controlling for other health-related factors, 30.9 percent of non-church attenders were hypertensive versus only 7 percent of regular church attenders.[46]

Christianity and Economic Benefits

We have seen that the Christian worldview provided impetus for science. Science begets technology, and technology creates jobs and general wealth. Given that we already find ourselves in a technological world created by others, what might be the role of contemporary Christian morality to economic prosperity? According to economist Kelly Mua, there is a strong link between Christianity and prosperity that exists "mainly by fostering religious beliefs that influence individual traits such as honesty, work ethic, thrift, and openness to strangers."[47] A team of economists using data from 66 countries encompassing the years 1981 through 1997 conclude: "We find that on average, religious beliefs are associated with 'good' economic attitudes, where ''good' is defined as conducive to higher per capita income and growth...Overall, we find that Christian religions are more positively associated with attitudes conducive to economic growth." [48]

A number of scholars have actually attempted to put a dollar amount on the benefits of Christianity to America. In his book *America's Blessings: How Religion Benefits Everyone, Including Atheists*, Rodney Stark estimates that Christianity benefits the American economy to the tune of $2.6 trillion per year. He arrived at that figure by asking: "What would it cost if America suddenly were transformed into a fully secularized society?"[49] That is, if there were no practicing Christians in America behaving according to Christian morality, how much might the costs to the U.S. economy be?

Because practicing Christians are less likely to be involved in crime and in drug and alcohol abuse, this represents a massive saving for the criminal justice system. Happier intact homes mean less divorce, illegitimacy, and parental abuse and neglect, leading to huge savings in welfare and far less criminal behavior. Religious schools and homeschooling not only provide superior moral training; they also produce children who get better grades and who are more likely to graduate. This means better job prospects, less unemployment, fewer deadbeats, and lower unemployment benefits being paid out. Better physical and mental health among Christians saves billions in health care costs. We have seen that regular religious attendees give more money to charity and volunteer their time much more than others, and more charitable giving and volunteering saves many millions of dollars in what otherwise would be a burden on the taxpayer.

A massive study filled with voluminous statistics by economists Brian and Melissa Grim arrived at three estimates the value of faith-based businesses, institutions, and churches to the American economy. Their most conservative estimate, taking into account only the revenues of faith-based organizations is $378 billion annually. Their second estimate, taking into consideration an estimate of the market value of goods and services provided by religious organizations and the contribution of faith-based businesses roots puts the value at over $1 trillion annually. Their third estimate includes those behaviors Stark included. In their own words: "Our third, higher-end estimate recognizes that people of faith conduct their affairs to some extent (however imperfectly) inspired and guided by their faith ideals. This higher-end estimate...places the value of faith to U.S. society at $4.8 trillion annually, or the equivalent of nearly a third of America's gross domestic product (GDP)."[50]

Charitable Giving

In Christian thought, the highest form of morality is love, as St. Paul's noted in I Corinthians 13: "...If I have the gift of prophecy and can fathom all mysteries and all knowledge, and if I have a faith that can move mountains, but do not have love, I am nothing. And now abideth faith, hope, charity, these three; but the greatest of these is charity" The love of God for man and the love of man for God must be manifested in an active concern for others made palpable by charitable giving of time, money, and blood donations. No other religious or secular body has ever been more forceful in pushing the idea of helping the unfortunate as Christianity. As American educator Carlton Hayes put it: "From the wellspring of Christian compassion, our Western civilization has drawn its inspiration, and its sense of duty, for feeding the hungry, giving drink to the thirsty, looking after the homeless, clothing the naked, tending the sick and visiting the prisoner."[51]

It is no surprise to find that practicing Christians live up to the "Love thy neighbor..." command far more than atheists. A national sample of 12,100 adults indicated "strongly that more frequent church attendance and greater participation in religious activities increase the levels and likelihood both religious and/or secular giving"[52] Another study of 30,000 people from 50 different sites across the U.S. found that people who attend church once or more per week were 25 percent more likely to donate money, and 23 percent more likely to volunteer time than their secular counterparts.[53] Yet another study across 29 states found that practicing Christians give far more time and money, and far more often, to both religious and secular causes than secularists.[54]

Caveats

Two caveats regarding the interpretation of the facts presented here are in order. First, all the secular benefits accruing from Christian beliefs are far from the only reasons for belief in God, and some theologians might dismiss these pragmatic factors as a secular version of Pascal's Wager (it is wise to accept God since you have much to gain if you do and much to lose if you don't). Belief in God comes from the depths of the heart, and one must voluntarily place Him there because he is God, and not because it is prudent or self-serving to do so. However, this is not an argument that an atheist would find at all credible. Thus, I am simply pointing out arguments that Christians can use to deflect any atheist claims that Christianity does no good in a secular sense for the individual or society. One wonders how the new atheists can make the patently false claim that religion "poisons" everything when confronted with massive evidence to the contrary. Perhaps some religions do poison everything. Dawkins has stated that the events of 9/11 gave birth to his militant atheism, but why blame Christianity for 9/11? And why place Christianity, a religion that showers the world with aid, in the same box with one that showers the world with bombs and bullets?

Second, theism overlaps with conservativism and Republicanism just as atheism overlaps with liberalism and Democratism. Studies consistently show a conservative/Republican advantage over liberal/Democratic individuals on all of the indicators of well-being presented here to almost identical degrees. That is, conservatives and Republicans are happier, more likely to be married, enjoy better physical and mental health, and give more to of themselves in terms of money, blood, and volunteering than their liberal Democratic counterparts.[55] So do we see this because most conservative Republicans are Christians, or because most Christians are conservative Republicans? Perhaps conservativism and Christianity are both indicators of the increasing wisdom humans acquire once they leave behind their youthful rebellious attachment to socialism/liberalism and atheism. There are numerous examples of famous individuals who were former strong liberals, socialists, or communists who became conservatives with maturity. Internet searches will reveal lists of them, but you won't find lists of famous conservatives who became liberals. I would love to see a plausible explanation for this from a committed leftist.

Chapter 4

Christianity, Western Democracy, and Cultural Marxism

> "No Human society has ever been able to maintain both order and freedom, both cohesiveness and liberty apart from the moral precepts of the Christian religion applied and accepted by all classes."
> John Jay, first Chief Justice of the United States Supreme Court

Christianity and Democracy

Along with science and capitalism, the other great benefit of Christianity to the secular world is democracy. Let me emphasize again that none of these benefits were ever intended or envisioned by the early Christians, but ideas, values, and beliefs have consequences latent within them. Ideas and beliefs—such as the belief that God is a God of reason who wants us to get to know him through his creation—shape motives and motives produce actions. It is only when the effects of these actions are manifest that we can start tracing them back to motives, and then back further to ideas, values, and beliefs. For instance, the idea of the equality of all humanity is a central idea of democracy and is something stated by St. Paul in Galatians 3:28: "There is neither Jew nor Greek, there is neither bond nor free, there is neither male nor female: for ye are all one in Christ Jesus." Paul did not mean this as a call for voting booths and bicameral parliaments; neither did he mean that secular distinctions among people should be disregarded. He meant that whatever secular distinctions existed, all people were God's creations and equally deserving of the glory of God and the promise of eternal life. All humans share the same origin, the same nature, and are called to share the same destiny regardless of their rank on Earth. As Malachi 2:10 tells us. "Have we not all one father? hath not one God created us?" It would be centuries before it was recognized that all people are equally entitled to all political and civil rights. These rights were first recognized in Christian societies and are yet to be seen in most non-Christian societies.

In St. Paul's time, severe inequalities or all kinds existed, including the practice of slavery. Even after the Emperor Constantine converted the Roman Empire to Christianity, slavery still existed throughout Europe. The Church gradually suppressed the slavery of Christians in Europe by the year 1000, although it was replaced by the less onerous institution of serfdom. In the 18th and 19th centuries, anti-slavery activism in Europe and America was founded on Christian morality and the idea of the brotherhood of all humanity; there were no abolitionist movements anywhere in the world that were not founded on Christian convictions; not one.[1]

The U.S. and U.K., the world's leading Christian democracies, engaged in slavery and/or the slave trade, and Charles Darwin rebuked both countries for doing so. However, he also noted that they sacrificed much to end it: "It makes one's blood boil, yet heart tremble, to think that Englishmen and our American descendants, with their boastful cry of liberty, have been and are so guilty: but it is a consolation to reflect that we have made a greater sacrifice than ever made by any nation to expiate our sin."[2] This was written shortly after Great Britain freed all colonial slaves at the cost of £20 million, which was 37 percent of the government's revenue in 1831.[3] In addition, there was an immense cost in lives and money of the 50-year patrol of Royal Navy warships that intercepting over 1,600 slave ships and liberated over 150,000 slaves.[4] This sacrifice of lives and resources was driven by a robust abolition campaign spearheaded by a coalition of non-conformist churches and the Church of England. The United States paid an even greater price in lives and resources to finally end slavery in the Civil War.

Judaism is also conducive to democracy, but it is incompatible with the other Hebraic faith, Islam. While Judaism and Christianity are often dogmatic about religious faith, Judaism and Christianity avoid political, civil, and social dogmatism, but Islam restricts free thought in all spheres of life. As Norman Graebner observes:

> Muhammad had crammed the Koran with political maxims, criminal and civil laws, and even theories of science; the biblical Gospel, on the other hand, imposed no demands on faith beyond the establishment of a proper relationship with God and men and men with each other. It was this quality in Christianity, among others, that permitted it to exist in a cultivated, democratic civilization.[5]

Alfred Stepan agrees with Graebner when he writes that most political and historical scholars find that Islam is incompatible with democracy: "According to this view, allowing free elections in Islamic countries would bring to power governments that would use these democratic freedoms [elections] to destroy democracy itself"[6] This was written in 2000 and was remarkably prescient. We witnessed the chaos and utter brutality that befell many Islamic Arab states after the "Arab Spring" in 2011 that many naïve Westerners thought would usher in democracy in the Middle East.

The Reformation and the Slow and Bloody Road to Democracy

There is no real separation of mosque and state in any Islamic country, where the law privileges Muslims over non-Muslims in all things. All laws passed by secular politicians must pass scrutiny by religious authorities. A somewhat similar situation existed in Christian Europe for centuries in which a cozy relationship existed between prince and priest. Thomas Jefferson noted that: "In every country and in every age, the priest has been hostile to liberty. He is always in alliance with the despot, abetting his abuses in return for protection to his own. It is error alone that needs the support of government. Truth can stand by itself."[7]

Religious dissenters had to tread lightly when the Church of Rome reigned supreme, but this changed after Martin Luther nailed his Ninety-Five Theses to the door of Wittenberg Castle Church in 1515, setting the Protestant Reformation in motion. Luther translated the Bible into the vernacular and taught that it, not the Pope and his priests, was the source of divinely revealed knowledge of salvation. (Let us not forget, however, that it was the early Christian community that was the source of both the Catholic Church and the scriptures) These ideas found fertile soil because they came in the midst of the Renaissance, a cultural movement that profoundly affected all intellectual life in Europe. The Renaissance was an age in which all kinds of political, philosophical, social, artistic, and scientific were changing. The primary impetus for this was the revival of ancient Greek philosophy, which was brought into Italy by Greek scholars fleeing Constantinople after it fell to the Ottoman Turks. Most importantly, the Renaissance placed human beings at the center of life. It was a time of questioning received orthodoxy which changed the intellectual landscape and encouraged many Church reformers, including Martin Luther. The dissemination of Luther's ideas was greatly aided by the mass production of Bibles made possible by Johannes Gutenberg's invention of the printing press.

The Protestant Reformation led to conflicts between Lutherans and Catholics for state sponsorship, which led to numerous civil and interstate wars that devastated much of the continent. To end religious strife, Europe's nations and principalities signed a treaty known as the Peace of Augsburg in 1555 and settled on the principle of *cuius regio, eius religio* ("Whose realm, his religion"). In essence, this principle meant that all individuals living in a given state must follow the religion of the state sovereign and resulted in the *de facto* division of Western Christian Europe into Lutheran and Catholic king-doms.[8]

The Peace of Augsburg still affirmed the unity of church and state and failed to address the issue of religious pluralism, which was becoming widespread among Protestants. The practice of any non-established religions was forbid-den, and those who did were branded heretics and faced banishment if they did not repent. The rise of Calvinism as a rival to Lutheranism brought more conflict, including the Thirty Years War that engulfed much of Western Europe from 1618 to 1648. This series of wars ended with a number of treaties collec-tively known as the Peace of Westphalia. The Peace of Westphalia was a pro-found turning point in the history of Western civilization marking the dim beginnings of the modern democratic nation state in the Western world. The Peace of Westphalia abolished the sovereigns right to control matters of reli-gious faith in their territories and provided a model for dealing with religious disagreements in a constitutional manner. The Peace of Westphalia meant that rulers no longer had the right to foist their religious convictions on their subjects or to interfere with their religious will.[9]

Atheists take these religious wars and make absurd claims, such as Richard Dawkins' claim in *The God Delusion* that, "Religious wars really are fought in the name of religion, and they have been horribly frequent in history."[10] Like-wise, Sam Harris boldly states in *The End of Faith*, religion is "the most prolif-ic source of violence in our history."[11] These chaps may be decent scientists, but they are terrible historians. Robin Schumacher looks at Philip and Axel-rod's three-volume *Encyclopedia of Wars*, to decisively refute that claim. Schumacher reports that the Encyclopedia lists 1,763 wars waged over the course of human history. "Of those wars, the authors categorize 123, as being religious in nature, which is an astonishingly low. However, when one sub-tracts out those waged in the name of Islam (66), the percentage is cut by more than half to 3.23%."[12]

Nevertheless, Christians must honestly admit the violence committed in the name of Christ, while soundly condemning it as anti-Christian. As Matthew 5:9 says: "Blessed are the peacemakers for they shall be called sons of God." This does not preclude "just wars" in defense against aggression, as Ambrose and Augustine made clear centuries ago. Christ does not wish to rule the Earth by military conquest: there is no universal caliphate to be won by vio-lent jihad in Christian theology. The religious wars for supremacy in Christen-dom in Europe in God's name were contrary His commands and an affront to Him.

Why Christianity is Important to Freedom and Democracy

It is ironic that while freedom requires breaking away from the tyranny of state religion, freedom requires a moral foundation that only religion can supply The American Humanist Association's motto, "Good Without God," assumes that an atheistic value system can supply the moral foundations for democracy, but we have seen that this is an egregious falsehood. "Good without God" will only last as long as society has a cadre of people nourished on Judeo-Christian values remaining on Earth; after they have gone and we are left with citizens who have been raised in a society that has given God the boot, watch out! Robert Winthrop, one time speaker of the House of representative, put it cogently: "Men...must necessarily be controlled, either by a power within them, or by a power without them; either by the Word of God, or by the strong arm of man; either by the Bible, or by the bayonet."[13] George Washington stressed this in his farewell address to the nation upon leaving his second term as President of the United States:

> Of all the dispositions and habits which lead to political prosperity, Religion and Morality are indispensable supports. In vain would that man claim the tribute of Patriotism who should labor to subvert these great Pillars of human happiness-these firmest props of the duties of Men and citizens...Let it simply be asked, Where is the security for property, for reputation, for life, if the sense of religious obligation desert the oaths, which are the instruments of investigation in Courts of Justice? And let us with caution indulge the supposition that morality can be maintained without religion. Whatever may be conceded to the influence of refined education on minds of peculiar structure, reason and experience both forbid us to expect that National morality can prevail in exclusion of religious principle.[14]

Only in a mature democracy with checks and balances and the rule of law does everyone have a chance to safely have their say. People in mature democracies can criticize their government with impunity, which the vast bulk of humankind could not do throughout history. The freedom of thought and of religious liberty enshrined in the First Amendment of the Bill of Rights recognizes that, in the domain of moral conscience, there is a power higher than the state that grants us these inalienable rights. However, G. K. Chesterton tells us that it is difficult to freely exercise these rights if there is no higher power than the government:

> But the truth is that it is only by believing in God that we can ever criticise the Government. Once abolish the God, and the Government becomes the God. The fact is written all across human history; but it is

written more plainly across that recent history of Russia; which was created by Lenin. There the Government is the God, and all the more the God, because it proclaims aloud in accents of thunder, like every other God worth worshipping, the one essential commandment: "Thou shalt have no other gods before Me." The truth is that Irreligion is the opium of the people. Wherever the people do not believe in something beyond the world, they will worship the world. But, above all, they will worship the strongest thing in the world.[15]

Alexis de Tocqueville, the great French social philosopher of American life, noted in his masterpiece on American society *Democracy in America* that America's freedoms and bounty rested on its religion: "there is no country in the world where the Christian religion retains a greater influence over the souls of men than in America; and there can be no greater proof of its utility and of its conformity to human nature than that its influence is powerfully felt over the most enlightened and free nation of the earth."[16] Even agnostics such as historians Will and Ariel Durant know the value of religion to society:

Even the skeptical historian develops a humble respect for religion, since he sees it functioning, and seemingly indispensable, in every land and age. To the unhappy, the suffering, the bereaved, the old, it has brought supernatural comforts valued by millions of souls as more precious than any natural aid. It has helped parents and teachers to discipline the young. It has conferred meaning and dignity upon the lowliest existence, and through its sacraments has made for stability by transforming human covenants into solemn relationships with God... *There is no significant example in history, before our time, of a society successfully maintaining moral life without the aid of religion."*[17]

In an earlier work, Will Durant echoed George Washington's fears about a nation's morality when it abandons religion:

The intellectual classes abandon the ancient theology and—after some hesitation—the moral code allied with it; literature and philosophy become anticlerical. The movement of liberation rises to an exuberant worship of reason, and falls to a paralyzing disillusionment with every dogma and every idea. Conduct, deprived of its religious supports, deteriorates into epicurean chaos; and life itself, shorn of consoling faith, becomes a burden alike to conscious poverty and to weary wealth. In the end a society and its religion tend to fall together, like body and soul, in a harmonious death. [18]

Christianity and Cultural Marxism

Such a death of American Christian culture is the goal of a pernicious philosophy called cultural Marxism. Cultural Marxism is a theoretical synthesis of Marxist and Freudian political thought dedicated to the idea that communism can be achieved incrementally rather than violently by slowly turning the culture into Durant's "epicurean chaos." Cultural Marxists realized after the failure of the expected revolutions in Western Europe following World War I that socialism (not to be conflated with communism, but rather seen by communists as a stopping point on the road to it) cannot be achieved in the West without destroying the two epicenters of morality—Christianity and the family. For the cultural Marxist, the agents of cultural revolution would not be Marx's proletariat but rather the intellectual wordsmiths in academia and the news and entertainment media. Their foot soldiers on the streets would be groups alienated from mainstream society such as radical activists in the black, feminist, and gay communities, who are convinced that they are victims of racism, sexism, homophobia, and religious bigotry. They are also, of course, victims of Donald Trump's "bogus" election and of capitalism.

Cultural Marxism was spawned by two Marxist philosophers in the early 20th century: Hungarian Georg Lukacs and Italian Antonio Gramsci. In 1919 Lukacs became the Deputy Commissar for Culture in the short-lived (133 days) communist regime of Bela Kun in Hungary. In this position, he was able to define what we recognize as the left's agenda for American education today. As Raymond Raehn explained Lukac's curricula: "Lukacs launched what became known as 'Cultural Terrorism.' As part of this terrorism, he instituted a radical sex education program in Hungarian schools. Children were instructed in "free love, sexual intercourse, the archaic nature of middle-class family codes, the out-datedness of monogamy, and the irrelevance of religion, which deprives man of all pleasures."[19] These are the Godless values the Russians and Chinese embraced with such disastrous results, and the values being foisted on American students today in slower more subtle fashion.

For instance, Kevin Jennings, head of the Obama administration's Office of Safe and Drug-Free Schools, is an American counterpart of Lukacs. He founded the Gay, Lesbian, and Straight Education Network (GLSEN) and is a supporter of the North American Man-Boy Love Association. GLSEN has received close to $1.5 million in government grants to promote its agenda in schools.[20] The content of the GLSEN agenda is revealed in a Family Research Council document called *Homosexuality in your child's school*.[21] Among the many practices listed are the promotion of "gender neutral" bathrooms, exhorting students to attend gay pride parades, cross-dressing days, and a seminar "for youth only," on "fisting" (placing the fist in the anus of another male). Among the books GLSEN recommends for the curricula is *Rainbow Boys,* in which a teen has homosexual sex, graphically detailed, with an adult male contacted via the Internet, and *Queer 13* describing a 13-year-old boy's sexual encounter with an adult male in a bathroom. These vile books promoting dangerous immorality have replaced religious and other wholesome works teaching morality and are couched in approving terms implying this is just a normal part of growing up. If this sounds too sick to be true, please take a look at the full list of recommended books for the educational curriculum on GLSEN's website.

In Great Britain, we have the example of the notorious (and very expensive) private boarding school founded by Alexander Neill. Neill explains his educational philosophy thus: "We set out to make a school in which we should allow children freedom to be themselves. In order to do this we had to renounce all discipline, all direction, all suggestion, all moral training, all religious instruction."[22] Summerhill has been rocked by numerous sexual scandals, such as young teens being urged to have sex with each other after mock weddings, unisex bathrooms and showers, and even allegations that Neill and other teachers slept with students. This is the kind of educational atmosphere lauded by cultural Marxists that Neill would have liked to have made the norm in British schools.

When Bela Kun's revolution failed, Lukacs fled to the Soviet Union and then to Germany, where he became a member of the Marxist think tank, called the Institute of Social Research, better known as the Frankfurt School. The School was dedicated to deconstructing the economic and revolutionary basis of Marxism and to reconstruct it with an evolutionary cultural basis. Lukacs' believed that any movement capable of destroying capitalism must be "demonic" and could only succeed when the individual believes not in "a personal destiny, but the destiny of the community" in a world one "*that has been abandoned by God.*" [23] God has told us that He will never abandon anyone, but anyone can abandon God, and that is the goal of the radical left.

Because the bulk of Frankfurt School was Jewish, with Hitler's rise to power and the persecution of the Jews, the School moved to Columbia University in New York. Many of its members were appointed to positions in other elite universities where they immediately began to apply "critical thinking" to every American institution. "Critical thinking" conveys a positive message of openness to all views, but as the cultural Marxist practices it, it is the unrelenting pursuit of the negative in order to vilify and obliterate any system of thought that is counter to theirs. Michael Walsh describes critical theory as: "At once overly intellectualized and emotionally juvenile, Critical Theory— like Pandora's Box—released a horde of demons into the American psyche. When everything could be questioned, nothing could be real, and the muscular, confident empiricism that had just won the war gave way, in less than a generation, to a central-European nihilism celebrated on college campuses across the United States."[24]

The most influential member of the Frankfurt School in America (Lukacs and Gramsci never darkened our shores) was Herbert Marcuse. Marcuse was the quintessential Marxist in his belief that tolerance is only for left-wing ideas and practices, writing: "Liberating tolerance, then, would mean intolerance against movements from the Right and toleration of movements from the Left. The scope of this tolerance and intolerance: ... "would extend to the stage of action as well as of discussion and propaganda, of deed as well as of word."[25] Marcuse envisioned a utopian socialist society which, "is to be ruled *despotically* by an enlightened group whose chief title to do so is that its members will have realized in themselves the unity of Logos and Eros, and thrown off the vexatious authority of logic, mathematics, and the empirical sciences."[26]

Marcuse's "toleration" mandate has formed the intellectual foundation for the academic left. Witness the attacks on conservative speakers in universities such as at the uber-liberal Berkley, while liberal, anarchist, and communist speakers are warmly welcomed. In many social science and humanities departments around the country Marcuse's goal of converting "illusion into reality and fiction into truth" has succeeded. As I have written elsewhere: "Marcuse's sophistry became so convincing to alienated minds that his Orwellian Newspeak defines much of the nonsense we see coming out of the liberal ivory tower. If you can convince people that censorship is tolerance, you can convince them of anything—freedom is slavery, ignorance is strength, black is white, $2 + 2 = 5$, and socialism is just great." [27]

Marcuse became the guru of free love by synthesizing the ideas of Marx and Freud in his best-selling *Eros and Civilization*, which became the bible of the left. In his book the vision of individual freedom was viewed as a life free of anxiety, and to achieve this one must be free of the constraints of morality; man "is free only where he is free from constraint, external and internal, physical and moral—when he is constrained neither by law nor by need."[28] Morality is for the cultural Marxist a constraining ball and chain rather than a protective safety catch. Channeling Lukacs, Marcuse wanted to remove any and all constraints on sexual behavior, including perverse behavior: "Against a society which employs sexuality as means for a useful end, the perversions uphold sexuality as an end in itself."[29] The "useful end" to which Marcuse alludes is the destruction of the traditional family, and he saw those who practice perversions as courageous rebels against capitalism and Christianity. Marcuse honestly stated that the ultimate goal of unbridled sexuality was the destruction of the family: "This change in the value of and scope of libidinal relations would lead to a disintegration of the institutions in which the private interpersonal relations have been organized, particularly the monogamic and patriarchal family."[30]

Following an unsuccessful communist attempt in Italy in 1919-1920, like Georg Lukacs, Antonio Gramsci left for the Soviet Union. While there he came to understand that faith in God and love of family were far more meaningful to ordinary people than slogans about class solidarity and other communist moonshine. As was the case with Lukacs, this led Gramsci to realize that the socialist revolutions failed in the West because the proletariat shares the Christian-based culture with the bourgeoisie, and therefore it was essential to capture the culture. To accomplish this, attacks on Christianity must be waged relentlessly and comprehensively: "Marxists must change the residually Christian mind. He wanted to alter the mind—to turn it to its opposite—so that it would become *not merely a non-Christian mind but an anti-Christian mind*." [31] Gramsci would be pleased to learn that the new atheists in our midst are likewise dedicated to doing exactly that.

Gramsci's rage against God was just as frenzied as any of the modern Four Horsemen. He called for the "suicide of Catholicism" and the "execution of God."[32] The failures of violent revolutions Gramsci had witnessed led him to the notion that the best way to achieve what he called "cultural hegemony" was to quietly and incrementally debase the culture without violence or bloodshed by undermining Western traditions and values by using the media, the law, and education to enfeeble Christianity and cripple the family. He called this strategy "the conquest of the system" by "the long march through the institutions."

Gramsci owed his stealth approach to the British socialist group called the Fabian Society, which was founded in 1884. It was named after the Roman general Fabius, whose slow and patient tactics against the superior army of Hannibal proved successful. In true eccentric British style, the society initially adopted a coat of arms depicting a wolf in sheep's clothing, which can still be seen in a stain glass window at the London School of Economics. Due to its obvious negative connotation, the coat of arms was replaced by a tortoise, representing the goal of a slow, imperceptible transition of society to socialism. Arch-atheist George Bernard Shaw, one of the Fabian Society's most famous members, described the Fabian strategy as "methods of stealth, intrigue, subversion, and the deception of never calling socialism by its right name."[33]

The "Long March" in America

Gramsci's "conquest of the system" involves capturing and reshaping institutions such as the schools, universities, the media and entertainment industries, the courts, and political parties, over time. To achieve this, Marxist must first convince non-Marxist leftists to get on board with an agenda acceptable to them such as "equality," "social justice," and "sexual freedom." It would thus be the disaffected journalists, entertainers, artists, teachers, and professors of society rather than its workers who would be instrumental in establishing an all-powerful state. Gramsci realized that once you have control of the entertainment industry, you have an open pipeline to promote as much sleaze as you want while casting aspersions on Christian morality and practices. Once you gain access to the press, schools, and universities, you have the same opportunities through the intellectual pipeline to push atheism, to distort American history, and to vilify capitalism and those terrible white males whose Christian values made the unparalleled success of the West possible.

Once you have the courts, you can remove all vestiges of religion from the schools and replace it with a Lukacs-like curriculum of free love with anyone or anything. For instance, in *Stone v. Graham* (1980) the liberal-dominated Supreme Court ruled it unconstitutional to display the Ten Commandments— the fundamental legal code of Western Civilization and the Common Law of the United States—on classroom walls. The Court ruled against God's commandments with these astonishing words: "Posting of religious texts on the wall serves no such educational function. If the posted copies of the Ten Commandments are to have any effect at all, it will be to induce the schoolchildren to read, meditate upon, perhaps to venerate and obey, the Commandments." Heaven forbid that schoolchildren might actually read, meditate upon, venerate and obey, the Ten Commandments! It might corrupt them and turn them into decent God-fearing adults, which would undermine leftist hedonism and prevent children from becoming worshipers of Big Brother. I have written about many such court cases in my book, *The Gavel and Sickle: The Supreme Court, Cultural Marxism, and the Assault on Christianity.*

Even better, if you can capture a political party that rewards idleness and penalizes success, and that turns the races, sexes, and sexual orientations against each other to gain political power, and you have the perfect recipe for turning the nation into a second-rate bloated socialist state incapable of doing anything except foisting further degradation and ruin on its people. We have such a party; the Democratic Party. In a 1944 speech, six-time Socialist Party candidate for President of the United States, Norman Thomas, noted that:

> The American people will never knowingly adopt socialism. But, under the name of "liberalism," they will adopt every fragment of the socialist program, until one day America will be a socialist nation, without knowing how it happened...I no longer need to run as a Presidential

Candidate for the Socialist Party. The Democratic Party has adopted our platform."[34]

Although there are many good Christians among Democrats and liberals who support moral ideas and lead decent lives, they are flirting with atheists. According to the Pew Research Center, 69 percent of those calling themselves atheists identify politically as liberal Democrats while just 10 percent of atheists identify as conservatives Republicans.[35] It is thus perhaps no surprise that when the 2016 Democratic National Convention in Philadelphia opened with a prayer, almost immediately the crowd booed and jeered the minister, as they booed God during the 2012 convention. They not only booed the minister during the invocation, but began chanting "Bernie, Bernie," rooting for Sanders the socialist savior, leaving little doubt that socialism is now mainstream in the Democratic Party, as Thomas predicted it would be. The only truly surprising thing is that a Christian minister was invited to offer a prayer at a Democratic Party event in the first place.

Anti-Christian and anti-family propaganda has penetrated deeply into Western educational systems. The classroom tactics of cultural Marxists to impugn religion and the family is sometimes subtle and indirect, but it can be much more open and aggressive. This tactic is illustrated by arch-atheist Richard Rorty, who was one America's most influential philosophers until his death in 2007. Rorty's narcissistic self-infatuation is evident when he proudly announces his contempt for "silly" religion and his desire to rip apart his student's relationship with their "frightening, vicious, dangerous parents" when they are "lucky" enough to find themselves in his "benevolent" classroom grip:

> When we American college teachers encounter religious fundamentalists, we do not consider the possibility of reformulating our own practices of justification so as to give more weight to the authority of the Christian scriptures. Instead, we do our best to convince these students of the benefits of secularization... So we are going to go right on trying to discredit you [parents] in the eyes of your children, trying to strip your fundamentalist religious community of dignity, trying to make your views seem silly rather than discussable. I don't see anything *herrschaftsfrei* [domination free] about my handling of my fundamentalist students. Rather, I think those students are lucky to find themselves under the benevolent *Herrschaft* [domination] of people like me, and to have escaped the grip of their frightening, vicious, dangerous parents.[36]

It is thus safe to say that the value of Christianity to Western democracies is understood all too well by its enemies, which is why getting rid of it is a major goal of theirs, as they have honestly stated numerous times in books and articles. Of course, not all radical leftists are cultural Marxist, and may not even be aware that such a philosophy exists. I do not claim that cultural Marxism is a conspiracy in the traditional sense wherein there is a cabal of secret conspirators directing the attack from the epicenter. It is not a hub-and-spokes conspiracy in which principal conspirators at the hub have entered into agreements with others at the spokes to take action to achieve their goal. Rather, it is more like a cancer—an unseen and largely undirected conspiracy of the dead Frankfurters—that has spread unknowingly over decades to invade almost every cell in American life. It has led to the tragic disintegration of American values of God, country, and family among large segments of the population.

The left has been strongly infected with this cancer and wants to "fundamentally transform" the United States, as Barak Obama put it. The journalistic meltdown over President Trump's strong defense of Western civilization and Christianity in his speech in Poland in 2017 reveals much about the left's contempt for Western values. Trump asked whether the West has the will to survive, and if we have enough confidence in our Christian values to defend them. The Poles were thrilled with Trump's sprinkling his determined defense of Western culture with references to Christianity and family values, but leftist journalists in America started pulling out their hair. Peter Beinart wrote a piece in *The Atlantic* titled "The Racial and Religious Paranoia of Trump's Warsaw Speech." The title highlights the left's mindless preoccupation with race and its anti-Christian and anti-Western values bias. No wonder Lenin called Western leftists his "useful idiots."

In conclusion, the radical left agrees with G.K. Chesterton and others we have quoted that socialism's big government agenda can only be realized when God is relegated to history's dustbin. Christianity and communism are polar opposites, as Will and Arial Durrant declare: "Heaven and utopia are buckets in a well: when one goes down the other goes up; when religion declines Communism grows."[37] If there is any doubt as to this, Karl Marx himself wrote: "communism begins where atheism begins."[38] The Four Horsemen of atheism may turn out to be the Four Horsemen of the Apocalypse. It is ironic that having defeated the tyranny of political and economic Marxism around the world in the Cold War we are losing the cultural war in our own backyards to cultural Marxism in a silent *coup d'état*. To be sure, the *coup d'état* is not yet a reality, so we Christians must come to understand that we are in a cosmic battle with good and evil to preserve our faith and our constitutional republic. We must fight the good fight against the radical left's agenda or become a state in which Big Government is worshiped rather than the Creator. Peter Hitchens, wrote about the radical atheist agenda and its consequences in a column in a 2012 article in Britain's *Daily Mail*. He is more aware of the danger than most because he lived it himself as a former socialist and atheist, and he fought many intellectual battles in televised debates with his now deceased brother, Christopher.

> The left's real interests are moral, cultural, sexual and social. They lead to a powerful state.... Many leftists fondly imagine they are rebels against authority, and liberators of mankind. It is because the left's ideas – by their nature – undermine conscience, self-restraint, deferred gratification, lifelong marriage and strong, indivisible families headed by authoritative fathers. Without these things, society becomes anarchic, chaotic, lustful and violent – unless it is very heavily policed and supervised."[39]

This cultural coarsening is what happens whenever and wherever we replace God with the State. Why would anyone want to replace the internal control provided by Christian morality with heavy-handed external police control, which is always in evidence in official atheist states, is as much beyond me as it is beyond Peter Hitchens, but the totalitarian streak runs deep on the hard left.

Having addressed the frightening and ugly nihilism of atheism and its terrible, soul destroying, consequences, we can turn to the more difficult task of God's existence. I take the existence of the Grand Designer as a given, but atheists obviously do not. An atheist looks only at *his* evidence with limited knowledge, and thus cannot comprehend how Christians can believe in God and the Bible. However, there are atheists who are seekers, and Hebrews 11:6 tells us that God rewards those who diligently seek Him. God wants us to be a witness to his love by acting lovingly to our neighbors. Loving one's atheist neighbor means in part that you argue humbly and patiently against ignorance so that they too can come to know God's love. As 1 Peter 3:15 says: "But sanctify the Lord God in your hearts: and be ready always to give an answer to every man that asketh you a reason of the hope that is in you with meekness and fear." It is not a quarrel with your atheist friends that you must have, but rather a gentle teaching.

But since the atheist believes that science is on his side and because it is the only verifiable way of knowing, science will provide him with a more satisfying and convincing argument than Biblical verses. After all, it was science that convinced even some of God's greatest enemies to accept God as the Creator of all. God needs no defending from anyone, but it would be a sin to deny any man or women who "asketh you a reason of the hope." I am completely aware that one cannot prove that God exists in any conclusive sense to everyone's satisfaction, but neither can we prove that He does not. All we can do is to reason to the best explanation from logic and the evidence of science, and then we may go to scripture. I begin by exploring the origin of the universe with an event that traumatized science: the Big Bang.

Chapter 5

The Big Bang and Fine Tuning
of the Universe

"Probably every physicist would believe in a creation if the Bible had not unfortunately said something about it many years ago and made it seem old-fashioned." Nobel Prize winning physicist, George P. Thomson

In the Beginning

Genesis 1:1 tells us "In the beginning God created the heavens and the earth." God's creation was *creatio ex nihilo* ("creation from nothing"). While these exact words are not found in the Bible, there are a number of passages from which this can be deduced. For example, Psalm 33:6 says: "By the word of the Lord the heavens were made, their starry host by the breath of his mouth," and John 1:1 "In the beginning was the Word, and the Word was with God, and the Word was God." Creation from nothing was deemed absurd by scientists and philosophers since nothing (no-thing) comes from nothing. Before the 20th century most scientists believed that the universe had no beginning, that it was static, eternal in time, and infinite in space and matter; it was simply a brute fact of existence that needed no jump start. This assumption was scientifically satisfying since it relieved scientists of getting into the messy metaphysical questions of the universe's origin, and what caused it to exist.

This view of the universe emerged in Europe the 13th century when scholars were exposed to Aristotle's ancient writings on the matter. Aristotle believed that everything that exists must have a cause, but he also believed in a past infinite universe that had been organized out of chaos by the Prime Mover. Sir Isaac Newton also accepted the infinite universe for religious reasons, even though it conflicted with *Genesis*. Gonzalez and Richards note that Newton "viewed the universe as the 'divine sensorium'—the medium through which God acted on the world. To be adequate to this task, the cosmos had to be infinite." He posited this because "For him, an infinite universe answered the question of why gravity did not cause the constituents of the universe to collapse in on one another."[1]

The steady-state universe began to unravel with Einstein's famous general theory of relativity. Einstein was unsettled to find that his equations predicted the expansion of the universe, which did not fit the accepted notion in science that the universe was static and past eternal. He "corrected" his equations by adding what he termed the "cosmological constant" representing a repulsive force to counter gravity's attraction, and thus leaving the universe static. He later called this the greatest blunder of his life, because his initial equations turned out to be right—the universe had a beginning and was expanding. Dark energy is now considered the cosmological constant that balances out gravity.

It was Belgian Catholic priest and mathematician/physicist, Georges Lemaitre, who noted in the early 1920's that all was not right with Einstein's cosmological constant. Like Newton, he reasoned that in a state of past eternity gravity would have long ago pulled all the matter in the universe together into one huge mass. Lemaitre drew the opposite (and correct) conclusion that to avoid this crunch the universe had to be expanding, and if it was expanding, it had to do so from a finite point in time. Simon Appolloni explains the reasoning: "Lemaitre concluded that the universe had to be anything but static and reasoned it must be expanding; what is more, all matter would stay separated [from the gravitational pull] as the expansion force slightly exceeded the gravitational force."[2]

Lemaitre reasoned that if the universe was expanding, then rewinding the cosmic clock we should arrive at a point when all matter was condensed into a single entity, which he called the "primeval atom." Modern physicists call this the singularity; a "point" of infinite density and infinite temperature, yet zero volume. Everything that exists in the universe, every last atom of matter, every physical force, and time itself was contained in this dense concentration of energy. Stranger yet, this singularity was not some tiny dot hanging around in space somewhere in a void because there was no "somewhere" for it to be, nor was it hanging around to pop into existence because there was no time before it popped. Because this sounded all too weird, almost all physicists at the time dismissed Lemaitre's reasoning.

In 1929-1930, American astronomer Edwin Hubble, working at the Mount Wilson Observatory in California, provided observational evidence for Lemaitre's expanding universe. Hubble showed that all galaxies are moving away from us and away from each other and that the farther away they were, the faster they are moving. This was determined by examining the wavelength spectrum of stars, with galaxies moving away from us becoming redder (more "red-shifted") as the wavelength is stretched. This effect is known as the Doppler Effect and is seen in all physical wavelengths. We understand it more clearly with sound, but it is equally true of color. We experience it every time we hear the sirens of emergency vehicles. As they come closer to us the sound waves are compressed, and as they recede they are stretched as the siren's pitch decreases. The inescapable conclusion from these observations was that some gigantic event caused the universe to expand with unfathomable force some 13.7 billion years ago, give or take a few million years.

This event has become known as the Big Bang. It is now accepted as settled science that this singular event brought matter/energy, time, and space into being in a split-second flash. This was not an explosion in the usual sense of the word, but an expansion of the universe creating space and time as it expanded at an unimaginable rate. The Big Bang was not an explosion as conventionally understood. Explosions throw matter apart in all directions which falls back randomly under the influence of the attractive force of gravity. They never result in matter clumping together in orderly patterns such as we see after the Big Bang forming into ordered galaxies, stars, and planets. The attractive force pulling matter back in had to be exquisitely calibrated to the "explosive" force driving it forward. How exquisite this balance? Physicist Paul Davies informs us that if the rate of expansion from the beginning differed more that 10^{-18} seconds we wouldn't be here. In his words: "The explosive vigour of the universe is thus matched with almost unbelievable accuracy to its gravitational power. The big bang was not evidently, any old bang, but an explosion of exquisitely arranged magnitude."[3]

In 2013, scientists estimated that the observable universe now stretches in all directions from us for 2.7×10^{23} miles.[4] For big number gurus, that's two hundred seventy sextillion, or one billion trillion miles, and it's still moving away ever faster. The universe had a beginning and a cause after all, and that cause has to be an entity that transcends time, space, and matter/energy since these things did not exist before the creation. As astronomer George Greenstein put it: "As we survey all the evidence, the thought insistently arises that some supernatural agency, or rather Agency, must be involved. Is it possible that suddenly, without intending to, we have stumbled upon scientific proof of the existence of a Supreme Being? Was it God who stepped in and so providentially created the cosmos for our benefit?"[5]

Interestingly, the Big Bang idea is much more ancient than most suppose. English theologian (Bishop of Lincoln) and mathematician Robert Grosseteste, perhaps the smartest man you never heard of, wrote a mathematical treatise called *De Luce (On Light)* in 1225 in which he explored the nature of matter and the universe. According to Bower and his colleagues: "Four centuries before Isaac Newton proposed gravity and seven centuries before the Big Bang theory, Grosseteste describes the birth of the Universe in an explosion and the crystallization of matter to form stars and planets in a set of nested spheres around Earth."[6] Grosseteste's dual role as scientist and theologian mocks the claim that science and religion are in conflict.

The Kalam Cosmological Argument for the Beginning of the Universe

The kalam cosmological argument is a modern form of the medieval Islamic argument for the existence of God. It relies on deductive logic rather than inductive observation, but subsequent scientific work has supported it. It asserts the notion that the universe had a beginning in finite time against the Aristotelian notion the universe is past eternal and that God merely invests it with order. The modern champion of the argument is philosopher William Craig, who offers the kalam argument in the form of the following syllogism (with my comments):[7]

1. ***Whatever begins to exist has a cause.*** The major premise comports with self-evident everyday experience; every physical object or system, or change in that object or system, has a cause preceding the effect. As self-evident as this may seem, there are objections to it. In what Craig described as something sounding like the "Gettysburg Address of Atheism," he quotes philosopher Quentin Smith as claiming that "the most reasonable belief is that we came from nothing, by nothing, and for nothing."[8] Furthermore, mathematicians and physicists were beginning to realize that while past infinity *may* be mathematically describable, it is not physically realizable. Astronomer Fred Hoyle tried to fit infinity into a mathematical model to avoid the question of whether the universe requires a First Cause. Hoyle was an atheist who attacked Christian beliefs at every opportunity, but it was a mathematical equation—Dirac's quantum mechanical equation regarding the fine balance between subatomic particles in nucleosynthesis that led him to question his atheism. He did not embrace Christian theism, but rather a purposive deistic universe. In 1994 he wrote: "It is because of this incredible chain of subtlety that I doubt the nineteenth century denial of a purposive universe."[9]

2. ***The universe began to exist.*** While the minor premise logically follows from the major premise, we have seen that the standard opinion before the Big Bang evidence came pouring in was that the universe was past eternal. A beginning of the universe made many scientists uncomfortable because it suggests that something must have caused the beginning. To be fully consistent a purely naturalistic perspective, scientists would have to say that the universe somehow created itself. Of course, they realized that nothing can be the cause of itself since it would have to have existed prior to itself to do so, which is absurd. Yet the universe is here, and it had a beginning. Astrophysicist Alexander Viilenkin said at a 2011 conference on "The State of the Universe" that, "All the evidence we have says that the universe had a beginning."[10]

The second law of thermodynamics argues against an infinite past. The second law states that an isolated system's—a system without an external source of energy—entropy, or disorder, always increases. Over time all such systems evolve towards thermodynamic equilibrium, which is a state with maximum entropy. If the universe was past-infinite, we would be in a state of thermodynamic equilibrium now, but we are in a splendid state and order because there is still lots of energy available. This will not always be the case. In some distant future billions of years from now, the universe will lose all of its energy and die a "heat death," meaning the intense heat energy of the Big Bang will have dissipated in an ever-expanding universe and it will enter into a deep freeze.

3. *The universe has a cause*. It was the conclusion of the syllogism that rattled many scientists hell-bent on leaving metaphysical entities such as a First Cause off the discussion table. If everything from a paper-clip chain to a space shuttle requires intelligence and agency, how much more intelligent and agentic must the creator of everything be? After all, that's what the word "universe"—from the Latin *universum;* "all things"—means. As Craig concludes: "A cause of space and time must be uncaused, beginningless, timeless, spaceless, immaterial personal being endowed with freedom of will and enormous power. And that is a core concept of God." [11]

Early Scientific Opposition to a Beginning

In the early 20th century, many scientists had an almost religious faith in the materialist laws of physics, which have proved themselves over and other again to be beautiful, true, and useful, but they could not fathom a beginning of everything. Hungarian cultural Marxist philosopher Georges Politizer, a compatriot of Georges Lukacs, vehemently denied the Big Bang because of what it implied for his Marxist materialism. He stated: "The universe was not a created object. If it were, then it would have to be created instantaneously by God and brought into existence from nothing. To admit Creation, one has to admit, in the first place, the existence of a moment when the universe did not exist, and that something came out of nothingness. This is something to which science cannot accede." [12] As agnostic astrophysicist Robert Jastrow points out: "This religious faith of the scientist is violated by the discovery that the world had a beginning under conditions in which the known laws of physics are not valid, and as a product of forces or circumstances we cannot discover. When that happens, the scientist has lost control. If he really examined the implications, he would be traumatized." [13]

Many scientists were indeed traumatized and railed against the idea of a beginning. Even the phrase "Big Bang" is a cynical one coined by Fred Hoyle when he was confronted with the idea. Scientists who were committed exclusively to a materialist philosophy likewise rejected the idea because it led to echoes of the "spooky" Genesis story of divine creation *ex nihilo*. Other scientists who railed against the idea of a universe with a finite past include astronomer Arthur Eddington, who said that "Philosophically, the notion of a beginning is repugnant to me." Eddington's opinion was not animated by anti-religious motives because he was a deeply religious Quaker. Appolloni tells us that "[Geoffrey] Cantor concludes '[Eddington] considered that no matter how far science advanced, God's creation remains ultimately mysterious and wonderful.' While Eddington seeks truth as a scientist, like Lemaitre, as a Quaker, the pursuit of truth (in all aspects of life whether scientific or religious) will always remain just that, a pursuit, not a realization"[14] We can agree 100 percent with this without denying the truth of creation.

Chemist Walter Nernst angrily proclaimed that: "To deny the infinite duration of time would be to betray the very foundations of science," and astronomer Allan Sandage, concluded that, "It is such a strange conclusion....it cannot really be true." Physicist Philip Morrison had more of the attitude of a true scientist by following the data where they lead: "I find it hard to accept the Big Bang Theory. I would like to reject it, but I have to accept the facts."[15] Allan Sandage, the "Grand old man of cosmology," later became a Christian, noting that "It was my science that drove me to the conclusion that the world is much more complicated than can be explained by science. It was only through the supernatural that I can understand the mystery of existence."[16]

Most commenters on the issue of scientists and the Big Bang seemed in those days were of the opinion that opposition to the Big Bang was (and is) motivated by the idea that a beginning implied a Creator, and such a notion cannot be allowed in science. However, an increasing number of scientists were accepting the theory, much to the consternation of Sir Fred, who complained in a 1949 BBC radio interview that: "The reason why scientists like the 'big bang' is because they are overshadowed by the Book of Genesis. It is deep within the psyche of most scientists to believe in the first page of Genesis." For Hoyle, *Genesis* influenced scientists' acceptance of the science behind the Big Bang, but it was more likely that the science of the Big Bang influenced their acceptance of *Genesis*. This is supported by the words of famous scientists themselves. Astronomer Robert Jastrow said, "Now we see how the astronomical evidence supports the Biblical view of the origin of the world. The details differ, but the essential elements in the astronomical and Biblical accounts of Genesis are the same: the chain of events leading to man commenced suddenly and sharply at a definite moment in time, in a flash of light and energy."[17] In a New York Times interview, Nobel Prize winning physicist Arno Penzias stated: "The best data we have (concerning the big bang) are exactly what I would have predicted, had I nothing to go on but the five books of Moses, the Psalms, the Bible as a whole."[18]

The Cosmic Microwave Background Radiation

Hubble's observations did not by themselves conclusively convince all scientists to accept the Big Bang theory. The "cincher" for most of them was the discovery of the cosmic microwave background (CMB) radiation. The CMB was discovered accidentally in 1964 by Arno Penzias and Robert Wilson, two scientists working at Bell Laboratories in New Jersey. They were working with a supersensitive radio telescope antenna designed to detect and measure radio waves from early balloon satellites. To do this, they had to eliminate all interference, such as radar or broadcasting signals from their receiver. After weeks of doing everything possible to eliminate interference, they found an annoying hiss that it was coming from every direction of the sky with equal strength. Penzias and Wilson finally concluded that radiation was coming from outside our own galaxy, but they could not explain it.

They turned for help a team of Princeton physicists led by Robert Dicke who were trying to find the radiation predicted to exist as a remnant of the Big Bang. It was predicted that the radiation would be found to be microwaves because of a massive redshift all the way back to about 380,000 years after the Big Bang. Because of this, and because it was coming from everywhere at once, they came to realize that, "Not only was it a real signal, it was evidence for the big bang itself."[19] According to scientists from the National Aeronautics and Space Administration, the fact that CMB radiation is detected everywhere we look and has a uniform temperature (2.725° above absolute zero Kelvin) to better than one part in a thousand "is one compelling reason to interpret the radiation as remnant heat from the Big Bang; it would be very difficult to imagine a local source of radiation that was this uniform. In fact, many scientists have tried to devise alternative explanations for the source of this radiation, but none have succeeded."[20] You have witnessed this background radiation yourself. The hissing and "snow" or static you see sometimes on your television is the echo of creation.

The Abundance of Light Elements

The third piece of important evidence for the Big Bang is the abundance of light elements in the universe. To appreciate this argument, we have to understand the origin of the elements. Scientists trace the history of the universe all the way back to "Planck time," which is an astounding 10^{-43} seconds after the Big Bang. At this time, all four fundamental forces of nature—gravity, electromagnetism, strong nuclear force, and weak nuclear force—were one. In the beginning, the universe was so hot (about 80 million trillion, trillion, degrees

Fahrenheit) that no atoms could form. At 10^{-35} seconds the universe had expanded "from something smaller than a proton to something the size of a grapefruit," and the strong and electroweak forces were unified." [21] With further cooling at 10^{-10} seconds came the unification of the electromagnetic and weak forces, and at 10^{-5} seconds, quarks, the first "matter," appeared. At first, the quarks zipped around in unbound states (they are never found this way today), but with just a little more cooling they were able to combine and form protons and neutrons.

Protons and neutrons are matter but have mirror images of themselves called anti-matter with the same mass. Matter has negatively charged electron and anti-matter has a positively charged positron (neutrons have no electric charge). As these particles whizzed around in the hellish maelstrom they annihilated each other in a flash of radiation, but also there were new particles of both kinds spontaneously arising from that same radiation. The laws of physics tell us that we should have expected equal amounts of matter and anti-matter, but because there were slightly more matter particles than antimatter particles (1 in 100,000,000), matter prevailed. If it did not, the universe would consist of nothing but pure energy.

At three minutes (a huge time jump on this scale) protons and neutron were able to form stable nuclei. If they had formed before this cooler time violent collisions would have immediately torn them apart. It was hundreds of thousands of years later when the temperature was cool enough that an electron could attach itself to a proton and neutron to form atoms. These atoms are hydrogen and helium with a smidgen of lithium, which have 1, 2, and 3 protons in their nuclei respectively. The abundance of the light elements is consistent with their creation in a Big Bang nucleosynthesis. The abundances of helium and deuterium (a rare--less than 0.02%--isotope of hydrogen that contains one proton and one neutron; the other isotope, protium, has one proton and no neutrons) is particularly important because it is much more abundant than could have been produced by stellar nucleosynthesis. Stars only destroy deuterium, which strongly suggests its synthesis in Big Bang nucleosynthesis. The 75/23 hydrogen to helium ratio is taken to be the ratio which existed at the time when the deuteron (a particle consisting of a proton and a neutron) became stable, thus halting the decay of free neutrons with the expansion and cooling of the universe.[21]

Heavier elements had to wait for the formation of stars from hydrogen and helium gases. These heavier elements require the extreme temperatures, and pressures found within stars and are cooked up in the process called stellar nucleosynthesis. This process produces elements up to iron; all elements heavier than iron are formed in the massive energy released by supernovae explosions in the process of supernova nucleosynthesis.

Cosmologists call the time before the formation of hydrogen atoms the cosmological "dark ages" because there was literally no light. The immense heat generated by the Big Bang created a soupy mix of subatomic particles with protons and neutrons scattering photons (the elementary particles of light) as a dense fog scatters the light from a car's headlights. When the protons and neutron were finally able to capture electrons to form atoms, photons were freed to travel through space, leaving behind the CMB radiation. With the emission of photons we get light, and thus cosmologists have been able to see back into the universe to about 380,000 years after the Big Bang.[22] See the Figure 5.1 produced by the National Aeronautics and Space Administration (NASA) of the timeline for the expansion of space. Thus, if anyone wants to dispute the origin of the universe with the Big Bang, they are going to have to contend with an enormous number of disparate observations that support it.

Figure 5.1 The expansion of the Universe / nasa.gov

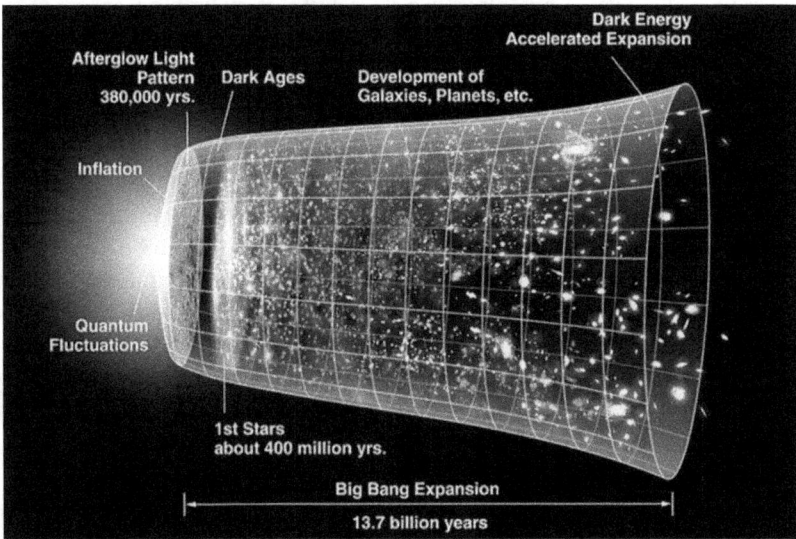

The Fine-Tuning of the Four Fundamental Forces Gravity

We live in a life-friendly planet, but the conditions for the existence of such a planet, never mind life on it, are so highly improbable that it leaves physicists and philosophers in awe. Each of the four fundamental forces of nature—gravity, electromagnetic, strong nuclear, and weak nuclear—have to be so fine-tuned that even the slightest variation in their values and the universe would not exist. To quote atheist physicists Stephen Hawking and Leonard Mlodinow: "The emergence of the complex structures capable of supporting intelligent observers seems to be very fragile. The laws of nature form a system that is extremely fine-tuned, and very little in physical law can be altered without destroying the possibility of the development of life as we know it. Were it not for a series of startling coincidences in the precise details of physical law, it seems, humans and similar life-forms would never have come into being."[23].

The Timeline for the Expansion of Space from the Big Bang

Gravity causes smaller cosmic bodies to orbit larger ones, such as the Earth and the other planets in our solar system to orbit the Sun and the moon to orbit the Earth. It is also the force that gathered the material of the Big Bang and made it coalesce in stars and planets. Once formed, the continued existence of stars became a balancing act between the force of gravity pushing in and the pressure from the explosive gases produced by burning hydrogen pushing out straining for release. If gravity was any stronger a star would collapse; any weaker and there would be no stars at all.[24] Gravity is thus very powerful at the level of big things like stars, but it is by far the weakest of the four forces. According to Robert Krebs, gravity is approximately 10^{38} times weaker than the strong force, 10^{36} times weaker than the electromagnetic force, and 10^{29} times weaker than the weak force.[25] It is only because the multiple trillions upon trillions of particles in large bodies add up that gravity has the power that it does.[26]

The law of gravity states that its strength increases proportional to the masses involved and decreases with the square of their distance apart. If gravity had been slightly weaker by the smallest degree at the moment of creation, it would not have been able to pull matter together to form stars and planets. If it had been slightly stronger to the same degree, it would have pulled matter back into a big crunch long before stars and planets were able to form.[27] To help us to understand the extraordinary fine-tuning of gravity, physicist Robin Collins asks us to imagine a dial broken down into one-inch increments that stretches right across the universe. This would be more inches than all the grains of sand on Earth. He noted that if we moved the gravity's setting just one inch out of those unimaginable trillions from its current setting, "That small adjustment of the dial would increase gravity by a billion fold." [28] If some malignant force were to move that dial, it would crush all the matter into the universe into a super dense mass.

Cosmologists tell us that gravity is in a cosmic tug of war with dark, or "vacuum energy." Recall that Einstein's cosmological constant allowed for a repulsive energy that was uniform across the universe. Most scientists used to believe that the cosmological constant was zero or even slightly negative, but we now know that the expansion rate of the universe is actually increasing, which can only mean that the cosmological constant is positive and that dark energy is pushing the universe apart. No one really understands what dark energy actually is or how it works, but one hypothesis is energy is produced by pairs of particles—one with a negative charge and one with a positive charge—that constantly pop into existence. Because they have opposite charges, they exist for only a fraction of a second before they collide and annihilate each other, which releases a tiny burst of energy. It is the sum of this energy that is hypothesized to cause the universe to accelerate faster. In today's expanded universe the galaxies are not packed so close together, so their gravitational pull is weakened, thus allowing the vacuum energy to play a more dominant role. Gonzalez and Richards state that "There is only one 'special time' in the history of the universe when the vacuum and matter energies are the same, and we're living near it. If the vacuum energy had become prominent a few billion years earlier than it did in our universe there would have been no galaxies. If it had overtaken gravity a little earlier still, there would have been no individual stars [and no us]"[29] The vacuum field is extremely weak as particle fields go, but the early universe still had to have a value large enough to allow the early universe to expand against gravity's pull. To quote Gonzalez and Richards again: "These particle fields require an extraordinary degree of fine tuning—at least 10^{-53} to get such a small, positive, non-zero, value for the vacuum energy."[30]

The Electromagnetic Force

The electromagnetic force is the combination of electrical and magnetic forces and is by far the best understood of the fundamental forces. The fundamental constituents of the electromagnetic force are massless photons, also known as electromagnetic radiation. Electromagnetic radiation refers to the parts of the electromagnetic field that radiate into space and form a spectrum of different wavelengths ranging from the shortest gamma rays with the highest energy to the longest to radio waves with the lowest energy. Other wavelengths include microwaves, infrared, ultraviolet, and X-rays, which are either neutral or deadly for life. If you examine a colored image of the electromagnetic spectrum, you will see a tiny sliver of wavelength color in the center we call visible light, without which life would be an impossibility. No wonder Genesis 1:3-4 says: "And God said, Let there be light: and there was light. And God saw the light, that it was good."

The electromagnetic force is the force that makes chemical bonding possible and gives matter its strength, shape, and hardness. If the electromagnetic bonding in the nuclei was even the slightest bit weaker, electrons could not be held in their orbits, and if it was slightly larger the electrons could not bond with the electrons of other atoms, so we would not get any molecules in either case. But we do have molecules for everything in life, so we might say that, except for gravity, the electromagnetic force is responsible for practically everything we encounter in life above the nuclear scale. Like gravity, electromagnetic radiation has an infinite range, although its strength, also like gravity, is proportional to the inverse square of the distance. Unlike gravity which only attracts, the electromagnetic force can attract or repulse. The electromagnetic force holds atoms and molecules together by the action of its attraction and repulsive charges and is so powerful that in comparison the contributions of the other fundamental forces as determiners of atomic and molecular structures is negligible.

As small as the relative contributions of the other forces may be with respect to this, they are still very important because without them the electromagnetic force would be useless. Theoretical physicist Paul Davies informs us that if the ratio of the nuclear strong force (discussed below) to the electromagnetic force had been different by 1 part in 10^{16} the stars could not have formed. He also tells us that if the ratio of the electromagnetic force to the gravitational force were increased by one part in 10^{40} only small stars can exist, and if it were decreased by the same amount there would be only large stars. "You must have both large and small stars in the universe: the large ones produce elements in their thermonuclear furnaces; and it is only the small ones that burn long enough to sustain a planet with life."[31]

The Strong Force

The strong nuclear force is by far the most powerful of the four forces, although it has the shortest interaction distance. It is the force that binds quarks together to form the protons and neutrons in the nuclei of atoms and underlies interactions between all particles containing quarks. Each atom is made up of a number of positively charged protons, and as we know, positively electrically charged objects brought close together will repel one another by the action of the electromagnetic force. Despite this repulsion, protons must have a way of sticking together or we would have no elements heavier than hydrogen or helium, and thus no life. It is the strong force that overcomes the proton's natural "shyness" and mate up with others. The strong nuclear force is also the force that powers the stars by crushing hydrogen atoms so tightly that their nuclei overcome their natural repulsion and fuse together, resulting in the massive amounts of energy that keep them, and us, alive. This force, along with the weak nuclear force, is called "nuclear" because their activity is confined to the nuclei of atoms.

One of the strange things about protons and neutrons (a neutron has no electrical charge) is that the mass of their nucleus is slightly *less* than the sum of their masses. This strange phenomenon exists because when protons and neutrons come together, a small portion of their mass is converted to energy.

This energy is the strong nuclear force that overcomes the electromagnetic repulsion and holds the nucleus together. Britain's Astronomer Royal Sir Martin Rees informs us that the mass converted to energy is only .007 of its mass, but if it was .006, a proton would not bond to a neutron to make helium and the universe would consist only of hydrogen. On the other hand, if it was .008, there would be ready and rapid fusion, and no hydrogen would have survived.[32]

The Weak Force

While gravity, electromagnetism and the strong nuclear force hold things together, the weak nuclear force plays helps to make things within atoms come apart by radioactive decay. This is not a bad thing since we don't want stability in many kinds of matter; we want certain things to flow, change, and burn. During what is called beta decay, a neutron is replaced by a proton, electron, and neutrino by the action of their constituent quarks. The stars could not exist without this process. It is this force that drives the fusion of hydrogen protons and neutrons to form deuterium. The energy generated from this fusion is the source of the heat we get from the sun. This vital action is extremely fine-tuned. The tiniest increase in the strength of the weak force would have driven the hydrogen-to-deuterium process faster, making stars use up their energy faster than their planets could cool, and thus life could not develop. A weaker force may have been too feeble to do much fusing at all, and all we may have in the universe is hydrogen. Because the energy generated from this fusion is the source of the heat we get from the sun—no heat energy, no life.

As weak as it is, the weak force plays a crucial role in producing life. We have seen that the heavier elements necessary for life are formed in giant stars and spewed into space in supernova explosions. Supernova explosions fuel the cosmic cycle by pollinating the new stars formed from its gasses containing the heavy elements. Such explosions would not occur if the weak force was not exquisitely calibrated. As Paul Davies explains: "If the weak interactions were slightly weaker, the neutrinos [neutrinos are similar to electrons, but they do not carry an electric charge] would not be able to exert enough pressure on the outer envelope of the star to cause the supernova explosion. On the other hand, if it were slightly stronger, the neutrinos would be trapped inside the core, and rendered impotent." [33]

Phase-Space and Initial Conditions

Phase-space is a concept of statistical mechanics and is the space of all possible states of a system and their velocities. In this case, the system is the entire universe and each point in that space refers to a different way that it might have begun. It considers all the simultaneous coordinates that space and velocity may have and is intimately connected to the second law of thermodynamics and the principle of entropy. As we have seen, entropy is the degree of thermodynamic "disorder" in a closed system, which is always increasing. Given this, there had to be an immense degree of order at the Big Bang because any universe capable of supporting life must begin with the lowest possible degree of entropy because the possibilities of high entropy universes are immensely greater. Mathematical physicist Sir Roger Penrose asks us to image all the possible way that the universe might have started off in the entire phase-space of the universe and the probability that the Creator could hit the exact point in the phase space in all its immensity to create a life-producing universe. He calculated the probability of the initial entropy conditions of the Big Bang by calculating the maximum entropy of the universe (thermodynamic equilibrium). This value is the logarithm of the total phase-space volume of all possible beginnings of the universe, or 10^{123}. Because logarithms and exponents are inverse functions, the total phase-space volume is $10^{10^{(123)}}$. Penrose's own words express it best (Note: W = original phase-space volume; V = total phase-space volume available.):

> How big was the original phase-space volume W that the Creator had to aim for in order to provide a universe compatible with the second law of thermodynamics and with what we now observe? It does not much matter whether we take the value $W = 10^{10^{(100)}}$ or $W = 10^{10^{(88)}}$ given by the galactic black holes or by the background radiation, respectively, or a much smaller (and, in fact, more appropriate) figure which would have been the actual figure at the big bang. Either way, the ratio of V to W will be, closely $V/W = 10^{10^{(123)}}$. This now tells us how precise the Creator's aim must have been: namely to an accuracy of one part in $10^{10^{(123)}}$ This is an extraordinary figure. One could not possibly even write the number down in full in the ordinary denary notation: it would be 1 followed by 10^{123} successive 0's. Even if we were to write a 0 on each separate proton and on each separate neutron in the entire universe- and we could throw in all the other particles for good measure- we should fall far short of writing down the figure needed.[34]

Penrose's calculations have presented problems for atheists, as evidenced by the title of a *Journal of High Energy Physics* article written by three physicists titled "Disturbing implications of a cosmological constant." These physicists noted that it is an unshakable given the universe could only make sense if it began in a state of exceptionally low entropy and added: 'there is no universally accepted explanation of how the universe got into such a special state. In this paper, we would like to sharpen the question by making two assumptions which we feel are well motivated from observation and recent theory. Far from providing a solution to the problem, we will be led to a disturbing crisis."[35] What is this "disturbing crisis" they found after examining all naturalistic explanations for such exquisite fine-tuning and finding them wanting? It is no less than forcing cosmologists to think the unthinkable: "Another possibility is an unknown agent intervened in the evolution, and for reasons of its own restarted the universe in the state of low entropy characterizing inflation." [36]

How improbable does "improbable" have to be before it becomes "impossible" in terms of the atheist's blind chance? Since all the parameter dials discussed here are related to one another, the improbability of a life-sustaining universe exceeds the available probability resources to the Nth degree. John Haught, who works at the intersection of science and theology, wrote of his analysis of fine-tuning: "So impressive is the still accumulating information about the many emergent levels of the world's fine-tuning for life that some scientists can hardly suppress a suspicion that something momentous, perhaps even purposive, is afoot in the cosmos."[37] Indeed, the more we find out about cosmic fine-tuning, the deeper the mysteries have gotten to be, and the more implausible a naturalistic explanation of it all seems to be. If all the parameters of the universe are so exquisitely fine-tuned, then perhaps they require a fine-tuner—namely God. Thus the "inference to the best explanation" is that atheistic account of the universe is logically preferable to the atheistic account. Robert Jastrow's account of how science caught up with theology on the matter of creation is both interesting and poetic: "For the scientist who has lived by his faith in the power of reason, the story ends like a bad dream. He has scaled the mountain of ignorance; he is about to conquer the highest peak; as he pulls himself over the final rock, he is greeted by a band of theologians who have been sitting there for centuries."[38]

But it is not only a moment of creation that the Bible beat science to the punch, but also the expansion of (spreading, stretching) of the universe, gravity, and the Earth's spherical shape. The Bible explains an expanding universe in poetic, if not scientific, terms in a number of places, such as Isaiah 40:22: "It is He that sitteth upon the circle of the earth, and the inhabitants thereof are as grasshoppers; that stretcheth out the heavens as a curtain, and spreadeth them out as a tent to dwell in." The Bible also describes the Earth as "hanging upon nothing," which implies the force of gravity, in Job 26:7: "He stretcheth out the north over the empty place, and hangeth the earth upon nothing." To appreciate the importance of these verses we have to realize that Book of Isaiah was written in the eighth century BC and the Book of Job in the sixth century BC. Greek philosopher such as Pythagoras and Aristotle reasoned that the world was round, and Eratosthenes proved it mathematically, but these men had their insights much later that Isaiah and Job. Almost all ancient cultures subscribed to a flat Earth, including the ancient Greeks, and reasoned that it was held in place by things such as elephants, turtles, or on the shoulders of the titan Atlas. I am not, of course, saying that we should take the Bible to be book of science. The Bible speaks to us in figurative terms primarily about how to lead a moral life, but it sometimes offers us gems such as these that provide a feast for thought.

Chapter 6

Earth: The Privileged Planet

'The most beautiful system of the sun, planets, and
comets could only proceed from the counsel and domin-
ion on an intelligent and powerful Being."
Sir Isaac Newton; considered the greatest scientist of all
time.

Location, Location, Location

Any real estate agent will tell you that it is a basic principle of their profession
that location is the major determinant of the desirability of a property. How
would you fine-tune your choice to find the nicest house, on the safest street,
in the safest neighborhood, and in the safest country in the world if cost were
of no concern? You would certainly like to be in an affluent country with a
peaceful and democratic reputation, and which has a low crime rate (say
Switzerland). After deciding on a country, you further refine your tuning down
to a location therein which neighbors are kind helpful, the weather is good,
and there are lots of opportunities for recreation, and you settle on a villa
overlooking Lake Lugano. If you were likewise asked to define a galaxy and
planet location where life itself is possible, you could do no better than the
Milky Way and Earth, because as far as we know, this is perhaps the only loca-
tions that fit the bill. We are in the right place with just the right kind of star,
just the right distance from it, with a stabilizing moon, and enjoy very helpful
neighboring planets.

Astronomers increasingly recognize that if the universe had not unfolded
exactly as it did, humanity would not exist. As the physicist and mathematician Freeman Dyson put it: "As we look out into the Universe and identify the
many accidents of physics and astronomy that have worked together to our
benefit, it almost seems as if the Universe must in some sense have known
that we were coming."[1] Let us start with our neighborhood called the Milky
Way galaxy to explore this extraordinary statement. Our galaxy's name is derived from Greek mythology. As the story goes, the god Zeus took the infant
Heracles, the offspring of one of his sexual dalliances with mortals, for his
sleeping wife, Hera, to breastfeed. Hera was ill-disposed to the half moral
Heracles and pushed him away while he was suckling. This caused milk to
spill into the night sky forming the Milky Way. We know today, of course, that

the Milky Way consists of billions of stars of numerous types in isolation and in pairs, triplets, and clusters. The Milky Way is what is known as a spiral galaxy; the other two major types are elliptical and irregular which, like ours, are salted with billions of stars.[2]

The formation of galaxies is the result of some very delicate fine-tuning. The first galaxies are thought to have formed about 200 million years after the Big Bang when the universe was a homogeneous mass of matter and energy of immense density. Physicists tell us that if you crush enough matter together it is destined to collapse into a black hole, so why didn't it? For matter to coalesce into galaxies there must be some contrast in matter density to enable matter to collapse under the pull of gravity to form galaxies. The formation of galaxies thus depends crucially on matter density variation from one location to another, but this variation must be very small. Astrophysicist Abraham Loeb tells us that: "The Universe we live in started with primordial density perturbations of a fractional amplitude~10^{-5}" [3] If the perturbations were smaller than this they will not amplify and form galaxies; if much larger then all matter would have certainly collapsed into a black hole. Note that Loeb's observation coheres with Roger Penrose's calculations in the previous chapter, namely, the universe would have quickly become a morass of black holes unless the Creator had not aimed at that one unique point in phase space to get the universe started with exceedingly low entropy (a black hole is a maximum entropy).

The Milky Way galaxy is in the top one or two percent of galaxies massive and luminous enough to have gravity strong enough to attract hydrogen and helium in massive amounts to construct the heavier elements needed for life, at least for complex, intelligent life, to exist. Our Galaxy has several neighborhoods containing globular clusters which are densely packed collections of perhaps millions of ancient stars revolving around the galactic core. Earth-like planets are unlikely to exist in globular clusters because their ancient stars are poor in the heavier elements necessary to build them. If there are such planets, the gravitation pull of the myriad of stars there would result in highly elliptical orbits, which would plunge planets both into each other and into extremes of heat and cold, both of which are unsuitable for complex life.[4]

The Galactic Habitable Zone

Our galactic neighborhood is in what is known as the Galactic Habitable Zone (GHZ), the "safe zone" of the city. The Milky Way is about 180,000 light-years across, and our relatively safe zone is about 27,000 light-years from its center, and tens of thousands of light-years away from the outer rim of the galaxy's spiral arm. Remember, a light year is the distance light travels in a year at 186,282 miles per second, so 27,000 light years is a *very* long way. Our solar system orbits the center of the galaxy about once every 200 to 250 million years traveling at about 500,000 miles an hour; a really wild ride.[5]

According to Gonzalez, Brownlee, and Ward, "The boundaries of the galactic habitable zone are set by two requirements: the availability of material to build a habitable planet and adequate seclusion from cosmic threats." [6] The center of the galaxy is a very dangerous place full of exploding supernovae and a gigantic black hole, so best not to build a house there. The GHZ band is far enough from the center to avoid the effects of deadly radiation of exploding stars or the possibility of drifting to close to the black hole and getting sucked in. However, we need to live close enough to benefit from the heavy elements supernovae explosions spew out into space. If it were any further out in the spiral arm of the galaxy, there would not be enough heavy elements to build Earth-like planets and we would be exposed to hazardous giant gas clouds the spiral arms often visit.[7]

All the stars in the galaxy's spiral arms are what astronomers call "metal-poor population II stars" [when astronomers talk about "metals" they mean the heavy elements] which inhibits planet formation, "and the few planets that exist there lack the requisites for life."[8] Fortunately, we are far away from the spiral arms, and orbit the center in an almost perfect circle (very low eccentricity). Most other solar systems do not evidence this orbital pattern, and thus very few of our neighbors enjoy the same level of safety. As Plaxo and Gross write in their astrobiology text about our "just right" orbit: "Such low eccentricity orbits are, however, relatively, rare, [they tend to be elliptical rather than circular] and the majority of Sun-like stars currently in our neighborhood spend a significant fraction of each galactic orbit far too close to the galactic center for comfort...less than 5% of all stars lie in the life-supporting zone." [9] Just because they exist in the life-supporting zone, however; does not mean that they contain life. There are a myriad of other conditions that have to be satisfied for the emergence of complex life.

Unlike our Sun, which is solitary, most stars (about 85%) are locked with two or more other stars resulting in wild gravitation pulls that make stable planetary orbits almost impossible in such systems.[10] This suggests that life-supporting zones in other galaxies are far less probable. Most observable galaxies in the universe fall into the elliptical category. They appear egg-shaped (hence their name) and have stars with rather random orbits (since many are conjoined). As Gonzalez and Richards describe them: "Elliptical galaxies, which have less gas and dust, contain stars with a wide range of orbits—most highly inclined and eccentric."[11] A highly inclined orbit means that an object has a very irregular orbit which is too varied to harbor complex life. The eccentric orbits would take them into the danger zone at the center of the galaxies where conditions would be like the center of our own; that is, littered with supernovae explosions and black holes. The situation in irregular galaxies appears even worse.

Thus, for a variety of reasons, elliptical and irregular galaxies cannot support complex life, but not any old spiral galaxy will do either. Astronomer Hugh Ross notes that such a galaxy can be neither too big nor too small. Galaxies more massive than the Milky Way spawn massive back holes with enough mass "to ignite potent relativistic jets of deadly radiation" and their immense gravitation forces chaotic "mergers with multiple smaller galaxies." Both too large and too small galaxies run into the problem of what is known as the co-rotation radius, which is "the precise distance from the galactic center at which at which stars rotate around the center at the same rate as the galactic arms."[12] The problem for larger galaxies is that the co-rotation is far too long for the heavier elements to reach any planets that may otherwise have the potential for advanced life. The problem for smaller galaxies is that the co-rotation radius is too short for life because planets will be too close to the galactic core's deadly radiation. As Gonzalez, Brownlee, and Ward put it: "We live in prime real estate."[13]

The Circumstellar Habitable Zone

If the solar system is in a prime real estate area, so is Earth's location within the solar system. We live in the Circumstellar Habitable Zone (CHZ). The CHZ is a band of space around the Sun which is hospitable to life because it can potentially hold water. Depending what parameters are included, the CHZ band is either between .85 and 1.75 or 0.5 to 3.0 astronomical units (AUs). One AU equals the distance between the Earth and the Sun, or 92,955,807 miles = 1.0 AU. Venus (barely) and Mars (at the far end) also lie within the CHZ, but neither has water.

If we were orbiting too much closer to the Sun, we may be caught in what is called a tidal lock. Tidal locking means that a body's rotational period equals its orbital period around its parent body. This occurs because the gravitational pull of a parent body—such as the Sun to the Earth or the Earth to the Moon—slows rotation until one side always faces the parent body and the other always faces away. Mercury is tidally locked to the Sun, and the Moon is tidally locked to the Earth. This results in an extremely hot surface on the side facing of a planet facing its star, and extreme cold on the side facing away, both being hostile to complex life forms. Unlike most planets, the Earth's orbit around the Sun describes an almost perfect circle, keeping it in the CHZ permanently. Venus's orbit is more circular than the Earth's, but it is close to being tidally locked; it has such a slow rotation that its day is actually longer than its year. That is, it rotates on its axis slower that it orbits the Sun. Earth's

24-hour spin rate keeps us from being both too long in the light and heat of the day or in the dark and cold of the night.[14]

The Sun

Let us take a look at our marvelous star we call the Sun. The Sun is a relatively young star, forming only about 4.6 billion years ago. It formed from an immense cloud of dust and gas called a nebular cloud composed mostly of hydrogen, but it would have also contained the heavier elements from the first stars that developed about two billion years after the Big Bang which subsequently became supernovae. The Sun formed at just the right time to benefit from the inheritance of the heavy elements bequeathed to it by these supernovae. At some point in our neighborhood, the gas cloud began to spiral around its center until gravity overcame the gas pressure and fused hydrogen into helium (nuclear fusion) to ignite our Sun into the flaming ball of plasma it is today. The cloud's material not used for the Sun coalesced into the planets, and the solar system was born. According to NASA, the ratio of the Sun's diameter to the Earth's is 109.1, which means that about 1,300,000 Earths should fit inside the Sun. The Sun has a core temperature of about 27 million degrees Fahrenheit and a surface temperature about 10,000 degrees Fahrenheit. It is composed of mostly of hydrogen (about 76%) and helium (about 22%), with traces of other of elements with heavier nuclei such as oxygen, carbon, neon, and iron.[15]

We have already seen that our Sun is something of an oddity in that it is only one of 15 percent of stars that is not partnered with other stars, but it has other properties that make it ripe for life on a nearby planet called Earth. We are all aware that the Sun's energy makes life possible, but perhaps not why or how. Sunlight is used as energy by plant life to synthesize foods from carbon dioxide and water in the process of photosynthesis. Humans eat these plants and animals that live on plants such as grass to get our own energy, so in a sense, we are eating cycled sunlight. We are also able to breathe thanks to sunlight because oxygen is a byproduct of photosynthesis, and the byproduct of taking in oxygen is the carbon dioxide we breathe out that plants need to live. When these plants die, over millions of years lying compressed deep within the ground we get the fossil fuels such as oil and gas we need to keep the economy humming.

Wind is another source of energy produced by the Sun. Wind is the movement of atmospheric gases around the planet caused by heat from the Sun. Heat warms the land and bodies of water at different rates because land and water absorb or reflect sunlight differently. This uneven heating results in changes in the atmosphere as hot air rises and cool air moves in to replace it. The flow directly moves around the pressure high/low systems because of the

rotation of the Earth. The Earth's rotation is causing the wind to deflect coun-
terclockwise in the northern hemisphere and clockwise in the southern hemisphere (this deflection is called the Coriolis effect). Although high winds can
cause a lot of damage, wind plays a vital role in keeping the air, land, and sea
fresh. It drives the ocean currents and aids plant life to disperse their seeds,
spores, and pollen. Wind-driven turbines are also playing an increasing role in
providing us with clean and renewable energy.

Stars are categorized according to their mass and luminosity. Luminosity is
a star's intrinsic brightness and energy output, which depends on its mass
and its temperature, and our Sun's is "just right" for life. The Sun is one of
only 9 percent of the most massive stars in our galaxy and is highly stable.
Despite its massive size relative to other stars in our galaxy, relative to other
stars in the universe it is classified as a "yellow dwarf." There are stars that are
hundreds of times more massive in the universe, but more massive stars have
a shorter lifetime and get more luminous more quickly, both of which are not
conducive to complex life. If a star is less massive, a planet must orbit closer
to receive its energy. But being too close can lead to tidal locking, and that is
also deadly to life.[16]

The Sun's luminosity varies only by one-tenth of a percent, which is very
important because more variety would lead to wild climate changes on Earth.
Many stars frequently undergo large random increases in luminosity and thus
release immense additional heat energy radiating to any bodies orbiting
them. We are fortunate that star is as massive as it is, but it cannot be so massive that it burns out before life has time to develop and manufacture an oxygen atmosphere and the water needed for an Earth-like planet. At the other
end of the spectrum, low mass stars are more likely to tidally lock any planets
it may have, and their unstable luminosity would sterilize life on an Earth-like
planet due to regular large and deadly stellar flares.[17] We are indeed blessed.
As Gonzalez and Richards write: "Taken together, then, the anomalies [mass,
luminosity, stability] suggest that the Sun is atypical in ways that enhance
Earth's habitability for technological life."[18]

The Moon

Although the role of the Sun for life is rather obvious, the role of our Moon is
less so. The Moon is an anomalously large moon in comparison to its parent
planet at almost one-third the size of the Earth. Evidence from the composition and age of the moon rocks brought back from the Moon indicate that it
was formed about 4.5 billion years ago by a collision at an oblique angle of a
Mars-size object with the embryonic Earth, which was still mostly molten
rock at this point. This "big whack," as astronomers have dubbed it, threw off
a massive amount of material that eventually coalesced to the bright body in

the night sky that songwriters rhapsodize about. But the moon does more for us than planting romantic notions in the minds of lovers and poets. The gravitational pull of the newly formed moon slowed down Earth's rotation, slowly lengthening our day from 5 hours to the current 24 hours. Rotation causes wind, and a rotational period of 5 hours would have meant constant cyclonic winds raging around the Earth. [19]

The Earth's axis (the degree to which it tilts toward or away from the Sun) varies little from its present angle of 23.5 degrees, but without the moon's gravity it would vary much more, and chaotically so. As it is, this stable tilt gives us our predicable four seasons and wind patterns. As Ward and Brownlee explain:

> This angle is nearly constant for hundreds of millions of years because of gravitational effects of the Moon. Without the Moon, the tilt angle would wobble in response to the gravitational pulls of the sun and Jupiter. The monthly motion of our large Moon damps any tendency for the tilt axis to change. If the Moon were smaller or more distant, or if Jupiter were larger or closer, or if Earth were closer to or further from the sun, the Moon's stabilizing influence would be less effective. Without a large moon, Earth's spin axis might vary as much as 90 degrees.[20]

Ever since Isaac Newton we have known that the ocean tides result from the gravitational attraction of the Sun and Moon. Tides are caused by the gravitational pull of the Moon which causes a slight bulge in the Earth and oceans that moves the oceans about. Tides help to clean and oxygenate the oceans and bring to them vital nutrients from erosion of the earth. The tides currents mix arctic water not able to absorb much solar energy with warmer water from regions that can; this mixing balances planetary temperatures making for a more predictable and habitable climate. If there were no Moon, the tides raised would be solely due to the Sun's gravitational pull and thus much smaller, which might have inhibited the development of life.

Physics professor Joseph Spradley concludes his article on the importance of the Moon for life on Earth with the following words:

> The apparently unique nature of our Earth-Moon system violates the contemporary materialistic faith that life is commonplace in the universe. For Christians, it supports the belief that God can work through natural and seemingly random processes to achieve his purposes in creation. It encourages a new appreciation for the special gift of life and an environment suitable for its survival. It echoes the words of Psalm 8:3–4, "When I look at your heavens, the work of your fingers,

the moon and the stars, which you have set in place, what is man that you are mindful of him, and the son of man that you care for him?"[21]

Jupiter, Saturn, and Mars

If few people have thought about the Moon's vital contribution to life on Earth, even fewer have considered the role of the gas giant, Jupiter. The planet Jupiter is 10 times larger than the Earth and 300 times its mass (mass basically refers to the amount of matter contained an object whereas size refers to its dimensions). A number of astrophysicists suggest that without Jupiter the Earth might not exist as the life-friendly planet that it is. The conventional wisdom has long been that Jupiter is both a maker and destroyer of planets. According to astrophysicists Konstantin Batygin and Greg Laughlin, our solar system is highly unusual. Noting that the most common mode of planetary formation generates planets with much greater masses than the Earth that are tightly packed closely around their parent star (closer than Mercury in our system) with short orbital periods, they set out to develop a model to explain our unique solar system. Jupiter was the first planet to form and was able to dominate the planet-building process thereafter. Where the rocky planets are today, there were nascent planets destined to be been bigger and gassier (like Jupiter) than the Earth, and uninhabitable like planets in other star systems.

Batygin and Laughlin's model posits that Jupiter migrated in and then back out of the inner solar system early in the solar system's history. The gravitational interactions during this long journal caused planets, such as those found in other star systems, to crash into each other with the debris either falling into the Sun or leaving the remnants to form the asteroid belt located between Mars and Jupiter. Jupiter itself would have fallen into the Sun if it maintained its inner trajectory but was rescued by the formation of Saturn. As the two planets came closer together, it caused a gravitational interaction (orbital resonance) and fixed their current orbits. This explains our "oddball" solar system and how these catastrophic events caused the debris to coalesce into the small rocky planets, including Earth. The authors conclude: "Most dramatically, our work implies that the majority of Earth-mass planets are strongly enriched with volatile elements and are uninhabitable."[22] In other words, these planets lack Earth's solid surface and optimal atmospheric pressure.

Jupiter and Saturn (indirectly as the savior of Jupiter), have contributed to the Earths habitability as well as to its formation. Some of the debris (asteroids) of the destroyed planets was flung off into space when it came too close to Jupiter's orbit. Millions of these asteroids and meteorites pummeled the early Earth over a period of about 400 thousand years in what is known as "the period of heavy bombardment," seeding it with vital life-essential elements. We needed an asteroid belt neither too large nor too small. A much smaller belt would have failed to bring the essential chemicals and minerals to us; a larger one may have pummeled us too much.

Needless to say, complex life would not have begun had the bombardment continued. Although there are far fewer asteroids today, we need protection from them, and the respective masses of Mars and Jupiter, the two planets marking the boundary of the belt, are most helpful in this regard. If Mars was more massive, as all models of planetary formation say that it should be, its gravity would sling more of these things our way but instead takes a number of hits for us.[23] Jupiter's powerful gravity functions as a giant vacuum cleaner sucking up asteroids that have been bumped out of orbit. Jupiter's clean-up role was in evidence when Comet Shoemaker-Levy 9 impacted it in 1994; had its gravity not sucked up the comet, it may have entered our neighborhood. The solar system's bully has become the Earth's bodyguard. The British geneticist J. B. S. Haldane's quip that "the Universe is not only queerer than we suppose, but queerer than we *can* suppose," appears apropos here. So many astronomically (literally) improbable events came together to form our livable planet that it is almost beyond human comprehension.

The Earth: Home Sweet Home

We finally arrive at our own rocky "pale blue dot," as astronomer Carl Sagan dubbed the Earth on viewing photographs sent back from the probe Voyager 1 from 3.6 billion miles away. The prize patch of the cosmic real estate we call the Earth was formed from the left-over materials from the creation of the Sun. Solar winds blew away most of the lighter elements (hydrogen and helium), leaving behind the heavier elements needed to form rocky planets. If we had been further away from the Sun, the solar winds would have been too weak to have this effect, and the light elements would have coalesced into gas giants such as Jupiter and Saturn. The Earth is also often referred to as the "Goldilocks" planet because, as far as we know, seems to be the only place in the universe that is "just right" for life. And not just for any kind of life, but for intelligent life that can plumb the depths of its own existence and discover the magnificence of the fingerprints of God. Gonzalez and Richards have calculated that the probability of getting an Earth-like planet by chance: "even in a universe with 10^{11} stars per galaxy and 10^{11} galaxies, totaling 11^{22} available attempts, the chances of getting one such system would still be one chance in 10^{158}. [24] But here we are; chance? Hardly. There are a whole host of things interacting with one another that must be very finely calibrated for intelligent life to be here, beginning with our planet's' just-right mass.

The Value of a "Just Right" Planetary Mass

There are so many things that set the Earth apart from other planets to make it habitable, and all of these things are interrelated. The first thing to look for in a planet's habitability is its mass, and just like Goldilock's porridge, the Earth's is "just right." The smallest planet yet discovered outside our solar system is 5.5 times more massive than the Earth. Such a huge mass means far greater gravity, which prevents the formation of mountains and continents. Any land that may form on such a planet would quickly become eroded by its seas, resulting in a giant water world.[25] But a planet must have sufficient mass to hold an atmosphere and greenhouse gases to allow for surface face water and for its warming, but not too much that it leads to a runaway greenhouse effect which completely evaporates all water. Furthermore, the right surface pressure and temperature must stay in the same range for billions of years to prevent atmospheric escape into space, as happened on Mars. Gravity must be sufficiently high to prevent this, but it can't be too high that the planet could not rid itself of the thick hydrogen-rich atmosphere that existed on the early planet. Astrophysicist Francois Forget tells us of the importance of this: "with a solid body slightly more massive than the earth, a potential 'super-Earth' may ultimately remain like Neptune, with a massive H^2-He envelope that would prevent water from being liquid by keeping the surface pressure too high."[26]

Besides giving us oxygen to breathe, the Earth's atmosphere provides protection for deadly solar radiation. The ozone layer, the prime protector from ultraviolet rays, is formed by oxygen floating at the top of the atmosphere layer. Ozone (or trioxygen) is formed when ultraviolet rays split oxygen atoms and three of them then become covalently bonded by sharing electrons. Water, carbon dioxide, and other gases in the atmosphere also help to absorb this deadly radiation and prevent the stripping away of the ozone layer. But before this radiation reaches Earth, most of it has been deflected by the magnetic shield that surrounds the Earth and extends about 40,000 miles out into space. Only the most energetic particles able to penetrate the shield and these tend to be channeled toward the poles and produce the beautiful auroras. Such a shield is most important in a planet's early life when its host star is more excitable and throws more of its material out into space, stripping planets of their atmosphere, as the Sun did to Mars.

If you saw the movie *The Core*, you will know that the Magnetic field is generated by a molten iron core at the center of the Earth surrounded by an ocean of hot liquid metal. The Earth's rotation causes this flow of liquid metal around the core producing a colossal dynamo-like effect that generates electric currents to produce the protective magnetic shield.[27] The movie showed some of the initial effects when the molten core stopped rotating and determined that within a year the field itself will have dissipated, leaving the Earth victim to deadly solar radiation. There was a lot of really bad science in the movie, but they got that one right.

Plate Tectonics

The Earth is a dynamic system like a river; always changing yet staying the same. We look at the majesty of a mountain range and think that it always existed, yet any mountains that existed early in the Earth's history would have naturally eroded away long before now. Geologists using a simple formula calculate that a "typical" mountain mass of 1.2 miles in height and 2.5 square miles wide would have completely disappeared in 123 million years; a short time in geological terms.[28] But we see mountains everywhere on the planet instead of a flat, lifeless water world; some gigantic force has to be continuously creating them. Plate tectonics is that force. Plate tectonics refers to the movement of plates of the outer shell of the Earth that drift on top of a thick, fluid mantle beneath the Earth's surface moving continents, creating mountain ranges, and causing earthquakes. This movement is generated by convection currents carrying heat from the Earth's interior to its surface. The Earth's heat comes partly from what is left over from its early molten state and partly from the decay of radioactive elements in the core and mantle.[29]

Both plate tectonics and the magnetic field depend on the process by which the less dense material of the Earth rises and more dense material sinks. Just as large-mass planets harbor too much gravity for mountains and continents to form, small-mass planets lack plate tectonics, which results in the same outcome. A planet with low mass leads to early cooling from its initial molten state, which leads to its crust solidifying and to a "stagnant lid" (no movement of its crust); too great a mass and plate tectonics may be too mobile. The Earth's plate tectonics have just the right amount of vigor, because it "falls within a zone of transition between 'hard' stagnant lid and mobile plate regimes."[30]

The "big whack" collision that formed the moon is thought to have helped to create both the magnetic field and plate tectonics. The collision generated such intense heat that liquid iron sank to Earth's center, thus providing the mechanism for generating magnetism. It also removed some of its crust, which is important because "a thicker crust may have prevented plate tectonics."[31] Without plate tectonics constantly pushing material upwards and maintaining volcanic activity the Earth would be a lifeless water world, as it once was. "The Earth is not unique because if its oceans. Any planet in the right part of the habitable zone will have those. What is unique about the Earth is that it has LAND. If the moon had not carried away most of the crust, there would be no ocean basins, no land, and no chance for life to evolve on land." [32]

It is interesting to note how Genesis 1:9-10 described first the appearance of water on the planet, and then the land: "And God said, Let the waters under the heaven be gathered together unto one place, and let the dry land appear: and it was so. And God called the dry land Earth; and the gathering together of the waters called the Seas: and God saw that it was good." It wasn't until 1963 that science conclusively accepted the "outlandish" idea that the Earth's interior actually moved to "let the dry land appear" and "that it was good."

Plate tectonics is also closely related our life-giving atmosphere by keeping volcanism active for a long time, which moves carbon in and out of Earth's interior. Like a "living" global thermostat, volcanoes regulate the amount of carbon dioxide in the atmosphere (and thus the carbon dioxide/oxygen ratio). Without this process, too much carbon dioxide (a greenhouse gas) would become trapped in the atmosphere, and the Earth would heat up so much that the Earth would become a hot, dead planet like Venus. Too little carbon dioxide and the Earth's heat would escape, and it would become a cold, dead, planet like Mars. The stage is set, then, by all of these non-living processes and mechanisms for life. Of course, life is far from a simple thing; it requires first and foremost a good supply of liquid water. But by itself water would produce nothing; life requires many other nutrients. These nutrients are available in abundance on Earth because once solar energy is converted to chemical energy the chemical constituents of these nutrients are changed, used, changed back, and reused in cycles. Just like the first law of thermodynamics tells us about energy, the nutrients involved in these cycles are never lost in these finely-calibrated cycles.

Despite the necessity of plate tectonics for life, earthquakes, tsunamis, and volcanoes are considered "natural evils" and arguments against an omnipotent and benevolent God by atheists because of the approximately 68,000 deaths that they and other natural events cause each year.[33] While the human and financial cost of these things is indeed horrendous, it is forgotten that without plate tectonics there would be no life at all—no land mass, no water cycle, no magnetic shield, and no functional carbon/oxygen ratio. As terrible and heart-breaking as the loss of life is, it pales in comparison to the 400,000 and 500,000 who are murdered ("moral evil") worldwide each year according to the UN.[34] Natural disasters are the inevitable result of the laws of God's natural design for life into which He does not interfere.

Water and the Hydrologic Cycle

Perhaps because of its abundance (70% to 75% of the Earth's surface is covered by it), few things are more unappreciated than water. Water makes up about 60 percent of a human adult's body, and it is vital its metabolism, temperature regulation, and the flushing of toxins. In liquid form (as we know, it is the only substance on Earth that exists naturally in liquid, solid, and gas form), it is the solvent required for biochemical reactions; that is, it dissolves and transports chemicals to and from a body's cells. In short, the chemistry of life could not exist without water. As simple as its H_2O structure is, it is one of the strangest molecules known to science. It is what is known as a "polar" molecule, which basically means that it has a tiny positive charge at one side (pole) and a tiny negative charge on the other. The ability of water to dissolve other molecules is due to its polarity. Astrophysicist Hugh Ross tells us of the importance of this yet another example of fine-tuning: "polarity of the water molecule if greater: heat of fusion and vaporization would be too great for life to exist; if smaller the heat of fusion and vaporization would be too small for life's existence; liquid water would become too inferior a solvent for life chemistry to proceed; ice would not float, leading to a runaway freeze-up."[35]

An atmosphere at the right temperature and supplying the right gravitational pressure on a planet's surface is needed to keep the liquid water from boiling away into space is needed for liquid water to exist. Through its role in temperature regulation, plate tectonics is important in sustaining the conditions required for surface liquid water to exist over billions of years.[36] But since, like every other solid body in the universe, the Earth began as an inhospitable ball of white-hot molten rock, where did all our water come from? According to Plaxco and Gross: "Jupiter's massive gravitational effects perturbed the orbits of icy, volatile-rich planetesimals (asteroids and icy comets) from the outer solar system and 'tossed' them into the inner Solar System, where they collided with—and provided the volatile [chemical elements and compounds] inventory of–the rocky inner planets."[37] The ice in the first planetesimals hitting the young volcanic Earth it would have instantly turned to steam, but as the Earth cooled below 100 degrees centigrade about 3.9 billion years ago, we attained the present amount of liquid water.[38]

The hydrologic cycle is a perfect recycling method of distributing fresh, clean water around the planet to plants, animals, and us. It also moves nutrients, pathogens, and sediment in and out of aquatic environments. We have to begin the cycle somewhere, so we begin with the power of the Sun lifting water from the surface through evaporation as gas. These gas molecules are too small and weak to bring with them to the clouds any of the contaminants muddying the waters, so they are pure H_2O. Clouds form from these molecules, and when the air cools to the point that it cannot support water vapor, droplets of rain, hail, sleet, or snow form from these molecules. Precipitation falls to the ground, replenishing the water supply, which is then ready to evaporate again, and keeping the cycle going via endlessly different paths that water can take on its pilgrimage of life.

If water is unappreciated, the stuff under our feet, dirt, and soil (dirt is dead soil) are even less so. The Earth's soil was produced over hundreds of millions of years as the forces of weather and the movement of the Earth have combined grind the rocky layer of the Earth into smaller and finer grains which has been infused with nutrients provided by dead plant and microscopic animal life. Without soil (and rejuvenated dirt) we would not be able to grow food, and the animals we eat would have nothing to eat themselves. Only a dynamic planet has soil, and it is the interaction of the tectonic and hydrologic systems combined with the early appearance of microorganisms could make it possible.[39] The coming together of so many highly improbable things renders it almost impossible not to see a Divine creative design at work. It certainly took an inordinately long time to get from hydrogen to intelligent human beings, but time is a human construct which presumably means nothing to a timeless God.

The Carbon, Oxygen, and Nitrogen Cycles

Every time countless animals and humans breathe we emit carbon dioxide, which in high enough concentrations may cause convulsions, coma, and death. It is also produced by the burning of fossil fuels. With all that breathing and burning going on, why hasn't the atmosphere become so overloaded that it kills us all? The answer is that plant life uses it for their lives, and they thank us by exhaling oxygen into the world to keep the oxygen/carbon cycle in tune. The leaves of plants are made up of small cells inside of which are structures called chloroplasts. Chloroplasts contain a chemical called chlorophyll which uses solar energy to split water molecules into hydrogen and oxygen which is then released into the atmosphere. This marvelous process is known as photosynthesis: "photo" from photon (particles of light) and "synthesis" (putting things together"). Plant and human life are thus bound tightly together in this wonderful world of ours, and it is inconceivable to think that there is no design behind such a finely-tuned exchange.

The nitrogen cycle is no less amazing. Nitrogen is important to us because it is vital to making the things that make us—amino acids, proteins, and the nucleic acids for DNA and RNA. Nitrogen makes up 78 percent of the gas in the atmosphere we breathe; oxygen is 21 percent, and the other one-percent is made up of other gases (not counting pollutants). The nitrogen/oxygen balance is a delicate one because by themselves they can be deadly for us to breathe. We also get our nitrogen by eating plant food and from the meat of plant-eating animals, thanks to lightning. Lightning (yet another "natural evil" that kills people) changes atmospheric nitrogen into nitrates, a form of dissolved nitrogen that falls in rain during thunderstorms and is the primary source of nutrients for plants. When plants and animals die, their nitrogen compounds are broken down by bacteria as the plants and animals decay with transforms nitrates back to nitrogen. This nitrogen is then released into the soil and back into the atmosphere, completing the cycle.

Are we Alone?

With all the incredibly precise fine-tuning in evidence in our special galactic neighborhood, perhaps we are tempted again to ask once again the question that every philosopher of the heavens has asked: "Are we alone?" Is it inexcusably egocentric based on any weight of evidence to claim that Earth is the only planet in the cosmos with complex, intelligent life (as opposed to simple life)? For a committed naturalist, it is. The narrative of naturalism has long been guided by the notion that there is nothing special about our planet. This cutting of Earth down to size is known as the Copernican Principle, which has little to do with Copernicus himself, because all he did was to remove Earth from the center of the cosmos. In doing so he humbled Earth a little, but he did not humble creation or the uniqueness of human beings made in God's image. It really doesn't matter anyway if we are not alone; the Creator could have literally salted the universe with intelligent life if that was his desire. His existence and majesty hardly rests on an affirmative answer to the question of human cosmic uniqueness.

But returning to the question anyway; there are far more parameters necessary for a life-bearing planet than I have addressed here. Hugh Ross lists an astounding 200 of them. Ross computes the probability of a planet falling within necessary parameters by chance as less than 1 in 10^{215} and states that "fewer than a trillionth of a trillionth of a percent of all stars will have a planet capable of sustaining advanced life. Considering that the observable universe contains less than a trillion galaxies, each averaging a hundred billion stars, we can see that not even one planet would be expected, by natural processes alone, to possess the necessary conditions to sustain life."[40] Astrobiologists Plaxco and Gross also weighed the probability of intelligent life on other planets given the hundreds of coordinated "accidents" that are required to get it going and concluded: "The range of values in Drake's parameters [an equation for estimating the probability of intelligent life outside the Earth] could adopt is so great, that despite the huge numbers of stars in the Universe, current scientific knowledge is entirely consistent with N=1. That is, Fermi [Enrico Fermi, the Italian-America Nobel Prize winning physicist] was right, and we are alone."[41]

Chapter 7

Cosmological Fine-Tuning and the Multiverse

"When these scientists talk about the multiverse, that's actually their way of talking about theology! It's their way of doing metaphysics without using the G-- word!"
Robin Collins, philosopher of science.

If you Don't Want God, Get a Multiverse

We saw in the last chapter how many scientists in the early 20th century were made uncomfortable by the theological implications of the Big Bang. Although all modern physicists accept the reality of the Big Bang, there are some who are just as uncomfortable with the religious implications of the exquisite fine-tuning they have discovered in nature over the last 75 years. The big problem that many physicists would like to avoid today is the incredible fine-tuning with such outrageously large improbabilities that suggests that some "super intellect has monkeyed with the physics, as well as the chemistry and biology, as Fred Hoyle once remarked. Rather than wrestling with the challenges fine-tuning poses, some physicists have instinctively turned to the extravagant speculation that our universe is but one of perhaps trillions of other universes in what they call a "multiverse." They have thus invented one metaphysical entity that we can never know to get rid of another who we can come to know. The crux of the matter, according to cosmologist Bernard Carr is: "If there is only one universe you might have to have a fine-tuner. If you don't want God, you'd better have a multiverse."[1]

Many people, theists, and atheists alike, believe that modern cosmology forces us to choose between God and the multiverse as an explanation for the remarkable fine-tuning of the constants and forces in our universe that makes it "just right" for life. The exquisite calibration—for which both atheistic and theistic scientists—rule out chance, means that the universe has a fine-tuner or else we have a multiverse of untold trillions of universes in which every possible variation of physical constants exists somewhere and we just happened to have won the cosmic lottery. I do not claim that physicists are attracted to research on the multiverse concept animated by atheism. All I am saying is that the concept is most attractive to atheists to counter the shock of the pairing of the theologian's Genesis with the scientist's Big Bang and then the subsequent discovery of so many exquisitely fine-tuned parameters.

Physicist Alan Lightman is one of those who says we must choose between God and the multiverse; noting that intelligent design (fine-tuning by a Creator God) does not appeal to atheistic scientists wedded to a materialist worldview: "The multiverse offers an explanation of the fine-tuning conundrum that does not require the presence of a Designer."[2] He adds that our universe only appears fine-tuned simply because we are here to observe it, period, full-stop, case closed. Of course, we are here to observe it, but the goal is to try to understand it at both a physical and metaphysical level, not to say that we cannot and then turn to speculations to relieve us from doing so. Lightman is an enthusiastic supporter of the multiverse hypothesis but concedes that it is a conjecture that cannot be proved. In an ultra-materialist mode, he writes:

> Not only *must* we accept that the basic properties of our universe are accidental and incalculable. In addition, we *must* believe in the existence of many other universes. But we have no conceivable way of observing these other universes and cannot prove their existence. Thus, to explain what we see in the world and in our mental deductions, we *must* believe in what we cannot prove" (my emphasis).[3]

Sounding very much like naturalism's pope speaking *ex cathedra*, Lightman concedes that the multiverse hypothesis cannot be proved, but also that all devout materialists *must* take the existence of trillions of unseen and unseeable universes as a matter of faith. He echoes Richard Lewontin's view noted in chapter 1 to the effect that scientists like Lightman are forced by their *a priori* commitment to an absolute naturalistic worldview in spite of absurdities they may encounter within it.

Beating the Odds for Intelligent Design with the Multiverse

What is this multiverse that Lightman says we must believe in? There are a number of different models, but all are based on finding a non-design explanation for cosmic fine-tuning. We have a finite universe capable of sustaining life, albeit one that is a virtual impossibility given the trillions of non-life sustaining alternate values the universal constants could have taken. Recall Roger Penrose's calculations of the precision of the "Creator's aim" necessary to create a universe compatible with the second law of thermodynamics. And that was just to get the whole thing started. The argument from design is basically that the probability of functional higher-order complexities produced by step-wise interactions of simpler constituent parts are highly improbable when considered against the vastly greater probability that they would produce a huge number of non-functional combinations, and thus design and purpose is a more logical answer for our existence than blind chance and purposelessness.

The multiverse hypothesis allows the design argument to be rejected because given an infinite multiverse and infinite time, we could insert an infinite number of probabilities into our equations and the notion of impossibility disappears; the impossible becomes probable, and the probable becomes inevitable. Hypothesize sufficient universes and you will beat the odds of finding one with its physical constants fine-tuned to such an incomprehensible degree such as ours. That is, in an infinity of universes at least one should contain all the "coincidences" that have led to complex and intelligent life on Earth. This looks very much like a "multiverse of the gaps" maneuver to me which seems to be saying that if you buy all the lottery tickets, you are bound to win the lottery. Be that as it may, the multiverse hypothesis is a serious weapon in the atheist armory, so it is necessary for Christians to engage it.

Max Tegmark, a brilliant and imaginative physicist, has spent decades exploring multiverse possibilities and has arranged different versions of the multiverse in hierarchical fashion such that subsequent levels encompass and expand on the lower levels. Each of these levels increasingly reveals how far into unreality some scientists will go to deny the Creator.

Level I is described as: "A generic prediction of cosmological inflation is an infinite 'ergodic' space, which contains Hubble volumes realizing all initial conditions—including an identical copy of you about 10^{10} (29) m [meters] away."[4] "Ergodic" refers to dynamic processes which, given sufficient time, will impinge on all points in a given space. An infinite ergodic universe must contain Hubble volumes in which all possible initial conditions (laws of nature) obtain. The Hubble volume is the observable volume of the universe, which extends from Earth to the maximum distance that light traveled since the universe became transparent about 380,000 years after the Big Bang. But because the universe is constantly expanding, light from the most distant regions will never reach us. According to Tegmark, given an infinite number of Hubble volumes that define universes having the same laws and constants as ours, there are Hubble volumes with similar, and even identical, configurations as ours, and thus each of us will have identical twins in these different universes. All of these supposed parallel universes arose when rapid inflation milliseconds after the Big Bang created different universes in bubbles of space/time with identical laws of physics. We will never be able to see these other universes or contact our identical twin(s) since they are beyond our Hubble volume.

The essence of Tegmark's Level II is the assumption that "different regions of space can exhibit different effective laws of physics and open up infinite possibilities."[5] As opposed to universes spawned in the Level I process where each universe has a different initial distribution of matter but the same laws of physics, Level II assumes that different regions of space exhibit different laws of physics in different localities, and thus there are infinite developmental possibilities for these universes. This model assumes that the Big Bang was just one of an infinite number of space-time bubbles arising within a larger system, like bubbles popping into existence as we run water in a bathtub, and our universe is just one of the bubbles.

Because our universe bubbled into existence from a pre-existing mega-universe, this eternally inflating mega-universe takes us back to a past eternal universe. Contrary to these past-eternal models physicists Audrey Mithani and Alexander Vilenkin have shown that these alternate universes, even if they actually existed, must have had a beginning. Past eternal universes must contain trajectories that stretch infinitely into the past, which they say is not possible. They write that: "Here we have addressed three scenarios which seemed to offer a way to avoid a beginning and have found that none of them can actually be eternal in the past." [6] The essence of their argument is that nothing can escape eventual massive entropy because a past eternity would have taken everything thermodynamic equilibrium by now.

Level III is about quantum mechanics universes, which essentially means that quantum events unfold in every possible way in different universes. Each quantum event splits the universe into copies of itself. In the strange world of quantum mechanics, you can have a simultaneous "event" and a "non-event" just as an atom is both decayed and not decayed at the same time. This is called a "superposition." Schrödinger's famous thought experiment in which a cat placed in a box for an hour with a radioactive atom and a vial of poison illustrates this. If the atom decayed in that hour it would trigger the release of the poison and the cat would die and would live if it did not. Such a situation produces a cat that is both dead and alive in quantum superposition. We cannot predict the cat's fate and can only know it by opening the box after an allotted time and making the observation. Tegmark argues that quantum superpositions are not confined to the micro world because we, and everything else, are made of atoms, and if atoms can be in superposition (in two states at once), then so can we. Tegmark informs us that "The only difference between Level I and Level III is where your doppelgangers reside. In Level I they live elsewhere in good old three-dimensional space. In Level III they live on another quantum branch in infinite-dimensional Hilbert space [a mathematical concept used to infer dimension beyond the familiar two and three dimensions of everyday reality]"[7]

Just when you thought that things couldn't get any weirder, Tegmark revs up the speculation throttle to the max with Level IV. In this level, multiple universes are made up of all mathematical structures which we can conceive of and governed by different equations from those that govern our universe. Level IV is Tegmark's favored level because he argues that any conceivable universe is subsumed within it, and therefore there can be no fifth level. He explains, that this level "can be viewed as a form of radical Platonism, asserting that the mathematical structures in Plato's realm of ideas…exist 'out there' in a physical sense, casting the so-called modal realism theory…in mathematical terms akin to what Barrow refers to as 'π in the sky.'"[8] This is Plato's ideal reality in which mathematical structures are real and the language we use to describe our subjective perceptions of reality is an approximation of the perfect mathematical "form" of reality.

There you have it; every mathematical structure has a physical reality outside of space and time and which no measurement or observation could ever falsify their existence. Tegmark believes in the radical Platonic notion that mathematics is the ultimate reality, and that the "hard" empirical things they describe are imperfect copies of their real form found only within their mathematical description. Tegmark really believes this, as his remarks in a *Scientific American* article make clear: "I argue that it means that our universe isn't just described by math, but that it is math in the sense that we're all parts of a giant mathematical object, which in turn is part of a multiverse so huge that it makes the other multiverses debated in recent years seem puny in comparison."[9] What Tegmark proposes as a test for Level IV ideas is to get mathematicians to dream up more mathematical structures "describing our world is the most generic one that is consistent with our observation." But testing theories in science always rests on the firm ground of induction from experimental data to theory; adjusting the theory as the data warrants, but mathematics is a deductive enterprise with its own notions of "truth" seeking that is separate from the empirical sciences.

M-Theory

The mathematical basis for the multiverse idea is the enormously complex M-theory, which has existed on the fringes of physics since 1968 as various versions of string theory. String theories are attempts to unify gravity with quantum mechanics by smoothing out the mathematical inconsistencies between quantum theory and the general theory of relativity. There are five major versions of string theory, and using mathematical transformations called dualities it has been shown that they could be related, which resulted in M-theory. M-theory is looking for a Grand Unifying Theory of the cosmic and quantum worlds. It asserts that the fundamental constituents of physical reality are not the point particles of standard physics such as quarks, but rather even tinier filaments of energy called "strings." These strings are said to vibrate with different oscillations that give rise to all particles and forces in the universe. They are said not to only vibrate in the familiar 3 dimensions of space and one of time, but rather 11 dimensions—10 spatial dimensions plus time that are 'folded" in on one another. All the extra postulated dimensions are curled up in what is called "internal space" in trillions of possible ways, each of which are assumed to be able to describe phenomena with its own restricted range.[10] It has been said that the number of possible solutions to the equations of M-theory may be as many as $10^{1,000}$, and that "Each solution represents a unique way to describe the universe. This meant that almost any experimental result would be consistent with string theory; the theory could never be proved right or wrong."[11] If there is a remote possibility of such an experiment, and if it should prove one's favored model wrong, one can adjust the equations to accommodate the findings.

Hawking and Mlodinow note in their book *The Grand Design* that the universe is indeed exquisitely fine-tuned. Like Tegmark, they want to attribute it to blind luck because if multiple trillions of universes exist, there must be a winner in the ultimate Powerball game despite the odds. Hawking and Mlodinow inform us that: "People are still trying to decipher the nature of M-theory, but that may not be possible,"[12] but continue as though it's not only possible but has been done and dusted. They go on to posit the existence of a many different universes by appealing the "laws" of M-theory (which they previously said may be undecipherable) as existing in the internal curled spaces. They write: "The laws of M-theory therefore allow for different universes with different apparent laws, depending on how internal space is curled. M-theory has solutions that allow for many different internal spaces, perhaps as many as 10^{500}, which means that it allows for 10^{500} different universes, each with its own laws."[13]

The number of universes predicted by M-theory is therefore incredibly large (remember that the best estimate of the number of atoms in the known universe is 10^{80}). However, 10^{500} is not enough to effectively address the fine-tuning for life phenomenon. If we take the product of all the probabilities starting with the "Creator's aim" in phase space and all the ratios, constants, forces, biological and chemical interactions (discuss in the next two chapters) that need to be precisely the way they are to allow human life, surely it would exceed 100^{500}. Thus, even such a number of hypothesized throws of the die cannot effectively account for the fine-tuning "problem," but perhaps string theorists can tweak the equations a little and add a zero or two to the exponent.

M-theorists write as though they ascribe intelligence, personality, and agency to mathematical equations since they appear to believe that their equations can bring universes into existence. Take Hawking and Mlodinow's bizarre notion (akin to Tegmark's) that the universe owes its existence to nothing but mathematical laws: "Because there is a law like gravity, the universe can and will create itself from nothing... Spontaneous creation is the reason there is something rather than nothing, why the universe exists, why we exist. It is not necessary to invoke God to light the blue touch paper and set the universe going."[14] By setting the laws of nature against God who created them, John Lennox accuses Hawking and Mlodinow of committing "a classical category error by confusing two entirely different kinds of entity: physical law and personal agency."[15] Laws are mathematical models that describe the behavior of forces or things that exist; they do not possess agency to bring those forces or things into existence; an abstraction has never created a concrete reality.

The divine law that Hawking and Mlodinow say created trillions of universes from "nothing" is gravity, which is something, not nothing; or is it? When asked to where gravity came from, Hawking answered: "M-theory."[16] So gravity was created by math squiggles on paper—can you feel Newton and Einstein rolling over in their graves? Tim Radford, science editor of Britain's *Guardian* newspaper, captures wonderfully the God-like nature with which M-theory has been endowed by Hawking and Mlodinow:

> M-theory invokes something different [from other theories of science]: a prime mover, a begetter, a creative force that is everywhere and nowhere. This force cannot be identified by instruments or examined by comprehensible mathematical prediction, and yet it contains all possibilities. It incorporates omnipresence, omniscience and omnipotence, and it's a big mystery. Remind you of Anybody?"[17]

Mathematics in Science

Strictly speaking, M-theory is not a theory in the scientific sense that it has been supported by empirical observations. It is a purely abstract mathematical theory with, as noted above, a ridiculously incredible number of possible solutions. This is not to criticize mathematics; the backbone of all science. Mathematics provides us with accurate quantitative information about the relationships among phenomena that exist in nature. The unreasonable effectiveness of mathematics has given it a mystical aura; as Roger Penrose said of it. "There is something absolute and 'God-given' about mathematical truth."[18] Mathematical truths represent the real world in abstract symbols and have been amazingly successful in doing so. Mathematical equations may represent some aspect of reality already known to the senses but not understood at the time, such as motion and gravity described by Newton, or electricity and magnetism described by Maxwell. On the other hand, they may describe something unknown but which can be tested experimentally and then known empirically, such as Einstein's general theory of relativity that predicted the bending of light by gravity. These and numerous other examples, justify the mathematical models as a faithful representation of empirical reality.

However, there are many string theorists who want to decouple mathematics from empirical validation, claiming that the validity of their mathematical models depends on the 'beauty" or "elegance" of their equations, and not at all on empirical findings. In other words, if physicists invent an imaginary world with clearly expressed and consistent mathematical rules, we can use these rules to gather imaginary mathematical "evidence" about that imaginary world. From this base, they can shape a falsifiable theory because the evidence derived from it looks the same to all observers who understand the rules of the math involved. Otherwise put, because the theory they propose is internally consistent and "beautiful" it must be valid.

The multiverse conjecture involving mathematical representations, elegant as they may be, is a creature of the imagination designed to try to explain away the reality of the fine-tuning of our universe. Mathematician George Ellis believes that "it is only the gaps in current theories that cannot tell us why the fundamental physical constants have the values they do that drive the multiverse theories." If we could explain them, "the drive for a multiverse explanation would fall away."[19] It seems to me that it is pretty lame to use a multiverse beyond our empirical reach to explain away things in this universe that are within our reach.

The math in string theory is so dauntingly difficult that it keeps the critical layperson at arm's length; I for one may as well be looking at hieroglyphics or ancient Chinese poetry in the original. I will thus call on Albert Einstein himself, who said: "As far as the laws of mathematics refer to reality, they are not certain; and as far as they are certain, they do not refer to reality."[20] I believe Einstein was saying that many mathematical models are linear and do not fully capture the chaos and complexity of nature and are thus only valid within certain limits. The British physicist Herbert Dingle, a former president of the Royal Astronomical Society, a formidable mathematician who engaged in many mathematical controversies with Einstein tells us how almost anything imaginable can be done with mathematics: "In the language of mathematics we can tell lies as well as truths, and within the scope of mathematics itself there is no possible way of telling one from the other. We can distinguish them only by experience or by reasoning outside the mathematics, applied to the possible relation between the mathematical solution and its physical correlate."[21] Recall how Einstein stopped the universe in its tracks on paper by inserting the "fudge factor" into his cosmological constant.

Kurt Godel's ontological proof of God's existence expressed in the language of mathematical logic is an example of what can be accomplished with mathematics. Godel was a mathematician of genius who has been described as the finest logician since Aristotle. The ontological argument was first proposed by St. Anselm, 11th century Archbishop of Canterbury, and expanded on by others over the centuries. Briefly, the argument goes like this: God is that which no greater can be conceived and nothing greater can be imagined, and if God does not exist then there is something greater than God that can be imagined. But we cannot, therefore, God exists. The argument is obviously much more involved than this, but this is the gist of it.

No one has ever found inconsistencies in Godel's theorem, and in 2014, computer scientists Christoph Benzmüller and Bruno Paleo fed Godel's proof into high-powered computer programs called "higher-order automated theorem provers" and proved him to be right.[22] They showed that his proof was correct by way of higher modal logic (modes of qualifying truth based on notions of necessity, contingency, and possibility). Would we expect any multiverse physicist to accept this? I doubt it. They would say that Godel's theorem was proved only by the internal consistency of the mathematics which is based on certain assumptions, and they would be right. We cannot prove God exists by mathematics any more than we can prove the existence of a multiverse. Mathematicians seek to describe and precisely measure defined features of nature. Since God is outside of nature, He lies outside of definition and measurement. We can describe a tree, a cloud, the movement of the planets, and a million other things with math because they are "things." They are material and natural while God is immaterial and supernatural, and thus not amenable to measurement. In mathematical terms, God is not a *theorem* to be proved; He is a self-evident *axiom* from which ultimately everything must be deduced.

Theories and Hypotheses in Science

Scientists earn their living seeking of new knowledge about the world. They do this in an orderly way by first making themselves masters of what is already known. This known knowledge has been organized in a systematic way by fitting facts into coherent and harmonious patterns we call theories. A great visual example of such a theory is one seen on the walls of university classrooms across the country is the periodic table. This powerful icon of science rests on the atomic theory of matter. Chemists knew about the properties of many of the elements displayed on these charts for centuries, but their relationships were not known until Dmitri Mendeleev placed them into a logical order in 1869. Mendeleev arranged the 63 known elements at the time in order of their atomic number, which is the number of protons in the nucleus of each element, starting with hydrogen. Mendeleev's genius was to recognize some elements had similar characteristics to others and grouped these in columns and found that they fit into regular intervals (periods) of eight elements that increased in atomic mass from left to right.

In addition to being looking backwards to fit known facts into a harmonious pattern, theories must also be forward-looking, telling researchers where they might look to fill in the gaps in their knowledge. Mendeleev's table had a number of gaps which indicated to chemists that there had to be other elements that fit the properties of others in its group. Chemists have done so, and the table has been adjusted to fit an additional 55 elements that have since been discovered or synthesized in labs. Thus, good scientific theories are always open to adjustment as new facts are discovered. Looking to fill the gaps in our knowledge takes the form of a series of statements that can be logically deduced from a theory called hypotheses, which are deductive statements about relationships between and among factors we expect to find based on the logic of our theories. Theories provided the raw material (the ideas) for generating hypotheses, and hypotheses support or fail to support theories by exposing them to empirical testing.

Science is often conducted in a messy and chaotic intellectual environment analogous to the homicide detective's new case in a physical environment. A detective confronted with a number of facts about a murder must fit them together to tell their story. At this point, the detective is rather like a Mendeleev with a bunch of chemical facts in need of an ordered explanation. Using years of experience, training, and good common sense the detective constructs a theory linking those facts together so that they begin to make some sense. An initial theory derived from the available facts then guides the detective in the search for additional facts in a series of "*if* this is true, *then* this should be true" statements (hypotheses). There may be many false starts as our detective misinterprets some facts, fails to uncover others, and considers some to be relevant when they are not. Good detectives, like good scientists, adjust their "whodunit" theory as new facts warrant. Detectives emotionally fixated on a particular suspect will do the opposite—adjust the facts to fit their theory. When detectives do this, the crime goes unsolved or the wrong person may be indicted. Even the most brilliant of scientists can have such an emotional attachment to their favored theory that nothing will convince them to the contrary. Witness the genius of Sir Fred Hoyle who went to his grave in 2001 still denying the reality of the Big Bang.

Is M-Theory Really a Theory According to the Criteria of Science?

In science a good theory is generally considered to possess the following characteristics:

(1). *Predictive Accuracy:* A theory must not only be backward looking to harmoniously fit known facts together, but it must also be forward-looking pointing to ways of finding new facts.

(2). *Predictive Scope:* Refers to the scope or range of the theory refers to how much of the empirical world falls under the explanatory umbrella of theory A compared to theory B. As the predictive scope of a theory widens, it tends to get more complicated.

(3). *Simplicity:* If two competing theories are equal in terms of the first two criteria, then the less complicated one is considered more "elegant."

(4). *Falsifiability:* A theory is never proven true, but it must have the quality of being falsifiable. If a theory is formulated in such a way that no amount of evidence could possibly falsify it, then it is not a scientific theory.

Given these universally accepted criteria for judging theories, does M-theory fit the bill? Given its lack of empirical support, it is better characterized as a hypothesis than a theory. Nevertheless, Hawking and Mlodinow inform us with certainty as if it had mountains of such support that: "M-theory predicts that a great many universes were created out of nothing. Their creation does not require the intervention of some supernatural being or god. Rather, these multiple universes arise naturally from physical laws."[23] They imply by this that M-theory possesses both predictive accuracy and predictive scope. But M-theory has not provided one scrap of empirical evidence; it is a gun that's never been fired so we cannot gauge its accuracy. The predictive scope is potentially enormous. If the laws governing the macro- and micro-worlds were ever united in ways that could be empirically verified it would be the elusive theory of everything. But it has not done this even on paper, so it fails here also. It is difficult to apply the term "simplicity" to M-theory because very few physicists or mathematicians understand it. As for the fourth criterion; there is no way, even in principle, that the theory could be falsified as it applies to the multiverse.

Failure to observe strings could falsify the theory, but could string ever be observed? The answer is that seems most unlikely. Sub-atomic particles are discovered by smashing atoms together in a collider at near the speed of light and analyzing the computer images formed by the debris. The smaller a hypothesized particle, the more the energy needed to detect it. The Large Hadron Collider is the world's largest particle accelerator built into a 17-mile underground circular tunnel on the Swiss-French border. It requires an accelerator tunnel of great dimensions to generate the high speeds necessary to detect sub-atomic particles, so what would have to be the circumference of a tunnel long enough to detect a string? There is a rather simple formula to calculate the radius of curvature needed for a collider given the energy of a particle, as well as for the strength of the magnetic field of the bending magnets that keep particles traveling on a circular trajectory. Physicist Frank Heile has done the math and shows that the radius would have to be 517 light years, which means that the diameter of such a collider tunnel would be 1,034 light-years, and that the magnetic power required would be quadrillions of times more powerful that the Earth's magnetic shield.[24]

Sir Roger Penrose, a friend of Hawking's and who worked alongside him for many years, describes Hawking and Mlodinow's ideas of the multiverse as "hardly science" and "not even a theory." He added that M-theory is "a collection of ideas, hopes, and aspirations. The book [*The Grand Design*] is a bit misleading. It gives you this impression of a theory that is going to explain everything; it's nothing of the sort. It's not even a theory."[25] Penrose is by no means the only one who derides the idea that M-theory is a scientific theory. In 2006, mathematical physicist Peter Woit wrote a book-length stinging criticism of string theory, likening it to that caricature of learning called postmodernism. The words "not even wrong" he uses in the title of his book implies a hunch masquerading as a theory since it does not make testable predictions of observations that we can determine whether they were wrong or not. Woit's says: "There is a striking analogy between the way superstring theory research is pursued in physics departments and the way postmodern 'theory' has been pursued in humanities departments. In both cases, there are practitioners that revel in the difficulty and obscurity of their research, often being overly impressed with themselves because of this."[26]

In 2017, Woit was even more convinced that string theory is not even wrong, stating that experimental results from the Large Hadron Collider had not shown any evidence of the extra dimensions string theorists had argued for as predictions of the theory. He states that: "The internal problems of the theory are even more serious after another decade of research. These include the complexity, ugliness, and lack of explanatory power of models designed to connect string theory with known phenomena, as well as the continuing failure to come up with a consistent formulation of the theory."[27]

Ellis and Silk add coal to the fire, noting that the mathematical elegance of M-theory generates grand but untestable hypotheses about multiverses existing pre-Big Bang in place of empirical science. They conclude that because M-theory is metaphysical, "theoretical physics risks becoming a no-mans-land between mathematics, physics, and philosophy that does not truly meet the requirements of any."[28] Ellis is a distinguished professor of mathematics and is not by any means denying the huge utility of math in physics, only in using it as a sleight of hand in an attempt to deny the obvious. The bottom line on M-theory, mathematically beautiful as the equations may be, is that its predictions have no chance to ever be observed experimentally. Even if other universes do exist with laws permitting spontaneous generation, it still does not explain the origin of life in the only universe we know to exist.

Ellis and Silk also argue that theories such as M-theory harm physics when their proponents argue for relaxing the criteria by which a theory is judged useful or not. They note:

> Faced with difficulties in applying fundamental theories to the observed Universe, some researchers called for a change in how theoretical physics is done. They began to argue--explicitly—that if a theory is sufficiently elegant and explanatory, it need not be tested experimentally, breaking with centuries of philosophical tradition of defining scientific knowledge as empirical. We disagree. As the philosopher of science Karl Popper argued: a theory must be falsifiable to be scientific.[29]

Tom Hartsfield joins the chorus of other physicists criticizing M-theory and explains why they do: "The fire igniting critics of string theory is not personal animus or professional jealousy. It's the idea that a single theory has become so entrenched and popular in its field that its failures cannot be addressed truthfully. Now, physicists ask that the rules be bent or changed just to accommodate it. To loosen the principles of our fantastically successful scientific method just to allow for one passing theoretical fad to continue would be a disaster."[30] Likewise, physicist Carlo Rovelli opines that theoretical physics has had a poor record in the last few decades because:

> It got trapped in a wrong philosophy: the idea that you can make progress by guessing new theory and disregarding the qualitative content of previous theories. This is the physics of the "why not?" Why not studying this theory or the other? Why not another dimension, another field, another universe? Science has never advanced in this manner in the past. Science does not advance by guessing. It advances by new data or by a deep investigation of the content and the apparent contradictions of previous empirically successful theories...But most of current theoretical physics is not of this sort. Why? Largely because of the philosophical superficiality of the current bunch of scientists.[31]

What if the Multiverse Exists?

I could go on for pages quoting eminent scientists criticizing M-theory as a "theory" too far, but as far as I am concerned, the multiverse physicists would do well to heed Isaac Newton, whose first rule of scientific reasoning is: "Nature does nothing in vain, and more is in vain when less will serve; for Nature is pleased with simplicity, and affects not the pomp of superfluous causes." But what if, against all the odds, M-theorists turn out to be right and the exquisite laws of nature in our universe turn out to be just local by-laws and other localities have different ones? What are the implications for theists' belief in the God of Christianity? Many atheistic scientists affirm that their existence would refute the design inference about cosmic fine-tuning which they say is the result of the "natural selection" among many trillions (or infinity) of universes. Some say that because of this we have to make a choice; an infinite number of universes ruled by blind chance or just the one we live in designed by the Creator. As philosopher Richard Swinburne puts it, "To postulate a trillion, trillion universes, rather than just one God, in order to explain the orderliness of our universe seems the height of irrationality."[33] While I agree with Swinburne's point, I also believe that there is no choice involved at all. If an infinity of universes exist, then I would say that it points to an infinitely creative God. Contrary to popular belief, according to Robin Collins, a number of ancient Christian theologians such as Nicholas of Cusa and Giordano Bruno, as well as scientists such as Newton and Leibnitz championed the notion a plurality of worlds. Collins writes: "Indeed, many felt that restricting God to creating one universe was contrary to the omnipotence of God."[34]

In a similar vein, cosmologist Bernard Carr writes that the so-called "choice" between God or the multiverse is wrong-headed for several reasons:

> In fact, this dichotomy between God and multiverse is clearly simplistic. It may be true that any physical mechanism for creating our Universe will create others. But if one has a sausage making machine, one still needs to ask who made the sausage-making machine. So, while the fine-tunings certainly do not provide unequivocal evidence for God, nor would the existence of a multiverse preclude Him. For if God can create one universe, He can presumably create many. Nevertheless, it is not surprising that the multiverse proposal has commended itself to atheists. Indeed, Neil Manson has described the multiverse as "the last resort for the desperate atheist." For if ours is the only universe, then one has a problem explaining the fine-tunings and might well be forced into a theological direction."[35]

Richard Dawkins' take on Hawking and Mlodinow's *Grand Design* is that physics has administered the *coup de grace* to God as if to proclaim that we need to choose between God and a multiverse. As I have argued, however, the "choices" are not mutually exclusive because even if a multiverse exists, it is more reasonably there by God's creative hand than by investing God-like power to spontaneous self-creation from nothing. A "pre-Big Bang" scenario just pushes back the beginning of His creation. As Keith Ward remarks, "it is logically impossible for a cause to bring about some effect without already being in existence...Between the hypothesis of God and the hypothesis of a cosmic bootstrap, there is no competition. We were always right to think that persons, or universes, who seek to pull themselves up by their bootstraps are forever doomed to failure"[36]

Renowned physicist Michio Kaku is a firm believer in the multiverse but sees a plan and an intelligent designer behind it all. He said in an interview reported in the British newspaper *Daily Express*, "To me it is clear that we exist in a plan which is governed by rules that were created, shaped by a universal intelligence and not by chance. Believe me, everything that we call chance today won't make sense anymore. The mind of God, we believe, is cosmic music, the music of strings resonating through 11-dimensional hyperspace." [37] Quantum physicist John Polkinghorne likewise has some respect for M-theory, but states that: "A possible explanation of equal intellectual respectability–and to my mind greater economy and elegance–would be that this one world is the way it is, because it is the creation of the will of a Creator who purposes that it should be so."[38]

Confronted with all the evidence we have from cosmology, all we can do is reason to the best explanation of why we are here, and that explanation points unerringly to a creator God. Frank Tipler, a former atheist, came to the same conclusion after 25 years of exploring quantum physics and cosmology: "When I began my career as a cosmologist some twenty years ago, I was a convinced atheist. I never in my wildest dreams imagined that one day I would be writing a book purporting to show that the central claims of Judeo-Christian theology are in fact true, that these claims are straightforward deductions of the laws of physics as we now understand them. I have been forced into these conclusions by the inexorable logic of my own special branch of physics."[39] The multiverse may be "the last resort for the desperate atheist," but if it exists it provides no comfort for them because it still needs the Creator. As long as there are stars in the sky, birds in the trees, love in the heart, and one or a trillion universes, we can know that He exists.

Chapter 8

Abiogenesis: The Search for
the Origin of Life

"In the presentation of a scientific problem, the other
player is the good Lord. He has not only set the problem
but also has devised the rules of the game – but they are
not completely known, half of them are left for you to
discover or to deduce."
Erwin Schrodinger, Nobel Laureate in physics

The Mystery of Life's Beginning

Physics is the most basic of the sciences, dealing as it does with the most
fundamental elements of reality. When physicists—particularly cosmologists
—feel that they have exhausted materialist/naturalistic resources, many of
them cross the permeable boundary between science and religion and pon-
der deep philosophical questions such as "What does it all mean?" They are
almost forced to do so. As we move away from physics to chemistry and biology, we enter more exclusively materialist territory, probably because the
work of scientists in these fields does not lead them to examine issues of ultimate reality. There is one exception, however, and that is origin of life (OoL)
researchers. The origin of life appears far more intractable than even the
origin of the universe. After all, we know that all matter is derived from humble hydrogen atoms forged by Big Bang nucleosynthesis being cooked into
heavier elements in stellar and supernova syntheses. Physics may be difficult,
but a few beautiful equations containing fewer than 10 symbols can describe
such things as gravity, force, and the relationship between matter and energy.
We cannot begin to describe the complexity of a single living human cell in
this way.

Scientific materialism proposes that just as matter and energy is ultimately
the same thing, life is continuous with, and arose from, inert matter. How did
this happen? No one has a clue. Nobel Laureate Francis Crick, the co-
discoverer of the DNA has stated that: "An honest man, armed with all the
knowledge available to us now, could only state that in some sense, the origin
of life appears at the moment to be almost a miracle, so many are the condi-

tions which would have had to have been satisfied to get it going."[1] Paul Davies made the same point: "Many investigators feel uneasy about stating in public that the origin of life is a mystery, even though behind closed doors they freely admit that they are baffled." [2] OoL researchers Trevors and Abel's article in *Cell Biology International* titled "Chance and necessity do not explain the origin of life," surveyed the many speculations that have been forwarded to try to explain the immense gap between prebiotic chemistry on a lifeless Earth to the stunningly complex DNA information code. They concluded that "Contentions that offer nothing more than long periods of time offer no mechanisms of explanation for the derivation of genetic programming. No new information is provided by such tautologies. The argument simply says it happened. As such it is nothing more than blind belief." [3]

Life from non-life is spontaneous generation; the only other possibility is Divine creation, as George Wald, Nobel Prize winner in Physiology or Medicine, admitted. But he then exposed his "blind belief," writing, "We cannot accept that [Divine creation] on philosophical grounds; therefore, we choose to believe the impossible: that life arose spontaneously by chance!" [4] Wald later became a deist upon contemplating cosmology (the remarkable fitness of the universe for life) and consciousness (mind as an immaterial phenomenon). In an article in the *International Journal of Quantum Chemistry*, he wrote: "It has occurred to me lately—I must confess with some shock at first to my scientific sensibilities—that both questions might be brought into some degree of congruence. This is with the assumption that mind, rather than emerging as a late outgrowth in the evolution of life, has existed always, as the matrix, the source, and condition of physical reality—that the stuff of which physical reality is composed is mind-stuff."[5]

Another Nobel Prize winner, biochemist and atheist Christian de Duve, wrote that, "If you equate the probability of the birth of a bacterial cell to that of the chance assembly of its component atoms, even eternity will not suffice to produce one for you."[6] Despite this, de Duve believed that this is indeed a lucky accident that happened, the proof being simply that we are here! To say that something occurred by accident or chance means that it did not happen by necessity or design. To say that something occurred due to necessity is to claim that it could not have been otherwise. In this context, it means that life just had to happen given the laws of physics and chemistry. Scientists use the term abiogenesis to mean the (unknown) process by which chemical (inorganic) evolution became biological (organic) evolution.

Obviously, abiogenesis is not a simple matter. In 1969, Dean Kenyon, with co-author Gary Steinman published a book titled *Biochemical Predestination* in which they proposed that abiogenesis was not only possible but was inevitable (predestined by physical and chemical laws). They argued that the chemical properties of amino acids attracted each other forming long chains that became the first proteins which eventually would lead to LUCA (the Last Universal Common Ancestor). The book was warmly received by biologists and chemists thrilled with the idea from leading biophysicists that life could emerge from non-life. For a very long time, biochemical predestination dominated the OoL landscape, partly because of Kenton's impeccable scientific credentials (PhD in biophysics from Stanford and Postdoctoral Fellow in Chemical Biodynamics) and partly, perhaps predominantly, because it ruled out an intelligent designer behind it all. Dean Kenyon is one of the foremost biophysicists of our time. After a long career trying unsuccessfully to determine how complex proteins and cells could self-organize naturalistically, he came to the conclusion that: "We have not the slightest chance of a chemical evolutionary origin for even the simplest of cells...so, the concept of the intelligent design of life was immensely attractive to me and made a great deal of sense, as it very closely matched the multiple discoveries of molecular biology."[7] A former atheist, Dr. Kenyon is now a practicing Christian dragged there by his science.

The Complexity of the Protein Making Process

The immense difficulties OoL researchers face can be appreciated somewhat by looking at the basis of life as it now exists. Your body consists of trillions of cells inside of which—with some exceptions such as mature blood cells—is a factory for making proteins. Your cells make thousands of different proteins for all the systems of your body. Proteins are constantly being made for substances you need to keep going, and the information needed to make them are carried on specific segments of DNA called genes within the nucleus of each cell. Genes are the blueprint, recipe, library, or construction manual (chose your own metaphor) for life because they contain all the information that instructs your cells what proteins to make and when to do it. This is an extraordinarily complex process and no explanation can begin to do it justice.

DNA consists of two strings of nucleotides tightly wrapped around a protein core and twisted around each other to form the familiar double helix ladder. Each nucleotide is built from a sugar and phosphate backbone, and a base (the rungs). There are four different bases: adenine (A), thymine (T), cytosine (C), and guanine (G), that bond in specific ways: C can only pair with G, and A can only pair with T. There are over 3 billion base pairs in the human genome, and a gene is a group of adjacent base pairs that code for the manufacture of a protein. Only about two percent of our DNA codes for proteins; many other segments regulate the behavior of the coding DNA, and new functions are being found all the time for what biologists used to call "junk genes."[8] According to one calculation, we have about 6 feet of DNA in each cell. If you multiply that by our approximately 100 trillion cells, we have about 12 million miles of the stuff, which is enough to reach to the moon and back 25 times.[9]

A heating system serves as a useful analogy for the genome's responsiveness to our needs. Your house's heating system's thermostat senses when the ambient temperature is below the desired setting and activates the furnace to restore the temperature to where you want it. The body's afferent nerves that carry nerve impulses from sensory organs to the brain may be thought of as a set of physiological thermostats that sense and transmit information about the state of your internal or external environment. When something is not right (say a cut finger), the "furnace" in the nucleus of the cell kicks on and an enzyme called DNA helicase unzips the double-stranded DNA into two single strands. An enzyme called RNA polymerase binds to the promotor region of a gene to signal the DNA to unwind so the bases on the DNA strand can be "read" to make a strand of messenger RNA (mRNA). Uracil is substituted for thymine as the base complementary to adenine at this time. When the RNA polymerase crosses a stop sequence in the gene, the mRNA strand is complete, it then detaches from DNA. The DNA helix is then reconstituted by the billions of free-floating nucleotides in the nucleus and the mRNA leaves the nucleus to take the message to the cell's protein factory.

Ever since I took a class in cell biology, I have been enthralled and mystified by the cell's marvel of design fitted into a space smaller than the period at the end of this sentence. The cell is a hive of non-stop chemical activity of mind-boggling complexity. It has been likened to a factory with the nucleus being the control center and the ribosomes being the construction guys that build the proteins on the assembly line. The Golgi apparatus bundles proteins and lipids as they are synthesized, and the lipid molecules that form the cell's membrane serve as a kind of foremen of the shipping department who decides what substances should leave or enter the cell. The factory floor is the cytoplasm and the power to run it all is provided by the mitochondria that convert oxygen and nutrients into energy in the form of adenosine triphosphate (ATP). The endoplasmic reticulum is part of the quality control mechanism that inspects the finished product to ensure that only correctly folded proteins are sent to their final destinations, and the lysosomes that break down waste in the cell and discards it are the janitorial staff. The cell is a perfect example of what scientists call irreducible complexity. Irreducible complexity means that any complex system requires all its parts be in place for it to function and that if any of the interacting parts were removed the entire system becomes non-functional.

The instructions for making proteins are transmitted to the cell by mRNA in the form of a triplet of bases (e.g., CAA, AGC, CCU, etc.) called *codons*. Codons can be thought of as three letter words that correspond to the word for a particular amino acid, the building blocks of proteins. There are four bases conveyed in units of three, so there are 4 x 4 x 4 = 64 possible arrangements of codons. This number is more than enough for the coding of the 20 standard amino acids. A sequence of codons provides a legible genetic "sentence" giving instruction for the building of a protein. Transfer RNA (tRNA) "reads" the coded message and picks up and transports the appropriate sets of amino acids that complement the codons (anticodons) on the mRNA strand. Codon and anticodon are then slotted into place by yet another form of RNA called ribosomal RNA (rRNA). When this is complete we have a protein, which is sent off from the cell to do its work by binding to a receptor protein. But proteins have to be folded in very specific ways if they are to fit into their receptors and function, and on rare occasions, mistakes are made in which they fold the wrong way. To counter this, the cell has a quality control system by which the protein is inspected, and if defective it is either repaired or stripped down to its component parts. DNA thus contains complex and specific information that results in the building of all forms of living things with astounding precision. Errors in this process not caught and rectified by the cell's elaborate surveillance system occur at about one error per 10 billion letters.

Finally, the cell is not a series of simple building blocks that click into place like Lego cubes, but rather systems within systems within systems. It would seem logical that all of these parts would have to arrive on the scene as a whole unit to be functional. If a protein evolved first, how did it arrange itself without the ribosomes; where was the ATP to energize the process? What if it needed repair and there was no repair mechanism? If the repair mechanism evolved first, what would have been its purpose if there was nothing to repair? There are many "chicken or the egg" question such as these, and there are ingenious answers; some plausible and some not, but every answer is shot down sooner or later. Of course, this is the nature of science; a mode of inquiry that never claims to have definitive answers. Figure 8.1 shows the marvelously intricate cell and its various parts.

Is there intelligence behind all that information contained in DNA? I have a book of matches in front of me that tells me to "Close cover. Keep away from children." Surely no one doubts that the simple information content consisting of 29 letters arranged in orderly sequence is the product of an intelligent mind. How likely is it that the 3 billion-plus letters arranged in an orderly fashion, and conveying immensely more complex information, is not the product of a mind with infinite intelligence? Former atheist Francis Collins, the head of the government's Human Genome Project, calls DNA the "language of God," and offers it as a compelling argument for the reality of God. As mentioned previously, it was the enormous complexity of DNA that moved long-term champion of atheism, Anthony Flew, to reject atheism, which he concluded does not fit reality and become a believer in an intelligent Creator, which does.

Figure 8.1 The Cell and its Structure
https://training.seer.cancer.gov/anatomy/cells_tissues_membranes/cells/structure.html

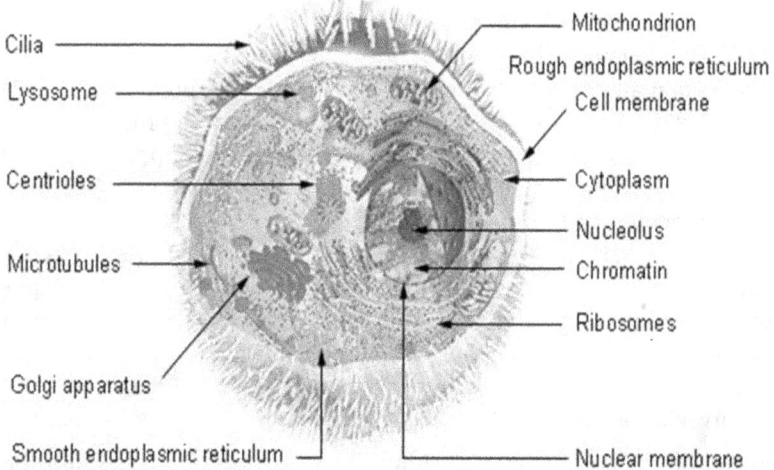

The amazingly complex and exquisitely orchestrated process of protein making is ultimately driven by information contained in the DNA. Physicist and information specialist Werner Gitt has looked at all the steps (many more than recounted here) and quantified the amount of information contained in DNA. Gitt writes that the binary (0, 1) information contained in DNA is "equal to the information contained in 750,000 typed A4 [regular typing paper] each containing 2,000 characters." [10] That's 1,500,000, 000 "on-off," "stop-go" bits of information required to keep you and me up and running! From a natural-ist point of view, this elegantly designed process, unmatched by anything even dreamed of by humans, is the result of multiple pure chance events cooperating with the laws of physics and chemistry. This is not a criticism since science *must* look for natural explanations regardless of an individual scientist's religious convictions; it cannot stop and conclude that God did it. We know that He did by "devising the rules of the game," as Erwin Schroding-er said in the epigraph of this chapter, but he left it up to science "to discover or to deduce." Perhaps by pursuing their theories more of them will come to appreciate God's handiwork and join with any number of physicists such as Albert Einstein in saying "The more I study science, the more I believe in God."

The Oparin- Haldane Hypothesis and the Miller-Urey Experiment

The earliest scientific speculation about a naturalistic OoL came around the time that the Big Bang was emerging as an alternative to the static universe in the early1930s. Russian Alexander Oparin and Briton J.B.S. Haldane separately concluded that life could not have formed from an oxygen-rich atmosphere that currently bathes the Earth because oxygen interferes with reactions that might have transformed simpler organic molecules into more complex ones by stealing electrons from hydrogen atoms. We see this occurring today when oxidizing turns metals into rust and when physicians warn us to take antioxidants to counter oxidation (free radicals stealing electrons) of our body's cells. They, therefore, posited that Earth's early atmosphere was "reducing;" that is, one in which there is little or no oxygen and one that easily produces chemical reactions. Such an atmosphere was considered to be rich in hydrogen and other compounds such as methane and ammonia that donate atoms to other substances; that is, they are reducing gases. Hydrogen, methane, and ammonia were considered the major components in the so-called "primordial soup" (Darwin's "warm little pond") by which chance and necessity produced the first molecules for life in the form of amino acids. These amino acids in turn formed chance Darwinian-like interactions with other substances necessary to build proteins. [11]

The appeal of a reducing atmosphere for OoL researchers is that it would not take a lot of energy to form the carbon-rich molecules vital to life. Unfortunately for the theory, geologists have found no carbonates (formed by carbon and carbon dioxide) in rocks dating back to the early Earth, indicating that most carbon dioxide was still locked in the atmosphere. Furthermore, in a reducing oxygen-free world there would be no ozone layer, and large amounts of ultraviolet radiation would reach the Earth's surface, "making delicate chemical reactions on the planet's surface very difficult."[12]

The reducing atmosphere hypothesis was widely accepted at the time, and in 1953 a famous experiment that became known as the Miller-Urey experiment was conducted. Harold Urey and his student Stanley Miller creating a closed system of flasks in the lab containing the reducing gases assumed to constitute the Earth's early atmosphere—water, methane, ammonia, and hydrogen. A Bunsen burner served as a heat source, and electrodes provided a continuous electric spark in the apparatus to provide the catalytic source to these molecules, mimicking the role of lightning in the real world. After about a week, a tar-like sludge was produced in the flask which contained five amino acids (a modern analysis of Miller's vials revealed that 22 amino acids had been produced). Later experiments have achieved similar results with a more accurate recreation of Earth's early atmosphere conditions. However, the distance from simple amino acids to DNA could be measured in light years.

Amino acids do not live, and their structure presents a problem called the *chirality problem.*

The Chirality Problem

Even if you can make amino acids, or even the more complex nucleic acids needed to build DNA and RNA under strict laboratory conditions, it's a far cry from making them self-assemble into chains to form a protein. Bruce Alberts and his colleagues say in their best-selling text, *Molecular Biology of the Cell,* that, "From a chemical point of view, proteins are by far the most structurally complex and functionally sophisticated molecules known." [13] Amino acids are monomers ("one part") that must bond together into large molecular chains called polymers ("many parts") to form functioning proteins in the process called polymerization, much like letters form into chains we call words. Unfortunately, proteins formed in the hypothesized prebiotic aqueous soup would tend to break apart rather than assemble. Many biological chemists point out that there is no evidence that a primordial soup ever existed, but even if it did: "Polymerisation into RNA requires both energy and high concentrations of ribonucleotides. There is no obvious source of energy in a primordial soup. Ionizing UV [ultraviolet] radiation inherently destroys as much as it creates."[14]

Because these molecules have already reacted, they are at thermodynamic equilibrium. In a system in a state of internal thermodynamic equilibrium, no further change occurs because there is no free energy intrinsic to the system that would allow them to do so. Free energy can only be supplied to a living system by a mechanism that can harvest energy from the environment so that it can counteract the decaying effects of the second law of thermodynamics; only then can the living system break free from the law's shackles. The problem is, of course, that a system must already be alive for it to possess such as mechanism.

An example of thermodynamic equilibrium is that of a steaming cup of coffee in contact with the temperature of your room. If left sitting the coffee will transfer heat to the room until coffee and room will approach the same temperature (thermodynamic equilibrium) and will maintain a constant temperature in the absence of further heat from *outside* the system. Low energy is associated with stability and not change. When a physical system reaches its lowest energy state, such as the coffee no longer transferring heat to the room, the system is in equilibrium, which by definition means that no further change can take place. The hypothesized prebiotic homogeneous soup would have had "no internal free energy that would allow them to react further. Life is not just about replication; it is also a coupling of chemical reactions." [15]

Getting nucleic or amino acids, sugars, and lipids to polyermerize to produce a functional protein appears an insurmountable problem at present. The biggest problem of getting amino acids to line up "just right" is the chirality problem, which presents the perhaps the greatest challenge to abiogenesis. Many molecules required for life exist in two mirror images of each other (they have the same elements and properties), just like your left and right hands ("chiral" come from the Greek for "hand"). One molecule is labeled D ("dextro") for right-handed, and the other L for "levo" or left-handed.[16] Your hands may appear to be identical, but you cannot fit your right hand into your left glove. Just like hands and gloves, chemical reactions that drive our cells only work with molecules of the correct "handedness."

All amino acids in living things are left-handed and all sugars in DNA and RNA are right-handed. However, when amino acids are found in nonliving material, or when synthesized in the laboratory (as in the Miller-Urey experiment), they come equally in D and L forms. Biologists call this a racemic or heterochirality. Thus, while there are an equal number of Ds and Ls in nature, a homochiral set of building blocks is necessary for life; that is, all amino acids must be left-handed and all sugars (ribose) must be right-handed if DNA and RNA are to be produced and work. The molecular locks of life can only be opened by molecular key with the proper handedness; nothing else will fit. Even one right-handed amino acid would destabilize the DNA in a helix so it would not be able to form long chains of information.

By the laws of nature, chemistry will always produce a racemic, so what is the probability that even a short protein of 100 amino acids could form from all left-handed monomers under the conditions thought to exist on a prebiotic Earth? You can go to an on-line calculator and do this yourself. Because the odds of an L or a D are 50-50, it is 0.5 x 0.5 x 0.5....and so on 100 times, which comes out to 10^{31}. Astrobiologists Plaxco and Gross, use a longer chain, and inform us that it "is highly improbable that a random chemistry could produce a polymer molecule that contained monomers of only one-handedness. To be precise, the probability of achieving homochirality in a 189-unit polymer from an equal-molar mixture of left- and right-handed monomers is 1 in 2^{189} (1in 8 x 10^{56})!" [17] Plaxco and Gross conclude that "The current genetic code seems far more highly optimized than one would expect were it simply an accident."[18]

The complexity of protein production does not end with polymer chains. Enzymes are needed to produce polypeptide bonds and ribosomes are needed to produce proteins. The linking of amino acids into polypeptide bonds and then proteins requires energy derived from ATP. All of this, and very much more, is governed by the rich and complex information contained in the genetic code, yet we are expected to believe that amino acid chains, which requires the coordinated functions of multiple molecules guided by the DNA code, somehow "just happened" in the past without ATP, without enzymes and ribosomes, and most importantly, without specific instructional information.

The RNA World Hypothesis

All living systems possess two things for them to be characterized as such: metabolism and reproductive capacity. The immense challenge abiotic researchers are confronted with is not only how inanimate matter could be converted into a chemical system we could call life under assumed atmospheric conditions on the prebiotic Earth, but also which came first, a self-replicating system or a metabolic system. In other words, before life existed, how did these things that are essential to all living systems, and produced only by these living systems, come into being? The complexity of OoL research may be gauged by the fact that 150 theories of abiogenesis were published between the 1957 and 2000, and many more have arrived on the scene since then. [19] The two most popular notions today are the RNA world hypothesis and the metabolism-first hypothesis.

Let us take the RNA world hypothesis first. DNA and protein work as a unit, with DNA storing information and protein doing the necessary enzymatic biochemical work. Because each requires the other, it presents a "chicken-or-the egg" dilemma. It is acknowledged by all OoL researchers that the DNA/RNA system is far too complex to have arrived spontaneously as a system, so which came first? RNA world proponents go back the idea of a primordial soup in which free-floating nucleotides came together to form an RNA molecule. This would solve the chicken-or-the egg problem since RNA can store genetic information and self-replicate like DNA and perform the required enzymatic activity of proteins.

The RNA world has many supporters, but there are just as many detractors. Biochemist Harold Bernhardt calls the RNA world hypothesis "the worst theory of the early evolution of life (except for all the others)." In his article, he points out that RNA is too complex to have arisen prebiotically and that the RNA molecule is inherently unstable. He states that the best ribozyme replicase (a molecule that catalyzes its own replication) created so far in the lab is about 190 nucleotides in length. There is no way to be certain whether such a replicase ribozyme existed in evolutionary environments, and Bernhardt says that this is "far too long a sequence to have arisen through any conceivable process of random assembly" He claims that it requires between 10^{14} and 10^{16} randomized RNA molecules "as a starting point for the isolation of ribozymic and/or binding activity in *in vitro* selection experiments, completely divorced from the probable prebiotic situation."[20] The efficiency and fidelity of the process of replication must be sufficient to produce viable copies at a rate exceeding the rate of decomposition of the parent molecule, which presents a major problem given the inherent instability of RNA.

Note that the experiment Bernhardt discusses is an experiment *directed* by intelligent beings working in ideal conditions with the best technology money can buy. Bernhardt quotes one of the reviewers of his article as writing that the relationship of such experiments and their "relationship to the prebiotic world is anything but worthy of 'unanimous support'. There are several serious problems associated with it, and I view it as little more than a popular fantasy." [21] Others have also cast aspersions on the RNA world hypothesis, stating that it is "an expression of the infatuation of molecular biologists with base pairing in nucleic acids played out in a one-dimensional space with no reference to time or energy."[22] Finally, after surveying the many difficulties with the RNA-first hypothesis, Jesse McNichol concluded in the journal *Biochemistry and Molecular Biology Education* that: "Because of these seemingly insurmountable difficulties, the idea of a 'perfect accident' insinuates itself into to logic of RNA world proponents." [23] Positing a perfect accident at some point in time is the starting point of many such theories.

Biologists Robertson and Joyce say that the RNA hypothesis does not really solve the chicken or egg problem: "To say that the RNA World hypothesis 'solves the paradox of the chicken-and-the-egg' is correct if one means that RNA can function both as a genetic molecule and as a catalyst that promotes its own replication." [24] No one has found a modern natural ribozyme that can catalyze such a reaction, and lab-made ribozyme replicase carries the reaction out much too slowly to keep up with the degradation of the parent molecule, indicating that it needs a source of outside energy for catalysis. It has been proposed that hydrothermal vents or black smokers, deep in the ocean serve this function, but others note that, "several issues relating to black smokers as sites of life's origin are problematic, among them their extreme temperature (more likely to break down organics than form them), their low pH, their short lifetimes and their lack of compartmentalisation, with its dismal consequence of irretrievable dilution into the ocean." [25] Note that a low pH reading means that a fluid is more acidic relative to its base content and is oxygen deprived.

Metabolism First Hypothesis

The other popular contemporary theory for the OoL is the metabolism first scenario. Metabolism first theory is animated by the well-known problems of the RNA world hypothesis; that is, RNA is inherently unstable and too complex to have arisen abiotically, and that the catalytic repertoire of RNA is too limited. To get around these problems, the metabolism first hypothesis proposes the spontaneous formation of simple molecules, such as the compound formed from carbon dioxide and water called acetate, triggered life. This is then presumed to lead to the accumulation of simple organic molecules that could serve as catalysts for more complex molecules.

To appreciate the problems of this model we have to understand what metabolism is. Metabolism refers to all of chemical processes that occur in your cells that enable you to grow and thrive; it converts the food into energy to fuel cellular processes such as building proteins and nucleic and is also a method of eliminating cellular waste. To do this, there must be a boundary between the cell and the outside world; biologists call this "compartmentalization."

This implies that the cell would have to come before metabolism. After all, what is the point of metabolism unless you have a compartmentalized organism (or at least a cell) for it to sustain?

British chemist, and lifelong OoL researcher Leslie Orgel, characterized the metabolism first scenario as a kind of "if pigs could fly" chemistry based on little more than the deficiencies of the RNA world hypothesis. He writes that "The most serious challenge to proponents of metabolic cycle theories—the problems presented by the lack of specificity of most nonenzymatic catalysts—has, in general, not been appreciated. If it has, it has been ignored. Theories of the origin of life based on metabolic cycles cannot be justified by the inadequacy of competing theories: they must stand on their own."[26]

Later research by Vasas, Szathmáry, and Santos showed that metabolic systems such as those proposed by metabolism first proponents are unable to retain information about their composition to allow them to evolve toward a metabolic pathway. In other words, they do not contain hereditary information by which they could pass on their composition to progeny. Commenting on the RNA and metabolism first scenarios, Vasas, Szathmáry, and Santos maintain that, "Both schools [RNA world and metabolism first] acknowledge that a critical requirement for primitive evolvable systems (in the Darwinian sense) is to solve the problems of information storage and reliable information transmission."[27] It really is all about information.

All life requires an energetic force, and thus metabolism first researchers, like their RNA world counterparts, suggest that life first arose in the hot vents deep in the ocean spewing out heat and various kinds of molecules. However, according to a 2017 paper in the journal *Advances in Biological Chemistry*, this scenario also runs into the second law of thermodynamics. The authors state that, "all molecules near the heat source, the hot water, will be equivalently heated up. They will then move away to cooler parts, and whatever reactions that occurred in the hot parts will just cease and cold, unreactive (dead) products will float off and dilute." [28]

Information

Vasas, Szathmáry, and Santos' point about information storage and transmission is a crucial one. Every living thing is a system composed of millions of separate parts that are interdependent in their functions. All molecules and cells in an organism are in cooperative relationships with all other molecules and cells by sending and receiving *information* on which they must act or else it all breaks down. Information transfer can only occur when both sender and receiver are "intelligent" enough to know what the information entails. Take the marvelous machinery of the Krebs cycle. This cycle is the cellular respiration system by which glucose is broken down in the presence of oxygen to produce cellular energy. Every movement we make and breath we take induces a series of complicated chemical reactions involving electrons changing a series of enzymatic molecules into others. It engages the many hundreds of mitochondria—the cells' power stations. Mitochondria have a sort of rotary motor that spins, turning out ATP. As noted previously, ATP is the fuel that energizes the body to do just about everything it needs to do. If you have ever seen a schematic image of the Krebs cycle, you will appreciate the marvelous complexity designed to make life possible. It is difficult to imagine how this system could have been cobbled together piecemeal by molecular tinkering, for from where did animals get the energy to move and breathe before it came online? No human bioengineer given an eternity of time could produce a better system.[29]

Mathematical information theory specialist Werner Gitt observes that the question of "'How did life originate?" is inextricably linked to the question "Where did the information contained in all those base sequences in the genetic code come from?"' He continues:

> Since the findings of James D. Watson and Francis H. C. Crick, it was increasingly realised by contemporary researchers that the information residing in the cells is of crucial importance for the existence of life. Anybody who wants to make meaningful statements about the origin of life, would be forced to explain how the information originated. All evolutionary views are fundamentally unable to answer this crucial question."[30]

Gitt went on to demonstrate in a sophisticated book-length argument of the impossibility of information arising from inert matter and tells us that this was the conclusion of multiple origin of life scientists at the International

Conference of the Origins of Life held in Germany. He put this notion in his Theorem 28: "There is no known law of nature, no known process, and no known sequence of events which can cause information to originate by itself in matter." [31] He later identifies the source of this incredibly sophisticated information content as God.[32] Gitt is too much of a scientist to offer this as a God-of-the-gaps argument. He is simply saying that whatever mechanistic process science might uncover, the vital information ruling them is non-material and has been provided by an intelligent designer we call God.

The Multiverse and Panspermia

To address the absurd improbability of life emerging from non-life, esteemed evolutionary biologist Eugene Koonin takes us back to the multiverse. Note the improbability he calculates for the simultaneous emergence of translation (the process by which the ribosome uses RNA as a template to make protein) and replication (DNA making an exact replica of itself): "the probability that a coupled translation-replication emerges by chance in a single O-region [observable region of the universe] is $P< 10^{-1018}$. Obviously, this version of the breakthrough stage can be considered only in the context of a universe with an infinite (or, in the very least, extremely vast) number of O-regions."[33] Let's not overlook the fact that this is the probability of getting just replication and translation; you still have to get these functions enclosed in a cell with all its complex interdependent parts and get their functioning started. Furthermore, you still have to show how translation-replication can emerge by natural means on this planet, but never mind the messy chemistry; just concentrate on the really big number of "O-regions," and we can get back to blind chance and it's problem solved!

In a lecture at the Royal Institute in London, Sir Fred Hoyle agreed that the complexity of life does not lend itself to chance:

> So, if one proceeds directly and straightforwardly in this matter, without being deflected by a fear of incurring the wrath of scientific opinion, one arrives at the conclusion that biomaterials with their amazing measure or order must be the outcome of intelligent design. No other possibility I have been able to think of in pondering this issue over quite a long time seems to me to have anything like as high a possibility of being true.[34]

Hoyle looked to the heavens as a way out of the conundrum, but not to God. What he looked to instead was the notion of panspermia ("seeds everywhere"). Panspermia asserts that the cosmos is teeming with life and that life hitched a ride on comets, asteroids, and meteors to get to Earth. In the book

Evolution from Space, Hoyle and his colleague Chandra Wickramasinghe wrote of the extremely low probabilities of getting the 20 amino acids to line up correctly and of obtaining a suitable sugar backbone for DNA/RNA, and then the probability of functioning enzymes. They then combined these immense probabilities: "there are about two thousand enzymes, and the chance of obtaining them all in a random trial is only one part in $(10^{20})^{2000} = 10^{40,000}$, an outrageously small probability....this simple calculation wipes the idea entirely out of court." [35]

It might just have ruled spontaneous chemical evolution "out of court," but panspermia, even if true, does not solve the OoL puzzle; it merely moves its origin elsewhere in the vastness of space where the same $10^{40,000}$ problem is encountered. But there is another problem. Hoyle and Wickramasinghe propose that not only inert substances such as nucleic acids arrived on cosmic spaceships, but also living things such as bacteria. As simple as this life form is, it still has a genome and lots of biological activity, and it has even been suggested that they can think in a rudimentary sense. [36] Surely this means that Hoyle and Wickramasinghe's astronomical improbabilities are more relevant for extraterrestrial bacteria than for terrestrial enzymes.

Ever the enigmatic thinker, Hoyle seemed to agree with this, and posited an "intelligent control" over the process of life, from space or from wherever. In Gert Korthof's summary and review of Hoyle's *The Intelligent Universe*, he quotes Hoyle's words: "Even after widening the stage for the origin of life from our tiny Earth to the Universe at large, we must still return to the same problem that opened this book—the vast unlikelihood that life, even on a cosmic scale, arose from non-living matter. It is apparent that the origin of life is overwhelmingly a matter of arrangement by intelligent control. Unintelligent natural selection is only too likely to produce an unintelligent result." [37]

Hoyle left unanswered the nature of this intelligent controller and did not invoke God. This is itself an indication of the enigmatic nature of this brilliant scientist because he has many statements in his books and articles in which we may envision him struggling with himself not to mention God while using metaphors that strongly suggest that he had God in mind. For example, writing of the fine-tuning required for manufacturing carbon and oxygen in the stars, he stated in the *Annual Review of Astronomy and Astrophysics*, that:

> If you wanted to produce carbon and oxygen in roughly equal quantities by stellar nucleosynthesis, these are the two levels you would have to fix, and your fixing would have to be just where these levels are actually found to be. Another put-up job? A commonsense interpretation of the facts suggests that a super-intellect has monkeyed with physics, as well as with chemistry and biology, and that there are no blind forc-

es worth speaking about in nature. The numbers one calculates from the facts seem to me so overwhelming as to put this conclusion almost beyond question." [38]

The issue that Hoyle was concerned with was why we see such an abundance of carbon (the fourth most abundant element in the universe) when it is so improbable for it to be cooked up in stars. Carbon is essential for life because carbon atoms form the backbone of almost all the important biological molecules (the familiar CHNOPS acronym for carbon, hydrogen, nitrogen, oxygen, phosphorus, and sulfur). Hoyle reasoned that we could only get an abundance of carbon through a process called the triple alpha process. To make a complicated process as simple as possible; to form carbon it is necessary for beryllium (element number 4) must fuse with helium (number 2) to build carbon (number 6). The problem is that radioactive beryllium exists for an average of 10^{-16} seconds, so in this unbelievably short time before beryllium decays, atoms of helium and beryllium must find each other and fuse. Physicist Gerald Schroeder informs us that, "If this reaction were foiled by mismatch, the universe would contain hydrogen and helium, and not much of anything else. The elements of life would not have formed." [39]

Who else but Almighty God could be the super-intellect that "monkeyed" with the laws of physics, chemistry, and biology to produce carbon? Ernst Chain, Nobel Laureate in medicine and physiology, sees that behind all this highly intellectualized OoL speculation is the desire to explain God away: "I have said for years that speculations about the origin of life lead to no useful purpose as even the simplest living system is far too complex to be understood in terms of the extremely primitive chemistry scientists have used in their attempts to explain the unexplainable that happened billions of years ago. God cannot be explained away by such naïve thoughts." [40] Why is it so difficult for some scientists to allow "a Divine Foot in the door"?

What can we conclude about OoL research thus far? There was considerable optimism among materialists after the 1953 Miller-Urey experiment that it would be relatively easy to kick-start life in the lab, but that optimism has slowly faded to pessimism. The close to 200 documented OoL theories checkmate one another, and it is fair to say that the years of experimentation and calculation since Miller-Urey by thousands of very gifted biologists and chemists have resulted in a clearer understanding of the overwhelming immensity of the problem rather than its solution. Such theories are confronted with numerous chicken-or-egg conundrums, and no sooner than one team of researchers think s they have solved some part of the problem another team comes along and takes their king. Others have resorted to "multiverse of the gaps" arguments which cannot be tested. But to say it once again; this does not mean that they must stop trying to discover the rules of physics, chemistry, and biology by which this "super-intellect" created all.

Chapter 9

Cracks in Neo-Darwinism:
Micro is not Macro

"There is a Divine Providence over and above the materialistic happenings of biological evolution." John Eccles, Nobel Laureate in Medicine and Physiology

Darwin's Doubters

Evolutionary scientist Scott Gilbert tells us that "The modern synthesis [of genetics and evolutionary theory] is remarkably good at modeling the survival of the fittest, but not good at modeling the arrival of the fittest."[1] This statement alerts us to the fact that we are moving away from the largely clueless science of abiotic "*arrival* of the fittest" to the "remarkably good" and supposed settled science of "the *survival* of the fittest." The enigmatic Sir Fred Hoyle had some serious problems with "remarkably good" Darwinism. In his 1999 book, *Mathematics of Evolution*, he writes in his own inimitable way saying that Darwinists have replaced God, who produced rabbits in ways too mysterious understand, to believe "that rabbits had been created by sludge, by methods too complex for us to calculate and by methods likely enough involving improbable happenings. Improbable happenings replace miracles and sludge replaced God."[2]

Hoyle's book explains in mathematical terms why so many Darwinian claims are outside the realm of possibility. He does not deny that small-scale changes within a species occur (microevolution); his argument is with large-scale evolution (macroevolution). He is adamant that species can only adapt within narrow limits; that is, the produce variation only within their kind. In other words, rabbits cannot become rhinos, even at their prodigious reproduction rate. Hoyle concludes: "The mistaken extrapolation from evolution in the small to evolution in the large that followed the Darwinian theory of 1859 led society into a bog which has only grown deeper in the passing years."[3] There are thus scientists who do not profess a belief in the Almighty who have bones to pick with Darwinian macroevolution.

Another dissenter is Nobel laureate physicist Robert B. Laughlin has written about evolution in a way as to suggest that there exists in biology an "evolution-of-the gaps" situation:

> Much of present-day biological knowledge is ideological. A key symptom of ideological thinking is the explanation that has no implications and cannot be tested. I call such logical dead ends antitheories because they have exactly the opposite effect of real theories: they stop thinking rather than stimulate it. Evolution by natural selection...has lately come to function more as an antitheory, called upon to cover up embarrassing experimental shortcomings and legitimize findings that are at best questionable and at worst not even wrong. Your protein defies the laws of mass action? Evolution did it! Your complicated mess of chemical reactions turns into a chicken? Evolution! The human brain works on logical principles no computer can emulate? Evolution is the cause!"[4]

Then we have Richard Lewontin, a scientific fundamentalist, who nevertheless describes Darwin's theory of evolution by natural selection as "hopelessly metaphysical, according to the rules of etiquette laid down in the Logic of Scientific Inquiry ... For what good is a theory that is guaranteed by its internal logical structure to agree with all conceivable observations, irrespective of the real structure of the world? If scientists are going to use logically unbeatable theories about the world, they might as well give up natural science and take up religion."[5]

How do we reconcile this with Theodosius Dobzhansky's oft-quoted statement that "Nothing in biology makes sense except in the light of evolution."[6] Dobzhansky was one of the true giants of 20th century biology and both a creationist and an evolutionist who believed that science does not preclude the process of evolution having either an author or an ultimate goal: an Alpha and an Omega. Hoyle, Laughlin, and Lewontin, were right, but so was Dobzhansky, because they had different versions of evolution in mind. For instance, Lewontin's claim about the theory of evolution does not mean that he doubts microevolution because, as he says, one cannot imagine any observation that would disprove natural selection as a cause of change in organisms. He only views the theory of natural selection as metaphysical rather than scientific because "Natural selection explains nothing because it explains everything."[7] Dobzhansky's view was also limited to the kind of factual evolution scientists are able to observe and study. The entire edifice of neo-Darwinism (the synthesis of Darwinism with genetics), however, claims more than it can demonstrate.

If anyone says that neo-Darwinism is "settled science" disputed only by religious fundamentalist, they will have to account for the more than well over
1,000 doctoral level scientists, mostly biologists, who signed a statement ex-
pressing their skepticism of it. The *Scientific Dissent from Darwinism* statement reads: "We are skeptical of claims for the ability of random mutation
and natural selection to account for the complexity of life. Careful examination of the evidence for Darwinian theory should be encouraged." Among the
comments of many scientists who signed the document was the following
from mathematician Colin Reeves: "Darwinism was an interesting idea in the
19th century, when handwaving explanations gave a plausible, if not properly
scientific framework into which we could fit biological facts. However, what
we have learned since the days of Darwin throws doubt on natural selection's
ability to create complex biological systems – and we still have little more
than handwaving as an argument in its favour."[8] Of course, a lot more scientists would sign a statement affirming their complete belief in Darwinism, but
head counts do not settle scientific issues. I mention the *Dissent* simply to
show that Darwinism is not in the same scientific league as theories such as
the atomic theory of matter, the germ theory of disease, or the laws of thermodynamics.

If these criticisms from top-rate scientists have merit, we have to wonder
why the theory of evolution from sludge to rabbits is treated as settled science. I have written positive articles and book chapters on evolutionary theory myself without giving serious thought to its problems. Not being involved
in basic evolutionary research, I have relied on information provided by
mainstream evolutionists. This is the way we all accept "settled science" in
any area because none of us have a truly intimate acquaintance with anything
beyond our own fields of inquiry. We defer to the specialist in their area of
expertise, but if we have doubts, we go to others in the same area of expertise
for second opinions. But anyone who doubts any aspect of evolution is looked
upon as a non-scientific nincompoop, maintaining that scientific arguments
against the Darwinian evolution are not possible. By saying this, they are
saying that the theory (as it applies to macroevolution) is not falsifiable. All
scientific theories are supposed to be falsifiable, so if Darwinian macroevolution is not, it must join the ranks of the likes of Marxism and Freudianism as
pseudo-science. When I began to have doubts about certain aspects of evolution, I went back to the source and reread relevant portions of Charles Darwin's *The Origin of Species.*

Charles Darwin: Atheism, First Cause, and Teleology

What about Charles Darwin himself, the man Richard Dawkins credits with
making it intellectually respectable to be an atheist? Although Darwin was

embittered toward Christianity by the loss of his beloved nine-year-old daughter, Annie, he never called himself an atheist; he often called himself an agnostic, and sometimes a theist, as in the following passage written some 33 years after the publication of *The Origin of Species*:

> Another source of conviction in the existence of God, connected with the reason and not with the feelings, impresses me as having much more weight. This follows from the extreme difficulty or rather impossibility of conceiving this immense and wonderful universe, including man with his capacity of looking far backwards and far into futurity, as the result of blind chance or necessity. When thus reflecting I feel compelled to look to a First Cause having an intelligent mind in some degree analogous to that of man; and I deserve to be called a Theist.[9]

In an 1879 letter to John Fordyce, Darwin denied the atheistic claim that a belief in evolution logically leads to atheism "It seems to me absurd to doubt that a man may be an ardent Theist & an evolutionist." His dear friend Asa Gray, a Harvard botanist with who he had a vast correspondence, was a case in point. Gray was both an evolutionist in his belief that species exhibit "descent with modification" and a theist in that he affirmed that God is creator of all. Darwin reiterated in his letter to Fordyce that he was no atheist: "I may state that my judgment often fluctuates [in his level of belief] … In my most extreme fluctuations I have never been an atheist in the sense of denying the existence of a God." However, he never warmed back up to Christianity. He denied the divine revelation of the Bible, and so his beliefs may be characterized as deistic, despite his assertion that he "deserve(s) to be called a Theist."[10]

According to biologist Stephen Freeland: "He [Darwin] did not reject the idea that the laws of nature (including natural selection) stemmed from an Ultimate Cause, nor did he deny that natural selection could lead predictably to sentience or humans; he simply denied that the pool of variation on which natural selection worked was directly manipulated by a higher hand"[11] Darwin wrote in *The Origin of Species* that, "To my mind it accords better with what we know of the laws impressed on matter by the Creator, that the production and extinction of the past and present inhabitants of the world should have been due to secondary causes, like those determining the birth and death of the individual."[12]

Darwin's "secondary causes" recalls St. Augustine's words in *De Genesi ad Literam* (V.4:11; my emphasis): "It is therefore, *causally* that Scripture has said that earth brought forth the crops and trees, in the sense that *it received the power of bringing them forth*. In the earth from the beginning, in what I might call the roots of time, God created what was to be in times to come." Augustine is saying that the natural properties of the earth that make crops and trees possible (matter has been granted the power by the Creator to act on other matter without requiring his micromanagement) are secondary to the primary cause that has been immanent in the laws of nature from the very beginning of the universe. There is little difference between Augustine and Darwin on this. Both talk about primary laws "impressed on matter by the Creator," and both recognize that the secondary causes of each thing of matter can change "in times to come."

Atheists such as Richard Dawkins view natural selection as a random process devoid of purpose: "Natural selection, the blind, unconscious, automatic process...which we now know is the explanation for the existence and apparently purposeful form of life, has no purpose in mind. It has no mind and no mind's eye. It does not plan for the future. It has no vision, no foresight, no sight at all."[13] Dawkins is at odds here with his hero Darwin, who did see a purpose and a goal in evolution. As Darwin put it in the penultimate page of *The Origin of Species*: "Hence we may look with some confidence to a secure future of equal inappreciable length. And as natural selection solely by and for the good of each being, all corporeal and mental endowments will tend to progress towards perfection."[14] Darwin was a teleologist (a believer in an end, purpose, or goal of evolution) and admitted as much. Furthermore, throughout his notes, articles, and books Darwin used the terms "Final Cause" consistently as the ultimate explanation and not as something which itself needs an explanation. Let us take a brief look at the basics of neo-Darwinian evolution.

Evolution According to Darwin

Microevolution is doubted by no one and is what Hoyle described as common-sense evolution. It is an established fact and of critical importance in many fields such as medicine, where evolutionary mutations in bacteria result in their resistance to medication. Macroevolution, however, is doubted and even categorically denied by many scientists, such as Hoyle. The problem emerges when evolutionists extrapolate the fact of small-scale evolution to explain entirely conjectural large-scale evolution. Microevolution may be defined as "variation within prescribed limits, of complexity, quantitative variation of already existing organisms," and macroevolution as "large-scale innovation, the coming into existence of new organs, structures, of qualitatively new genetic material."[15] Darwinists maintain that the accumulation of small quantitative changes of microevolution *within a species*, eventually results in the large qualitative changes of macroevolution that result in totally new species. The orthodox notion is that it is through this process of small accumulations that a small shrew-like creature became the ancestor of all mammals, including us. This was supposed to have happened fairly quickly (in evolutionary terms) after the extinction of the dinosaurs 65 to 66 million years ago, making it easier for mammals to survive and reproduce in large numbers.[16]

Darwin's basic idea was that populations of plants and animals grow until they strain the ability of the environment to support all members. The production of excess offspring results in a struggle for existence in which only the "fittest" survive. Darwin noted that individuals within populations exhibit a considerable degree of variation with respect to phenotypes (disease resistance, aggressiveness, color, size, speed, cunning, etc.). The precedents (or initial conditions) of natural selection are: (1) there must be phenotypic trait variation in a breeding population with (2) consistent fitness differences between the phenotypes, and (3) heritability of the phenotypic trait(s). The result of this process is a change in the trait frequency distributions across generations. As the theory goes, variants of a trait sometimes gave their possessors an edge in the struggle for survival in prevailing environmental conditions. The edge, whatever it may be, meant that those possessing it would be more likely than those not possessing it to survive and reproduce, thus passing the genetic edge on to future generations.

The arrival of a new advantageous trait is the result of a genetic mutation, which is a change in the DNA sequence of a gene caused by errors during a normal process of DNA replication which the cell's repair mechanism did not catch. Most mutations are neutral, but many others are deleterious in that they reduce the fitness of an organism and increase the susceptibility illness and disorders. Occasionally a beneficial mutation arises that increases an organism's fitness by increasing its reproductive success. If the mutation is sufficiently advantageous it will arrive at what biologists call "fixation." This is a situation whereby a mutant allele (one of a pair of genes—one from each parent—located at the same location on the same chromosome) arises in a population and completely replaces the other allele after a certain number of generations; that is, it becomes fixed.

Skin color and lactose tolerance are examples of alleles (alternate forms of a gene) that have gone almost to fixation in Europe. The people who moved out of Africa into Europe about 40,000 years ago brought their dark skin with them, which is advantageous in sunny latitudes but not in less sunny Northern Europe. In 2012, a team of geneticists found that Europeans have two alleles that lead to depigmentation, and thus to pale skin. People who moved into northern latitudes could not get enough sunlight to synthesize vitamin D, so natural selection favored the evolution of two genetic solutions; the pale skin that absorbs sunlight more efficiently than darker skin, and lactose tolerance which enables them to obtain the vitamin D in milk products.[17] Darwin called this type of process *natural selection* because it is nature (the environment) that "selects" the favorable variants and preserves them in later generations. The above example is, of course, an example only of natural selection "within kind."

Macroevolution and the Problem of Time

At a 2016 Royal Society Meeting in London, theoretical biologist Gerd Muller accused Darwinism of evading the "big questions." He concedes that microevolutionary theory performs very well and has provided abundant tests and predictions that have been well confirmed. If evolutionary explanations would be confined to this level, he explains, there would be no controversy. However, he chides evolutionists for habitually taking the success of smallscale evolution as the "explanation of *all* evolutionary phenomena" and points out that "a wealth of evolutionary phenomena remains excluded. For instance, the theory largely avoids the question of how the complex organizations of organismal structure, physiology, development or behavior—whose variation it describes—actually arise in evolution."[18]

We have seen that orthodox Darwinists posit that a tiny shrew-like creature became our ancestor through this process of the accumulation of small advantageous mutations when conditions became favorable after the extinction of the dinosaurs. Nowhere in the Darwinian literature have I found a discussion of how many small accumulations would be necessary for the almost incalculably complex differences that exist between shrews and Shakespeare. Although 65 to 66 million years ago is assuredly a long time, in evolutionary time it is exceedingly small, and hardly enough time to make game-changing mutations, as a number of articles in molecular biology journals attest.

Molecular biologists Gauger and Axe's experiments with the evolutionary divergence of enzymes involved introducing directed mutations to determine how long it would take to make a conversion with the required minimum of seven or more nucleotide substitutions. They estimated that it would take 10^{30} generations to get a paralogous (different but descending from the same ancestor) protein with a new fold (recall that the way a protein folds gives it its shape and function). This is a timescale way beyond life on Earth, never mind a "piddling" 65 million years. As of 2016, the universe was 4.23×10^{17} seconds old, or 432 followed by 15 zeros; 10^{30} is 1 followed by 30 zeros. In other words, two enzymes cannot be reconfigured through a gradual process of mutation and selection as standard Darwinism claims that they can if they were given all the seconds that have ticked by since the Big Bang to do it.

Gauger and Axe cite others who have arrived at similar conclusions (the rejection of chance) but who nevertheless stick doggedly to the chance and necessity process of Darwinism. They continue: "We agree with their rejection of chance, but we argue here that the Darwinian explanation also appears to be inadequate. Its deficiencies become evident when the focus moves from similarities to dissimilarities, and in particular to functionally important dissimilarities—to innovations. The extent to which Darwinian evolution can explain enzymatic innovation seems, on careful inspection, to be very limited."[19]

In the journal *Theoretical Biology and Medical Modelling*, John Sanford and his colleagues developed mathematical models to determine "the waiting time" to form a specified string of nucleotides in a hominid population of 10,000 individuals by the Darwinian mutation/selection process under ideal conditions. As we have seen, nucleotides are biological information systems that encode the information in cells like letter encode information in books. The researchers note that a typical human gene is about 50,000 nucleotides long, a new gene that would contribute to moving us on the way to becoming what we are today from whatever primordial entity we are hypothesized to have been millions of years ago would require many thousands of positive mutations within the ancestral gene. Note that a typical protein-coding sequence may be about 3,000 nucleotides long, but the whole gene complex (promoters, regulators, enhancers, etc.) controlling the expression of that protein is what the authors' had in mind when they wrote the typical gene is 50,000 nucleotides long. The profound problem is how long would it take in just one gene, and the authors' answer is staggering.

> For nucleotide strings of moderate length (eight or above), waiting times will typically exceed the estimated age of the universe–even when using highly favorable settings. Many levels of evidence support our conclusions, including the results of virtually all the other researchers who have looked at the waiting time problem in the context of establishing specific sequences in specific genomic locations within a small hominin-type population. In small populations, the waiting time problem appears to be profound, and deserves very careful examination. To the extent that waiting time is a serious problem for classic neo-Darwinian theory, it is only reasonable that we begin to examine alternative models regarding how biological information arises.[20]

Mutations and Devolution

John Lennox observes that experiments of the selective breeding with many thousands of generations of fruit flies (they live a maximum of 50 days) produce nothing but weird fruit flies with features that are maladaptive rather than adaptive. Moreover, they quickly achieve genetic homeostasis; that is, their gene pool runs out of variation capacity. He also notes that studies of 30,000 generations of E. coli (the equivalent of about a million human years) produce harmful *de*volutionary results, losing many of the building blocks of RNA, rather than beneficial evolutionary results. He quotes biochemist Michael Behe as saying, "The lesson of E. coli is that it's easier for evolution to break things up than to make things."[21]

Although they reproduce asexually, relatively simple organisms such as bacteria have an easier shot at gaining favorable mutations than humans because they reproduce far more rapidly and have exponentially larger populations. Bacteria do evolve adaptations that make them resistant to antibiotics, but these are adaptations "within kind," and no new body parts have evolved to make them other than what they were when they first arrived on the living landscape about 3.5 billion years ago. Populations of mammals did become much larger after the dinosaurs were no longer around to feast on them, so mutations rates would have gotten much greater. However, evolution requires adaptive mutations, not maladaptive ones, and the latter are many times more common. Thus, while elevated mutation rates helps advantageous traits to spread through a population faster, it also hurts by increasing mutation load and thus overall fitness. In other words, increases in mutation rates will result in an increased mutation load and higher rates of genetic death. This would seem to rule out rapid mutation as an explanation of the evolution of humankind. As three microbiologist put in the journal *BIO-Complexity*.

> Of the many amino acid differences (often hundreds) that distinguish any two enzymes with different functions, if more than a tiny fraction of these are important for making those functions different, then it may be effectively impossible for undirected mutations to stumble upon the right combinations for functional conversions...The problem for evolutionary explanations is that the very special circumstances needed to achieve even weak conversions in the lab translate into highly unrealistic evolutionary scenarios.[22]

And this is just the difficulty of the mutation and natural selection of lowly enzymes or unrealistically small strings of nucleotides. How about the literally millions of such mutations, with intermediary mutations more likely to be maladaptive than adaptive, required to go from Hoyle's "sludge" to the intellectual genius of Fred Hoyle himself? This becomes exponentially unlikely when we realize that to produce a new phenotypic trait such as an arm or an eye in accordance with Darwinian scenarios requires genetic innovation to control metabolic pathways, and such innovation requires countless *coordinated* sequences of enzymatic steps, not innovation in one isolated enzymatic function.

Necessity and Information

Chance must be rule out as an explanation of macroevolution, but what about necessity, the other half of the interplay between chance and necessity that neoDarwinists place their faith in? The chance half means that there just happens to be a genetic variant in a mating population that just happens to be advantageous in a particular environment at a particular time. The necessity, if it can be called that, is the process of natural selection that generates order in the genome by preserving the useful and eliminating the harmful. Without this winnowing process mutation would yield only disorganization and extinction because of the many disadvantageous mutations. However, natural selection is not a force like gravity or electromagnetism in the sense that it acts on something to produce an effect. It does not *induce* variation; it is a process that *reacts* to it by preserving favorable variants. Natural selection is a consequence of the Darwinian "struggle for survival," not its cause.

But neo-Darwinists want more from necessity than mere reaction. The term "necessity" implies that something is predestined and could not be otherwise, such as the fact that apples always fall downwards. Necessity is based on the belief that life is nothing more than complicated chemistry. As we saw in the previous chapter, origin of life researchers have long insisted that the organic emerged necessarily from the inorganic, but the more advances they make in trying to demonstrate this, the more mysterious life gets. If the laws of chemistry and physics work on molecules in nature to produce a Shakespeare from a shrew, these laws must also work in the laboratory to produce far simpler changes, but as we have seen, they don't. They do not because necessity is no more the answer to Darwinian dilemmas than is chance.

The big issue is one of information. Evolutionary biologist George Williams notes that: "Evolutionary biologists have failed to realize that they work with two more or less incommensurable domains: that of information and that of matter... The gene is a package of information, not an object. The pattern of base pairs in a DNA molecule specifies the gene. But the DNA molecule is the medium, it's not the message."[23] DNA is a communication system written in code. The base triplets are encoded into mRNA and decoded into amino acids and proteins by tRNA and rRNA. The three-letter code for the amino acid arginine is AGC, but AGC per se is not arginine; it is the instructions for making it. There are no laws of physics or chemistry that say those three letters must code for that particular amino acid. As physicist Vincent Bauchau put it:

> The sequence on a string of DNA is not determined by the laws that govern the physical and chemical properties of DNA. If it was so, the string could not contain any information. For DNA to work as carrier of genetic information, it was necessary that this molecule acquires the

capability to change its sequence arbitrarily...there is nothing from chemistry or physics that can be used to derive the function of DNA. This function is irreducible.[24]

Physicist and information theorist Hubert Yockey tells us the reason why many other principles of biology are not reducible to physics and chemistry:

> The reason that there are principles of biology that cannot be derived from the laws of physics and chemistry lies simply in the fact that the genetic information content of the genome for constructing even the simplest organisms is much larger than the information content of these laws. The existence of a genome and the genetic code divides living organisms from nonliving matter. There is nothing in the physico-chemical world that remotely resembles reactions being determined by a sequence and codes between sequences.[25]

Thus, we see two remarkable things about the DNA code: (1) It has the ability to change itself in response to environmental conditions—this is a necessary requirement for evolution to occur, and (2) The information content in the genome is far greater than the information content of physico-chemical laws. What is *not* remarkable about this ingenious code of codes is to say that it had an Intelligent Designer and is not the result of blind chance or physio-chemical necessity.

Macroevolution, Speciation, and the Cambrian Explosion

At the heart of most scientific and philosophical objections to macroevolution is *speciation*, the formation of new and distinct species. Species are groups of interbreeding animals that cannot reproduce with animals not of their kind. It is easy to demonstrate local adaptions within a species, but all but impossible to demonstrate speciation, although evolutionists beg to differ. A book produced by the National Academy of Sciences (NAS) contained the following statement: "A particularly compelling example of speciation involves the 13 species of finches studied by Darwin on the Galápagos Islands, now known as Darwin's finches."[26] Notwithstanding the fact that finches remained finches and can interbreed, none of these so-called "species" are distinct; they simply vary in small morphological differences within their kind (they are ecomorphs). As two evolutionary biologists put it in a 2015 *Biological Reviews* article:

> We suggest that morphological clusters represent locally adapted eco-morphs, which might mimic, and have been confused with, species, but these ecomorphs do not form separate gene pools and are ephem-

eral in space and time. Thus, the pattern of morphological, behavioural and genetic variation supports recognition of a single species of *Geospiza*, which we suggest should be recognized as Darwin's ground finch.[27]

Thus, the NAS was pushing a fiction on us that they knew to be false, which led law professor Phillip E. Johnson to write, "When our leading scientists have to resort to the sort of distortion that would land a stock promoter in jail, you know they are in trouble."[28]

The trouble with speciation is that, if true, we should find innumerable transitional fossils, as Darwin said, but we do not. N. Heribert Nilsson, an evolutionist at Lund University in Sweden, expresses his disappointment that his life's work for the search of transitional forms:

"My attempts to demonstrate evolution by an experiment carried on for more than 40 years have completely failed... The fossil material is now so complete that it has been possible to construct new classes, and the lack of transitional series cannot be explained as being due to the scarcity of material. The deficiencies are real, they will never be filled."[29] Stephen J. Gould, one of the most eminent paleontologists of the 20th century, admitted that:

> The extreme rarity of transitional forms in the fossil record persists as the trade secret of paleontology. The evolutionary trees that adorn our textbooks have data only at the tips and nodes of their branches...in any local area, a species does not arise gradually by the gradual transformation of its ancestors; it appears all at once and 'fully formed.' Yet Darwin was so wedded to gradualism that he wagered his entire theory on a denial of this literal record. "[30]

Gould was not anti-evolution; he wrote those lines to argue against Darwinian gradualism and to promote his own theory of punctuated equilibrium. The gist of the theory is that mating populations are at evolutionary equilibrium for many generations, but this stasis is occasionally punctuated by rapid bursts of change. Although Gould did not specify a specific mechanism for this, more recent work has proposed a molecule called Hsp90 (heat shock protein 90) that appears to hold mutations in abeyance (concealing them) as long as all is well in a species' world. However, when the environment changes drastically, such as with radical climate change, Hsp90 loses its ability to function properly and the mutations express themselves and are passed on to future generations. Of course, it is only advantageous mutations that would be of use, and we know that neutral and deleterious mutations are much more common. One study demonstrated this, finding results that sounded more like devolution than evolution:

> Using fruit flies, the researchers were able to fool the insects into thinking that their climate was changing. They soon found that radical changes occurred in the insects in just a few generations as they tried to adapt to changes in the environment. When the genetic variations usually suppressed by Hsp90 began to express themselves, major changes developed in the insects' body plans. Some insects began to sprout weird limbs from different wings, some thick-veined wings, others deformed eyes or legs.[31]

When formulating his theory, Gould had in mind the conundrum of the Cambrian explosion in which, after waiting for animals to arrive on the planet for three billion years, they seemed to arrive all at once with no ancestral forms to be found in the geological record. As biologists Peterson, Dietrich, and McPeek explain the Cambrian conundrum in the journal *Bioessays*:

> Beginning some 555 million years ago the Earth's biota changed in profound and fundamental ways, going from an essentially static system billions of years in existence to the one we find today, a dynamic and awesomely complex system whose origin seems to defy explanation. Part of the intrigue with the Cambrian explosion is that numerous animal phyla with very distinct body plans arrive on the scene in a geological blink of the eye, with little or no warning of what is to come in rocks that predate this interval of time.[32]

They conclude by indicating what this means for Darwinian macroevolution: "Thus, elucidating the materialistic basis of the Cambrian explosion has become more elusive, not less, the more we know about the event itself, and cannot be explained away by coupling extinction of intermediates with long stretches of geologic time, despite the contrary claims of some modern neo-Darwinists."[33] The Cambrian conundrum has been recognized for quite some time. In *The Origin of Species*, Darwin recognized the problem posed to his theory by the sudden appearance of numerous animal forms with no ancestors to be found in the fossil record. As Darwin wrote, "If numerous species, belonging to the same genera or families, have really started into life all at once, the fact would be fatal to the theory of descent with slow modification."[34]

No Anti-Darwinism in Class: It may make Students Think about God

With so many secular scientists pointing out flaws in Darwinian macroevolution in top tier biology journals, why are schools forbidden to teach them? Phillip Johnson provides a wry answer given by a Chinese paleontologist: "In China we can criticize Darwin but not the government. In America you can criticize the government but not Darwin."[35] Johnson was commenting about the brouhaha that followed the Kansas Board of Educations' decision to omit macroevolution from the curriculum and to include intelligent design. A number of scientific and secularist organizations filed suit against the board, and after a series of hearings a federal judge ruled against the board in *Kitzmiller v. Dover Area School District* (2005). In a 139-page ruling, Judge John Jones ruled that intelligent design (ID) is not science, and that it violated the establishment clause of the First Amendment.

I have two major objections to this ruling. First, it is sheer arrogance for a non-scientist to state that the science that questions macroevolution published by both ID proponents and non-proponents in peer-reviewed scientific journals is not science. Second, the establishment clause forbids only the United States Congress from establishing a national religion, as its wording plainly states: "Congress shall make no law respecting an establishment of religion." Jones' ruling is tantamount to equating the Kansas Board's decision with Congress doing just that. Nevertheless, Jones' decision was made in accordance with the Supreme Court's belief that any reference to God should be purged from the public square. I have documented how the Court has managed to use the establishment clause to eviscerate the free exercise clause that forbids Congress from prohibiting the free exercise of religion in my book *The Gavel and Sickle.*

Atheist philosopher and law professor Thomas Nagel, who wants to "liberate us from religion," nevertheless argues in his book—*Mind and Cosmos: Why the Materialist Neo-Darwinian Conception of Nature Is Almost Certainly False*— that ID should be taken seriously and deserves our gratitude for challenging a scientific worldview that he considers entirely ideological.[36] Evidently, the courts consider it acceptable for the schools to inculcate only a naturalist and atheistic worldview as fact at the expense of the intellectual excitement of the give and take of contending views. Immunologist Scott Todd tells us that the commitment to naturalism is why, *despite* evidence to the contrary, that ID is excluded for the academy: "it should be made clear in the classroom that science, including evolution, has not disproved God's existence because it cannot be allowed to consider it (presumably)." He then tells us why it's not allowed: "*Even if all the data point to an intelligent designer, such an [sic] hypothesis is excluded from science because it is not naturalistic.*"[37] I have always thought that science was about reasoning to the best explanation and not to just to the best *naturalistic* explanation.

Intelligent Design and Theistic Evolution

Neither proponents of ID nor theistic evolution (TE) deny microevolution; they simply deny that it is undirected and purposeless. ID scientists investigate biological patterns that show signs of intelligence, and thus direction and purpose. It takes the mind-boggling improbabilities of life forming from non-life as powerful signs of intelligence, and places special emphasis on the irreducible specified complexity of DNA, the cell, and many other biological features.[38] As Geneticist Joseph Kuhn notes "Irreducibly complex systems involving thousands of interrelated specifically coded enzymes do exist in every organ of the human body. At an absolute minimum, the inconceivable self-formation of DNA and the inability to explain the incredible information contained in DNA represent fatal defects in the concept of mutation and natural selection to account for the origin of life and the origin of DNA."[39]

ID's powerful arguments have attracted many former Darwinists, such as Gunter Bechly, an eminent German paleontological evolutionary biologist. Because of his standing as the leading evolutionist in Germany, Bechly was chosen to organize as museum exhibit to celebrate the bicentennial of Darwin's birth in 2009. Among the many exhibits, Bechly had a weight scale erected showing a dozen anti-Darwinian books in one pan, and Darwin's *Origin of Species* in the other. Naturally, Darwin's book left the combined weight of the other books dangling in the air. This was a powerful visual symbol; all contrary evidence is impotent against the weight of Darwin's theory. However, Bechly decided to read those dangling books and began to have gnawing doubts about his commitment to Darwinism. The upshot was that he rejected Darwinism and became a Christian. Bechly is an example of a scientist who follows the data to where they lead instead of blindly sticking with ideological orthodoxy. As he put it:

> I am a philosophical theist and strongly oppose atheism, materialism, naturalism, and scientism. I have not become a theist *in spite* of being a scientist but *because* of it. My "conversion" was based on a critical evaluation of empirical data and philosophical arguments, following the evidence wherever it leads. I am skeptical of the Neodarwinian theory of macroevolution and support Intelligent Design theory for purely scientific reasons.[40]

Theistic evolutionists (TE) seem relatively unimpressed with the idea of irreducible complexity and chide ID proponents for limiting God's reach. Kenneth Miller, a cell biologist and devout Catholic, represents this view:

In various ways, objections to evolution take a narrow view of the ca-
pabilities of life—but they take an even narrower view of the capabili-
ties of the Creator. They hobble His genius by demanding that the material of His creation ought not to be capable of generating complexity.
They demean the breadth of His vision by ridiculing the notion that
the materials of His world could have evolved into beings with intelligence and self-awareness. And they compel Him to descend from
heaven onto the factory floor by conscripting His labor into the design
of each detail of each organism that graces the surface of our living
planet.[41]

TE accepts a chain of inorganic material events creating complex life but
affirms God's guiding hand in the process. In other words, God's chosen
method of bringing life into existence was the evolutionary process in which
He endowed nature with the creative power to organize itself. Certain TE
scientists are obsessed with providing an adequate naturalistic explanation
for God's guiding hand in evolution, and some have appealed to quantum
phenomena. For instance, quantum physicist Robert Russell makes the TE
case in his idea of NIODA (non-interventionist objective divine action) in
which he sees continuous creation arising indirectly from "God's direct action
of sustaining in existence quantum systems and their properties during both
their time evolution and their irreversible interactions."[42] Another quantum
physicist, Amit Goswani, also sees God operating at the quantum level "The
idea of a God as an agent of downward causation has emerged in quantum
physics."[43]

Both ID and TE camps see the Creator's providential plan and purpose unfolding over time. Whether by direct intervention (special creation) of by the
unfolding of His laws, we are here to glorify in His name. Whatever science
eventually discovers, there is absolutely nothing it could show that would cast
doubt that only a Divine Hand could possibly be responsible for the immaterial information coded in the book of life. No one knows how He did it, but by
inference to the best explanation tells us that He did. Let us give the final
word to Albertus Magnus, 13th century scientist, philosopher, and theologian:
"In studying nature we have not to inquire how God the Creator may, as He
freely wills, use His creatures to work miracles and thereby show forth His
power; we have rather to inquire what Nature with its immanent causes can
naturally bring to pass."[44]

Chapter 10

Answering the Tough Questions:
God of the Gaps, Free Will, and
the Problem of Evil

> "God is not an alternative to science as an explanation, he is not to be understood merely as a God of the gaps, He is the ground of all explanation: it is his existence which gives rise to the very possibility of explanation, scientific or otherwise."
> John Lennox, mathematician and philosopher

God of the Gaps Revisited

Natural science points unequivocally to the existence of God and social science and history conclusively show that Christianity produces happier, healthier, wealthier, and more moral people and societies. These are positions easy to defend since there is such an abundance of evidence supporting them that one must but a blind eye to the telescope to deny them. We now engage more philosophical topics for which there is little that we could call empirical evidence. These issues are free will, which is central to Christian thinking, and the problem of evil, often called "the rock of atheism." The free will and the problem of evil issues are intimately connected, but before I turn to them, I take a longer look at God of the gaps arguments because it is both the argument made most often by atheistic scientists and the easiest of the three topics to engage and refute.

Beginning with the Enlightenment, there was an explosion of scientific knowledge which some thought would bury God. As more knowledge was acquired about the world, more scientists came to the opinion that we don't need God to explain the universe and assumed that it would eventually explain everything. In response to this onslaught, many theists resorted to God-of-the-gaps arguments by pointing to gaps in scientific knowledge and inserting God into them. The 19th century Scottish evangelist and biologist Henry Drummond was annoyed with all such efforts which were fairly common at the time: 'There are reverent minds who ceaselessly scan the fields of nature and the books of science in search of gaps—gaps which they fill up with God. As if God lived in gaps!"[1] God must never be considered a placeholder for what we do not yet know.

Modern scientists have developed a tolerance for the intoxicating effects of science as they get nearer to the bottom of Heisenberg's glass and see God. Many of them see advances in fundamental science as pointing toward, not away, from God. They have observed the incredible fine-tuning of the laws of nature, the equally incredible information content of DNA, and intricate nanotechnology of the living cell and have ventured beyond science to try to come to terms with why the universe has the properties that it does. Except for multiverse proponents, scientists have ruled out chance as beyond the available probability resources. More scientists are sounding like Joseph J. Thomson, a Nobel Prize winning physicist: "As we conquer peak after peak we see in front of us regions full of interest and beauty, but we do not see our goal, we do not see the horizon; in the distance tower still higher peaks, which will yield to those who ascend them still wider prospects, and deepen the feeling, the truth of which is emphasized by every advance in science, that 'Great are the Works of the Lord'."[2]

If we claim that some phenomenon that cannot currently be explained by science means that God did it, if or when science does explain it we have opened to door for the atheist to claim that this automatically excludes God. Isaac Newton's appeal to God as a divine fiddler who was needed now and again to stabilize planetary orbits was demolished by Pierre Laplace, and thus left Napoleon and a great many others wondering where God was. I am reminded of the words of warning written by the great German theologian Dietrich Bonhoeffer; God did "do it" because he did it all, but he is not Newton's stop-gap. Upon reflecting on a physics book, he was reading, Bonhoeffer wrote:

> It has again brought home to me quite clearly how wrong it is to use God as a stop-gap for the incompleteness of our knowledge. If in fact the frontiers of knowledge are being pushed back (and that is bound to be the case), then God is being pushed back with them, and is therefore continually in retreat. We are to find God in what we know, not in what we don't know; God wants us to realize his presence, not in unsolved problems but in those that are solved.[3]

Is Intelligent Design Guilty of God of the Gaps Reasoning?

Intelligent design (ID) is often accused by atheists, and by some theists, of engaging in God of the gaps arguments because they claim that it makes no falsifiable predictions. This is strongly denied by ID scientists. In his magisterial 611-page book *Signature in the Cell,* Stephen Meyer informs us that ID theory "merely claims to detect the action of some intelligent cause (with power at least the equivalent to those we know from experience) and affirms this because we know from experience that only conscious, intelligent agents produce large amounts of specified information."[4] Meyer lists a number of hypotheses that can be derived from the theory, including the possibility of someone effectively demonstrating that "large amounts of functionally specified information do arise from purely chemical and physical antecedents." Such a demonstration would surely falsify one of ID's hypotheses.[5]

A design inference in ID theory is not triggered by any phenomenon that we cannot yet explain, but rather from what we know about cause and effect. It is triggered when an event defies probability and when it conforms to a meaningful specified functional pattern, such as the DNA code. ID by no means rejects microevolution; it recognizes it as the only reasonable naturalistic explanation for the life forms we see around us. In fact, ID uses the same methodological principle that Charles Darwin adopted for explaining historical events. That is, when trying to explain past events, scientists should first identify causes known to produce the effect at present and then extrapolate that cause to past events; if it works now, it probably worked then. As Meyer explains: "Since the observed process of natural selection can produce a small amount of change in a short time, Darwin argued that it was capable of producing a large amount of change over a long period of time. In that sense, natural selection was "causally adequate.'"[6] However, ID challenges Darwinism to account in naturalist terms for the unimaginable amount of information required to get life going in the first place. It cannot content itself by saying, as Richard Dawkins did in *The God Delusion,* that it was "a lucky chance." Surely this is an evolution-of-the-gaps argument.

Even though the probability of such things as fine-tuning of the universe and the origin life arising from naturalist sources exceeds the probability limits, some scientists still embrace Dawkins' "lucky chance" and yet they see God's hand in it. Physicist Paul Ewart views chance as creatively freeing the world from determinism and that God's higher purpose operates independently of random processes at a lower level: "God is willing to let the dice fall where they may without micromanaging every outcome. His sovereignty then rests in bringing to pass his overall aim on a macroscopic scale."[7] "God's use of chance provides him with a creation far richer in possibilities than could be possible in a deterministic universe."[8]

Although I cannot conceive of all the wonders of the universe being attributable in any way to chance, I recall Einstein's criticism of the indeterminacy of quantum mechanics, "God does not play dice with the universe." Niels Bohr's reply is a little lesson in humility: "Albert, stop telling God what to do." It is no part of finite man to presume to know exactly how an infinite and transcendent God decided to create everything. God can work through seemingly natural and random processes, all of which are astronomically improbable to achieve his purpose. To deny that the Lord cannot "work in mysterious ways His wonders to perform" is to deny his omnipotence and to question His judgement. Let us not forget the words of Isaiah 55:8-9: "For my thoughts are not your thoughts, neither are your ways my ways, saith the Lord. For as the heavens are higher than the earth, so are my ways higher than your ways, and my thoughts than your thoughts."

Perhaps God purposely created the universe in such an incredibly unlikely way so that we never stop looking for signs of His fingerprints. If there is intelligent life on other planets, if there are trillions of other universes, and if life arose abiotically, it only adds to the majesty of God. This is so because all these things we currently find utterly improbable or even impossible, may at some distant future be found true. And if they are, we can rejoice that they will be found to be the fruits of the grand design inherent in the natural laws of the universe that He set in motion for us to discover. God did not create a universe incapable of being described in natural terms, nor one that required Him to twiddle the dials occasionally. God's role in creation is at a different level from the laws of nature. He is the agent that designed it all and who gave us the intelligence and motivation to figure it all out. God's hand is seen in the secondary causes through *His* laws of nature. The "how" questions of nature are the domain of science for which we need no God of the gaps; the "why" questions are the domain of God's agency and purpose.

Free Will and Determinism

The issue of freedom of the will has bedeviled philosophers for millennia without resolve. Since the great minds of all ages have not come to a consensus on the matter, we can hardly claim to resolve it here. But it is an issue central to Christian faith and must be addressed. Christianity affirms that we have been endowed by the Creator with the ability to make free choices, and that those choices must be such that they are faithful to His commands. On the other hand, atheism contends that free will is an illusion and that our thoughts and behavior are fully determined by our genes and our past experiences.

Let us define free will succinctly as the ability to choose a course of action independent of any outside influence, and determinism as the doctrine that says one's choice of action is not really free but is the necessary result of a sequence of outside causes channeled through our genetic makeup and prior experiences. The Greek philosopher Epicurus deduced free will from Democritus' atomic theory within which the "swerve" of an atom can occur without cause. Roman philosopher Lucretius developed his theory of free will based on the same idea: "The atoms do not move in straight or uniform lines; there is in their motion an incalculable declination or deviation, an elemental spontaneity that runs through all things and culminates in man's free will."[9] The modern version of this argument is based on Heisenberg's principle of uncertainty (unpredictability), which some believe has destroyed determinism and affirmed the unfettered freedom of the will. But as far as we know quantum events have little or no importance in everyday life and, besides, would you want the kind of freedom in which no one can probabilistically predict your behavior? The random, unstructured firing of neurons is one of the defining features of schizophrenia and being in that unfortunate condition is not my idea of freedom. Sociologist Max Weber wrote of this kind of freedom as the "privilege of the insane."[10] If free will means action without a cause, all actions would be unpredictable and chaos would reign.

Free Will and the Mind/Brain Issue

Human actions are intentions designed to result in a desired outcome. They require a conscious *mind* which forms the intention and an acting agent to carry it out. The contents of that mind form intentions, and physical brain states reflect those intentions. The brain is a very complicated piece of biological machinery, but it cannot understand why what it perceives gives rise to an intentional action; only a mind can do that. Those who deny the existence of free will identify the physical mechanisms of the brain with the physical operations and deny the reality of the mind, or will claim that if mind exists at all, it is epiphenomenal. I maintain that it is the conscious mind that gives meaning to the brain's physical activity. The brain cannot bootstrap itself into meaningful activity by purely internal processes; it must interact with information content from outside itself in a reciprocal causal way. This conception is akin to Newton's third law of force that underlies the dynamics of all processes in the universe. That is, if x affects y, then y affects x and both experience the effects of the other; there are no one-way streets.

It is useful to think of mental causation as we think of DNA; i.e., as information. Mental information is stored in the neural structures of the brain as biological information is stored in DNA. In their packaged form, both are temporarily "material," or at least materially housed. When my thoughts are communicated to other parts of the brain, or outwards to other minds, they are converted from their material substrate to immaterial energy. When stored by self or other, they are again embodied in matter. Or to analogize, when I am writing at my computer, what I intend to say precedes the electrical patterns that are engaged within the physical computer, and then my thoughts become physically embodied and manifested on the screen. The content of the information is decidedly not the result of the electrical patterns emanating from the computer. Likewise, my thoughts precede the electrical patterns of my brain where the information content of my immaterial thoughts are stored, but they are not caused by those patterns. When I decide which keys to hit to make manifest the thoughts that "come to mind" on the computer screen by "firing up" a specific sequence of electrical activity, my mental state has acted causally on a material object.

When I "fire up" a specific sequence of electro-chemical activity swinging from neuron to neuron in the synaptic jungle of my brain, these activities are merely neural correlates of my mind. If I change my mind to form a different sentence, a different sequence of firing takes place. In other words, this is downward causation in which the physical events in my brain are caused by me; my thoughts are not pre-determined by them even though I need them to think. We cause these brain states in top-down fashion in response to what we are thinking or doing (recall my discussion of the brain "lighting up" in response to falling in love in chapter 1). Every mind state is also a brain state, but mental properties are they are not reducible to neural properties without remainder.

A materialist might grant me that but counter by saying that there are certain physical or chemical laws that make the soup and sparks in my brain that require me to believe in certain logical facts such as 2+2 = 4 or if I drop a rock it will fall to the ground. In doing so, he has admitted the existence of the immaterial because laws are not things; they have neither matter nor energy. How do these laws make me decide to believe things that are not logical necessities such as if despite my horrible culinary skills, I believe it will please my wife immensely if I cook dinner for her tonight? Laws are simply mathematical descriptors of how things work; they don't make them work. As the Oxford mathematician John Lennox said in one of his YouTube debates: "The laws of arithmetic tell me that 2 + 2 = 4, but that never put four pounds in my pocket." A better question for materialists would be to ask who made the universe in such a brilliantly fine-tuned intelligible way that it can be described by elegant mathematical laws.

We have said that everything in the universe has a cause; we are of that universe, so what we think and do assuredly has a cause. Agreeing to this does not commit us to determinism since we are capable of causing our own thoughts and behaviors. If we are not responsible for own behavior, then praise and blame alike are pointless, as are concepts of theology such as human uniqueness (made in the image of God), sin, faith, love, and morality. It might well be that a "soft" determinism is necessary for free will. If I did not think that the things I do produce meaningful consequences, why would I do anything? All rational action, instruction, coaching, training, tutelage, and guidance are deterministic in the sense that they are designed to produce effects. We preach, discuss, and write books and articles under the assumption that we can change the minds of others, who we assume are quite free to accept or reject what we propose. I know that I am a free agent and that living according to that position is necessary, but I also know that my agency is constrained and/or enabled by my temperament, upbringing, knowledge, conscience, physical and cognitive abilities and disabilities, and the formal and informal constraints imposed on me by others. But without a belief in free will or agency—our ability to shape our own worlds—our minds would be imprisoned in a deadly *que sera, sera* fatalism.

Some folks believe that any kind of causal talk about our behavior detracts from our freedom and dignity, which I find to be counterintuitive. Let us say that I know you have found a wallet in a store containing a considerable sum of money and I predict that you will turn it in at the counter. Have I, by predicting your behavior, impugned your free will and thus insulted you? I have certainly made a deterministic prediction about you based on my knowledge of your moral character, but rather than insulting you I have praised your character, and praiseworthiness and blameworthiness are the pillars that support the free will concept. If, on the other hand, I said that although I have known you for several years, you are a free, autonomous agent and therefore I do not know whether or not you will turn it in, I have insulted your moral character by implying that you might decide to keep the wallet.

Free Will and God's Omniscience

The 16th century French theologian John Calvin denied free will. Calvin argued that because God is omniscient He knows everything that you will do before you do it, and thus you are not free to do otherwise. Central to Calvinist theology is the belief in predestination whereby some people have been selected by God from eternity past for salvation and all others are predestined to eternal damnation. The latter may lead the life of saints and hear the Gospels from birth to death to no avail because God gives the faith to really believe to the elect alone. There is no hope of salvation in the act of choosing God, because God chose you before you were born for salvation or damnation. Calvin wrote: "Hence we maintain that, by his providence, not heaven and earth and inanimate creatures only, but also the counsels and wills of men are so governed as to move exactly in the course which he has destined."[11] If this is the case, we cannot be held responsible for sinful choices that flow out of our wills because we "governed as to move exactly in the course which God has destined?"

Calvin also asserted that: "Men do nothing save at the secret instigation of God, and do not discuss and deliberate on anything but what he has previously decreed with himself, and brings to pass by his secret direction." [12] This is a God of the gaps argument raised to the Nth power. Since Calvin's God is the author of every sinful act we perform--God did it! I am not responsible for my actions, not because of my genes and environment as atheists claim, but because my deliberations and decisions are initiated by the "secret instigation of God." Such a fatalistic theology delivers Christianity into the hands of atheists since God is the author and instigator of evil and therefore is not worthy of our love and devotion.

Because an omniscient God knows what you will do does not mean that He made you do it. Humans exist in the arrow of time in which there is a before, a now, and an after. If I predict this week what you will do in circumstance X (call this "time 1"or "before") and you do exactly that next week ("time II" or "now"). I can say at ("time III" or "after") that "I knew it," although I did not make you do it. I must wait until time II to see if my prediction proved to be correct. God, on the other hand, is outside of time such that there is no before or after; only an eternal now in which a human past, present, and future exist simultaneously in the eternal: "I was, I am, I will be." God thus knew what you would do because he knows everything, but he still invested you with a free will to choose to do otherwise in time as humans experience it.

The Compatibilist Option

The notions of free will and determinism best employed by Christians against atheist denials of free will is to tie the notions together in a philosophical position called compatibilism, a position that insists that free will and determinism can peacefully coexist. Compatibilism does not deny that events initiated by humans have a chain of events leading to them which we may call causal, but it avers that as long as a person is free from external coercion they have the free will to initiate the event or not and the ability to clip the chain at any point. The courts of all civilized societies are compatibilist in the sense that they hold people responsible for their actions yet leave space for a variety of mitigating factors (mental disease or defect, coercion, among other things) when passing sentence on criminals.

Regardless of where one sits on the free will/determinism issue, we assuredly agree that all sane human beings engage in goal-directed behavior. A strict determinist might say that this is not an indication of any sort of free will because animals also engage in goal-directed behavior dictated by their natures. We do not invest them with free will since they are instinctively compelled to engage in behavior that assists them to survive and propagate. A compatibilist would reply to this that humans have the unique ability to take ownership of their natural desires and to control them. They have the ability to actively reflect on their desires to form judgments concerning their desirability in light of other moral and pragmatic considerations. To give a simple example: suppose the "animal" appetitive desire to eat a donut overcomes me (call this a "first-order" desire). The rational part of me then leads me to forgo the pleasure for the sake of future considerations of health (a "second-order" desire). In taking control of my first-order desires—which are more "natural" in that we share them with all other animals—I believe that I am as free as it is possible to be in a world of cause and effect.

One might think that compatibilism is a cop-out because two logically inconsistent positions cannot both be true. But compatibilism can appeal to Niels Bohr's principle of complementarity; i.e., the wave-particle dual nature of light, to buttress its position. There was much initial resistance among physicists to this counterintuitive wave-particle duality, but it as it became more and more empirically endorsed it led to modern quantum theory. Albert Einstein and Leopold Infeld had the following to say about this supposed conundrum:

> But what is light really? Is it a wave or a shower of photons? There seems no likelihood for forming a consistent description of the phenomena of light by a choice of only one of the two languages. It seems as though we must use sometimes the one theory and sometimes the other, while at times we may use either. We are faced with a new kind of difficulty. We have two contradictory pictures of reality; separately neither of them fully explains the phenomena of light, but together they do.[13]

Human beings exhibit this same duality. Substitute human action for light, and free will and determinism for waves and particles, and we can likewise conclude that neither free will nor determinism alone is sufficient to understand human action; we need both concepts to do so. Just as there is no longer any paradox in the wave-particle duality of light in physics, there should be no paradox about humans being both free agents and determined. Determinism gives us the only kind of free will worth having. It is a free will that follows the reasoned dictates of our natures and lays on our shoulders the responsibility of owning our actions.

The Problem of Evil

As mentioned previously, the problem of evil in the world is considered the "rock of atheism." The existence and experiencing of evil at the hands of others or by natural disasters has probably done more to break religious faith than all atheistic arguments combined. Who can fathom why an omnipotent and benevolent God permits murder, torture, rape, wars, slavery, the Holocaust, disease, earthquakes, volcanic eruptions, hurricanes, and countless other evils that cause so much suffering? How do we square the existence of an omnipotent, omniscient, and omnibenevolent God with the evil that exists in the world? The atheist argument is that an omnipotent God would prevent evil if He is benevolent. If He cannot, he is not omnipotent; if He could prevent evil and does not, He is not benevolent. In any case, the atheist argument boils down to the argument that it is logically impossible for both the Christian God and evil to coexist. The area of philosophical theology that attempts to deal with the problem of evil is known as theodicy, a term derived from the Greek *theos* ("God") and *dike* ("justice").

Theodicy seeks to explain why it is not impossible for both an omnipotent and benevolent God and evil to exist. Theodicy has been defined an attempt to justify or defend God in the face of evil, but God needs no justification or defense from His creations any more than our parents need justification or defense for their marriage and our existence. What is in need of justification and defense is our Christian belief in the Creator against atheist onslaughts that we are irrational in our beliefs because the existence of evil gainsays such beliefs. Christians must address the problem of evil if they are to uphold the rationality of their world view.

Atheists are fond of asking theists why there is evil in the world, but why don't theists ask atheists why there is good in the world? The daily news is full of evil acts, both moral and natural, precisely because they are atypical. For every mother who murders her child there are millions who are gently nurturing their children; for every flight that crashes there are millions that land safely; for every evil act there are millions of loving ones. Evil gets all the ink and pixels because, while evil is assuredly everywhere, it is not the norm—good is. For St. Augustine evil was the turning away from the light of God and that evil had no objective reality: "For evil has no positive nature; but the loss of good has received the name 'evil.'"[14]

Augustine was not arguing that evil is not an experienced reality; he was simply arguing that it is the negation of the good spawned by the fall of man from the original state of righteousness. There are other things that we experience—such as cold and darkness—that are negations with "no positive nature." Yet there must be objective positive standards by which we judge things we experience as evil, cold, or dark so that they can be distinguished. Heat exists; it is that which transmits energy from one thing to another by the kinetic motion of particles. Cold has no such properties; it is a word we've invented to describe a condition we experience if we don't have enough heat for our liking. Likewise, light exists in the form of streams of photons; darkness is the absence of light. Physicists don't measure darkness; they measure the amount of light present, and darkness is a term we use to describe a space without light. We feel evil like we feel cold when little heat is present, we experience it like we experience darkness when photons are minimal, and we feel evil when the love of God is absent in humans.

Free Will and the Problem of Evil in *The Brothers Karamazov*

In the passionate 19th century novel *The Brothers Karamazov* there is a chapter titled "The Grand Inquisitor." In this chapter, Russian author Fydor Dostoevsky provides the finest example in literature of the meaning of free will for Christians and how it is tied to the problem of evil. Dostoevsky's premise is that without God humans cannot be free. He did not mean an unfettered freedom immunized from all conscience to do whatever one pleases, but rather the freedom to choose to partake in communal life and to embrace its moral obligations. We have seen that the premise that one cannot be free without God became a brutal truth in his beloved Russia when it succumbed to atheistic communism 37 years after Dostoevsky's death. It was Dostoevsky's belief that man must choose between Christ or atheism despite the evils of the world, a choice he had faced himself and made in favor of Christ.

In the Grand Inquisitor, the intellectual Ivan Karamazov delivers a devastating critique of theism citing the most wanton gratuitous evil done against defenseless children. Ivan is not an atheist, but is consumed with doubt, and maintains that even if God exists, he is a malicious and hostile God because he permits the evil that washes the world in tears. Ivan has a desire for faith but he considers it impossible for him to attain, primarily because evil in the world precludes a benevolent God. Ivan describes in sadistic detail the suffering of children to his brother, Alyosha, a novice monk, and then enters into the parable of the Grand Inquisitor.

The parable begins in Spain at the height of the Spanish Inquisition when Jesus Christ appears on the streets of Seville and begins performing miracles. He is immediately recognized by the people, who begin to flock about Him. This was witnessed by an old cardinal—the Grand Inquisitor—who orders Jesus' arrest. In His cell that night Jesus receives a visit from the cardinal who reprimands Him for returning and hindering the work of the church. The Grand Inquisitor explains to Christ that He has placed an intolerable burden of freedom upon man by expecting flawed humans to voluntarily choose to follow Him, and that the church has rectified this by removing the awful burden of freedom and has provided the miracle, mystery, and authority that man craves. The cardinal then informed Jesus that now man has willingly submitted his freedom to the church in exchange for happiness and security and that this work must not be undone.

The cardinal further berated Christ for refusing the three temptations offered by Satan during Christ's 40 days in the desert: refusing to turn stones into bread (miracle); refusing to cast Himself from the pinnacle of the Temple to be saved by angels (mystery), and the offer of sovereignty over the Earth (authority). Had Jesus accepted these temptations, said the cardinal, people would have absolute certainty of his divinity and would have worshiped him, and they would have security of sure knowledge instead of the freedom to accept Him or not. Because He did not, the church had to assume His power, because under Christ's way only the strong and the faithful would achieve salvation and what then would become of the millions too weak to accept responsibly for their freedom of choice? Christ's insistence that man must freely to choose to follow Him allows for the evils committed by those who choose not to. Christ does not want followers bought and paid for by miracle, mystery, and authority, but by faith in the revealed truth. Jesus remains silent all through the cardinal's monologue and kisses him on his wizened lips at its end, and the stunned cardinal sets Him free with the admonition not to return.

Alyosha did not take Ivan's tale in the way Ivan had intended. He viewed it as praising Jesus rather than reviling him because Jesus' silence signaled His patient confidence that all evil will eventually be rectified. The characters of Alyosha and Ivan illustrate differences in attitude toward suffering of the true believer and the doubter. While both show concern for the suffering of others, Ivan's concern is manifested only by intellectualizing it. He collects anecdotes of cruelty from newspapers and books and using them as a sword against God. Alyosha, on the other hand, goes out among the suffering to see what he can do to alleviate it. His faith in God lends itself to an active concern for well-being of others, kindness, and morality based on a solid foundation. Ivan's doubt leads to the rejection of conventional morality, coldness towards his fellow man, and a crippling existential despair. He wanted to believe, but he suffered from having Bacon's "little philosophy" or Heisenberg's "first gulp of natural science," both of which tend to have the effect of intellectually moving one away from God.

Evil and Soul-Making Theodicy

Augustinian theodicy attempts to absolve God of all responsibility for evil based on human free will. Augustine maintained that God created finitely perfect human beings who fell from perfection by the use of free will to turn from God, and it was this act of rebellion that causes evil and suffering. Man created evil by rebelling against God and suffers as a consequence. God could have constructed human nature such that evil simply was not an option and still given us the ability to make choices; just not moral choices. But God wants moral choices above all and that requires moral freedom, and moral freedom necessarily entails the possibility of evil. A world in which free will exists is to be preferred over one that does not, regardless of the benefits that such a world may offer. I will risk being the victim of evil rather being an automaton. If God in his love for us were to coerce us into behaving morally at all times it would erase our freedom and stifle character building; how would we know what good is without experiencing evil? God could not have given us free choice without that entailing the possibility of evil.

John Hick, one of the most distinguished theologians of the 20th century, rejected Augustinian theodicy as relying on a too literal reading of the fall. Hick argued that if Adam and Eve were created as perfect beings and living in infinite plenitude, they would not have rebelled against God. Hick opts for the theodicy of the second-century philosopher and theologian Irenaeus, which claims that God is responsible for evil, but is justified because of its benefits for human development. Irenaean theodicy maintains that humans were not created in a perfected state but are in an evolutionary process of development from morally imperfect beings to morally perfected beings.

Hick's theodicy is premised on a truly omnibenevolent and omnipotent God and the corollary to this that he sees—universal salvation. Only if all souls eventually achieve salvation does the evil suffering of humans throughout history make sense. Hick states that God created the world to serve as a "vale of soul-making" which entails "human goodness slowly built up through personal histories of moral effort has a value in the eyes of the Creator which justifies even the long travail of the soul-making process."[15] An objection to this seemingly interminable process of soul-making might be that if the moral and spiritual development of human beings is the goal, why has God wasted over four billion years setting the stage for it on Earth? This objection again fails to remember that the arrow of time—before, now, after—is experienced only by humans, and not by God, who is timeless. Irenaean theodicy is thus forward looking to a future perfection of the personality through human striving in faith in God and love of humanity in a process that extends into postmortem existence rather than Augustine's backward-looking to the fall for which countless generations of humans bear no responsibility.

The essence of Hick's theodicy is that morality and characters can only be built by experiences evil and responding to it positively in the spirit of "That which does not kill me strengthens me." An extreme example of this is given by Holocaust survivor and psychiatrist Viktor Frankl who writes of his experiences of suffering and the opportunity for growth it provides in the Auschwitz concentration camp in his book *Man's Search for Meaning.*

The way in which a man accepts his fate and all the suffering it entails, the way in which he takes up his cross, gives him ample opportunity – even under the most difficult circumstances to add a deeper meaning to his life. It may remain brave, dignified and unselfish. Or in the bitter fight for self-preservation he may forget his human dignity and become no more than an animal. Here lies the chance for a man either to make use of or to forgo the opportunities of attaining the moral values that a difficult situation may afford him. And this decides whether he is worthy of his sufferings or not.[16]

However, it is surely true to say that most victims of this atrocity were devastated or destroyed (literally), so what purpose is there in that? Hick says the suffering of others also serves a purpose for the observer in that it serves to develop sympathy and compassion, which may help present and future victims of evil. A world in which humans cannot harm others would also be a world in which they cannot make the moral choice to help one another. I find this to be rather immoral on its face; shouldn't humans be treated as valued ends in themselves and not as a means to the end of another's character building? What right has one person to expect the suffering of another for his or her moral benefit? However, I am partial to Irenaean theodicy because of its universalism—all will eventually be saved. It has the taste of "the best of all possible worlds" (and world's to come), so it is emotionally satisfying, but that doesn't mean that it is the reason that God permits moral evil.

The Problem of Natural Evil

The free will and soul-making arguments apply only to moral evil; the choices made by free agents. Natural evils—fires, hurricanes, tornadoes, earthquakes, volcanic eruptions, diseases, famines, and other such occurrences—cannot be justified in this way, and thus they are said pose a greater threat to belief in a benevolent God than moral evil. Philosopher and theologian Richard Swinburne falls back on a soul-making theodicy by showing that natural disasters provide additional opportunities to develop sympathy and to give aid and comfort to victims: "The pain makes possible those choices that would not otherwise exist."[17] I believe this to be a desperately weak argument, but I also believe that a natural evil theodicy is easier to formulate and defend than a moral evil theodicy.

God has created a world that functions according to natural laws; laws that we can discover and incrementally come to know His creation more intimately. These natural laws make our world "just right" for complex and intelligent life, but there are trade-offs which are sometimes disastrous. We have seen that the many of these natural evils—earthquakes, tsunamis, and so forth—

are caused by plate tectonics generated by convection currents carrying heat from the interior of the Earth to the surface. God could prevent these things by stopping the rotation of the iron core, but then there would be no sentient beings to experience good or evil. God can't suspend His laws of nature when people have made their home near a fault line, volcano, or floodplain without becoming Newton's tinkerer. The suffering caused by the operation of natural laws can be viewed as unfortunate by-products of laws built into creation so that humans can freely come to know and love God.

Natural laws ensure regularity and consistency in a world of cause and effect without which we could never discover natural laws. If cause A only resulted in effect B when no humans were present, we would be living in a world of miracles, which are by definition the suspension of natural law. A world in which natural laws guarantee consistency permits intentional action, moral deliberation, and scientific investigation. A world of miracles in which a man, for instance, falls from a 10-story building and gets up unscathed, is inimical to both moral and rational activity because it would be the Grand Inquisitor's world of miracles, mystery, and authority. The universe declares the power and glory of God, but a miracle world would declare it so obvious that we would have no choice but to believe. God is not a supernatural Santa Clause who grants us every wish for safety and security; He wants us to take responsibility for ourselves in a world of predictable cause and effect. Many of the putative natural evils that atheists naively trot out as proof of God's non-existence are necessary for sentient life to exist.

This is my feeble attempt at a theodicy of natural evil, but all theodicies ultimately fail because they are the attempts of humans presuming to know the mind of God and seeking to justify Him by human standards of good and evil, which cannot be done. After science, logic, and reasoning paint a picture of God and His creation, theodicists conflate God's actual plans with those they think they should be. No one can understand the mind of God because there is none like him. They take the pessimist position that lives have been lost because of moral and natural evil and forget the fact that He gave life to us all in the first place. They are attempting to answer questions that only God can answer. It is therefore wise to heed St. Augustine's advice when confronted with different interpretations of Scripture used to support a particular theodicy:

> In matters that are obscure and far beyond our vision, even in such as we may find treated in Holy Scripture, different Interpretations are sometimes possible without prejudice to the faith we have received. In such a case, we should not rush in headlong and so firmly take our stand on one side that, if further progress in the search of truth justly

undermines this position, we too fall with it. That would be to battle not for the teaching of Holy Scripture but for our own, wishing its teaching to conform to ours, whereas we ought to wish ours to conform to that of Sacred Scripture.[18]

This is the "scientific" way to look at evidence and thus I could not agree more. However, I believe that the best answer to the problem of evil is not answered in any learned theodicy but in the promise of Revelation 21:4: "And God shall wipe away all tears from their eyes; and there shall be no more death, neither sorrow, nor crying, neither shall there be any more pain: for the former things are passed away." **AMEN!**

Chapter Footnotes

Chapter One: Science Points the Way to God

1. Laplace, in Keyser, C., 1915, p. 28.

2. In Jennings, B, 2015, p. 59.

3. Lennox, J., 2009, p. 46.

4. Lewontin, R., 1977.

5. In Singh, S., 2004, pp. 361-362.

6. wie y ski, A., 2016.

7. In Christian, J., 2011, p. 608.

8. In Duck, M., and Duck, E., 2014, p. 32.

9. Lennox, J., 2009:25.

10. Ibid, p. 27.

11. Ibid, p. 28.

12. In Holt, 1997.

13. In Marsh, 2012, p. 72.

14. In Lennox, J., 2009, p 20.

15. In Coyne and Heller, 2008, p. 42.

16. Walsh, A., 2018.

17. Kennedy, D. 1907, p. 265.

18. Ibid, p. 265.

19. Davies, P., 2007.

20. Collins, F. 2007.

21. Stark, R., 2003, p. 154.

22. Plank, M., 1949, p. 184.

23. Crick, F., 1994, p. 3.

24. Esch, T. and G. Stefano, 2005.

25. In Weitnauer, C., 2013, p. 28.

26. Planck quoted in Olsen, 2013, p.382.

27. Jeans, J., 1930, p. 137.

28. In Schafer, L., 2006, p. 509.

29. Lipton, P., 2000, p. 185.

30. Meyer, S., 1999, p. 27.

31. Craig, W., 2008, p. 39.

32. In Maurin, A., 2013.

Chapter Two: Christianity, Rationality, and Militant New Atheism

1. Pew Research Center, Religious Landscape Study, 2016.

2. International Christian Concern, 2017, p.11.

3. Shackelford, K., 2016.

4. Walsh, A., 2018.

5. Leiter, B., 2014, p. 39.

6. Schulzke, M., 2013.

7. Hitchens, C., 2003.

8. Markham, I., 2010, p.141.

9. Lewontin, R., (1997.

10. Nagel, T., 1997, p. 130.

11. In Hewlett, M., 2008, p. 184.

12. Weber, M., 1930, p. 13.

13. Aikman, D., 2012, p. 5.

14. Freedom House, 2015.

15. Harrison, P., 2012.

16. Ecklund, E. & Park, J., 2009.

17. Gross, N., & Simmons, S., 2009.

18. Easton, J., 2005.

19. In Kainz, H., 2010, p.21.

20. Shalev, B., 2003, pp. 57–59.

21. In Margenau and Varghese, 1997, p. 139.

22. Einstein, A., 1941.

23. In Dimitrov, 2010, p. 168.

24. In Isaacson, W. 2007, p. 390.

25. Wiker, B., 2005.

26. Flew, A. and Varghese, R., 2007, p. 33.

27. McGrath, 2010, p. 81.

28. Ziegler Hemingway, M., 2008.

29. Ibid.

30. Pew Forum on Religion & Public Life, 2009.

31. Dawkins, R. (nd). From debate with John Lennox.

32. In Cammaerts, E., 1937, p, 211.

Chapter Three: Christianity, Atheism, and Morality

1. Wilson, E., 1993, p. 219.

2. Lewis, C., 2001, p. 8.

3. In Lennox, J., 2011, p. 99.

4. In Craig, W. and Meister, C., 2010, p. 18.

5. Nietzsche, F., 1997, p. 14.

6. Nietzsche, F., 1990, pp. 80-81.

7. In Jal. M., 2010, p. 136.

8. Hazard, J., Butler, W. & Maggs, P., 1977, p. 470.

9. Hosking, G., 1985, p. 213.

10. Hitchens, P., 2010.

11. Solzhenitsyn, A., 2006, p. 577.

12. In Bennetts, M., 2014.

13. Xu, Q., 2014, p., 142.

14. Phillips, T., 2014.

15. Hewitt, T., 2016.

16. Overy, R., 2004, p. 281.

17. Tatara, C., 2013, pp. 43-44.

18. Hulme, C. and Salter, M., 2001, p. 5.

19. Craig, W., 2010, p. 29.

20. Kenny, M., 2008.

21. Bingham, J., 2016.

22. Smith, G., 2017, p. 11.

23. Pew Research Center; Religious Landscape Study, 2016.

24. Kristeva, J. 1989, p. 5.

25. Dervic, K., et al, 2004, p. 2303.

26. Rasic, D., et al, 2009, p. 32.

27. Pascal, B., 1958, p. 257.

28. Call, V. and Heaton, T., 1997.

29. Wilcox, B., 2004.

30. Day, R., and Acock, A., 2013.

31. Bahr, H. and Chadwick, B., 1985.

32. Wilcox, B., 2004.

33. King, V., Ledwell, M., and Pearce-Morris, J., 2013.

34. Ellis, L. and Walsh, A., 2000, p. 205.

35. Dollahite, D. and Thatcher, J., 2005, p. 5.

36. Fragile Families Research Brief, 2005, p. 2.

37. Kruk, E., 2012, p. 49.

38. U.S. Department of Health and Human Services, 2011.

39. Wood, R., Goesling, B., & Avellar, S., 2007, p. 48.

40. Weitoft, G., Hjern, A., Haglund, B. and Rosén, M., 2003, p. 289.

41. Ellis, M., Vinson, D., and Ewigman, B., 1999.

42. Hummer, R., Rogers, R. Nam, C. and Ellison, C., 1999.

43. Strawbridge, W., Cohen, R., Shema, S., and Kaplan, G., 1997.

44. Hall. D., 2006.

45. Sørensen, T., Danbolt, L., Lien, L., Koenig, H., and Holmen, J., 2011.

46. Walsh, A., 1998.

47. Mua, K., 2016.

48. Guiso, L., Sapienza, P., and Zingales, L., 2003.

49. Stark, R., 2012, p. 163.

50. Grim, B., and Grim, M., 2016, p. 2.

51. Schmidt, A., 2004, pp. 147-148.

52. Forbes, K., & Zampelli, E., 2013, p. 2487.

53. Brooks, A., 2003.

54. Brooks, A., 2004.

55. Walsh, A., 2017.

Chapter Four: Christianity, Western Democracy, and Cultural Marxism

1. Drescher, S. and Engerman, S., 1998.
2. In Richerson, P. & Boyd, R., 2010, p. 565
3. Blackburn, R. 2000.
4. Sherwood, M., 2007.
5. Graebner, N., 1976, p. 264.
6. Stephan, A., 2000, p. 48.
7. Jefferson, in an 1814 letter to Horatio Spofford.
8. Straumann, B., 2008.
9. Ibid,
10. Dawkins, R., 2006, p. 316.
11. Harris, S. 2005, p. 27.
12. Schmacher, R., 2012.
13. Winthrop, R., 1852.
14. Washington, G., 1796.
15. Chesterton, G., 2001, p. 57.
16. de Tocqueville, A., 1994, p.199.
17. Durant, W. and Durrant, A., 1968, p. 43 and p. 51.
18. Durant, W., 1935, p. 71.
19. Raehn, R., 2004, p.2.
20. Heyer, W., 2011.
21. Sprig, P., 2006.
22. Neill, A., 2012, p. 84.
23. Minnicino, M., 1992, p.6.
24. Walsh, M., 2015, p.1.
25. Marcuse, H., 1969, p. 109.
26. Kolakowski, L., 1981, p. 416.
27. Walsh, A. 2018, p. 13.
28. Marcuse, H., 2002, p. 252.
29. Ibid, p. 50.
30. Ibid, p. 201.
31. In Malachi, M., 2008, p. 250.

32. In Grelle, B., 2016, p. 34.

33. In Stormer, J., 1964, p. 26.

34. In Walsh, A., 2018, p. 11.

35. Lipka, M., 2016.

36. Rorty, R., 2000, pp. 21-22.

37. Durant, W. & Durrant, A., 1968, p. 51.

38. In Sheen, F., 1948, p. 69.

39. Hitchens, P., 2012.

Chapter Five: The Big Bang and Fine Tuning of the Universe

1. Gonzalez, G. and Richards, J., 2004, p.260

2. Appolloni, S., 2011, p.23.

3. Davies, P.1984, p. 184.

4. Scharf, 2014, p. 211.

5. In Strobel, L., 2002, p. 189.

6. McLeish, T. et al, 2014, p.161.

7. Craig, W. 2008.

8. In Strobel, L., 2002, p. 122.

9. In Bussey, P., 2016. p. 70.

10. In Grossman, L., 2012, p.7

11. In Strobel, 2004, p. 132.

12. In Yahya, H. 1999, p. 19.

13. Jastrow, R., 1981, p. 19.

14. Appolloni, S., 2011, p. 29.

15. All cited by R. Jastrow, 1978, p. 122 and 123.

16. In Strobel, L., 2004, p. 84.

17. Jastrow, R., 1981, p. 19.

18. In Schaefer, H., 2003, p. 49.

19. Trefil, J. and Hazen, R., 2007, p. 318.

20. National Aeronautics and Space Administration.

21. Trefil, J. and Hazen, R., 2007, p. 321.

22. Bromm, V., and Larson, R., 2004.

23. Hawking, S. and Mlodinow, L 2010, pp. 160-161.

24. Bussey, P., 2016,

25. Krebs, R., 2006, p.133.

26. Exponential numbers such as these are a lot larger than they seem for those not used to working with them. Astrophysicist Hugh Ross (1993, p. 115) provides us with an analogy that helps us to understand the immensity of 10^{37}. "Cover the entire North American continent in dimes all the way up to the moon, a height of about 239,000 miles (In comparison, the money to pay for the U.S. federal government debt would cover one square mile less than two feet deep with dimes.). Next, pile dimes from here to the moon on a billion other continents the same size as North America. Paint one dime red and mix it into the billions of piles of dimes. Blindfold a friend and ask him to pick out one dime. The odds that he will pick the red dime are one in 10^{37}."

27. Gonzalez, G. and Richards, J., 2004.

28. In Strobel, L., 2002, p. 161.

29. Gonzalez and Richards, 2004, p.:205.

30. Ibid, p. 205.

31. In Lennox, J., 2009, p. 70.

32. In Lemley, B., 2000, p.64).

33. Davies, P. 1982, p.68.

34. Penrose, R., 2016, pp. 445-446.

35. (Dyson, L., Kleban, M., and Susskind, L., 2002. p.1.

36. Ibid, p. 19.

37. Haught, J., 2008, p. 38.

38. Jastrow, R., 1992, p. 107.

Chapter Six: Earth: The Privileged Planet

1. Barrow, J. and Tipler, F., 1986, 318.

2. Gonzalez, G. and Richards, J., 2004.

3. Loeb, A., 2010, 8.

4. Plaxo, K. and Gross, M., 2006.

5. Astronomy Essentials, 2015.

6. Gonzalez, G., Brownlee, D. and Ward, P., 2001, p. 62.

7. Ibid, p 209.

8.   Plaxo, J. and Gross, M., 2006, p. 35.

9.   Ibid, p. 36.

10. Ibid, p. 34.

11. Gonzalez, G. and Richards, J., 2004, p. 151.

12. Ross, H., 2016, pp, 32-33.

13. Gonzalez, G., Brownlee, D. and Ward, P., 2001, p. 67.

14. Kopparapu, R. et al, 2014.

15. National Aeronautics and Space Administration, 2017.

16. Gonzalez and Richards, 2004.

17. Tarter, J. et al, 2007.

18. Gonzalez, G. and Richards, J., 2004, p.137.

19. Spradley, J., 2010.

20. Ward, P. and Brownlee, D., 2000, p., 223.

21. Spradley, J., 2010, p. 273.

22. Batygin, K., & Laughlin, G., 2015, p. 4217.

23. Ross, H., 2016, p. 46.

24. Gonzalez, G. and Richards, J., 2004, p. 327.

25. Beaulieu et al, 2006.

26. Forget, F., 2013, p. 180.

27. National Aeronautics and Space Administration, 2016.

28. Trefil, J and Hazen, R., 2007, p. 355.

29. Ibid, p. 362.

30. Valencia, D., O'Connell, R. and Sasselov, D., 2007, p. 47.

31. Gonzalez, G. and Richards, J. 2004, p.6.

32. Hoffman, N., 2001.

33. Centre for Research on the Epidemiology of Disasters, 2015.

34. United Nations Office on Drugs and Crime, 2014.

35. Ross, H., 1993, pp.112-113.

36. Cockell, C., et al, 2016.

37. Plaxo, K. and Gross, M., 2006, p. 53.

38. Trefil, J. and Hazen, R, 2007, p. 379.

39. Ross, H., 2016.

40. Ross, H., 1994, pp. 169-170.

41. Plaxo, K. and Gross, M., 2006, p. 247.

Chapter Seven: Cosmological Fine Tuning and the Multiverse

1. In Folger, T., 2008.

2. Lightman, A., 2011, p. 38.

3. Ibid, p. 40.

4. Tegmark, M., 2009, p.1.

5. Ibid, p.1.

6. Mithani, A., & Vilenkin, A., 2012, p. 6.

7. Tegmark, M., ibid, p. 8.

8. Ibid, p. 12.

9. Tegmark, M., 2014.

10. Hawking, S. and Mlodinow, L., 2010.

11. Folger, T., 2008.

12. Hawking, S. and Mlodinow, L., 2010, p. 117.

13. Ibid, p. 118.

14. Ibid, p. 180.

15. Lennox, J., 2011, p. 36.

16. Ibid, p. 39.

17. Radford, T., 2010.

18. Penrose, R., 2016, p. 146.

19. Ellis, G., 2011, p.295.

20. Einstein, A., 1923, p. 28.

21. Dingle, H., 1972, pp. 31-32.

22. Benzmüller, C., and Paleo, B., 2014.

23. Hawking, S. and Mlodinow, L., 2010, pp, 8-9.

24. Heile, F., 2016.

25. Penrose, R., 2010.

26. Woit, P., 2006, p. 207.

27. Cited in Horgan, 2017.

28. Ellis, G., and Silk, J., 2014, p.321.

29. Ibid, p. 321.

30. Hartsfield, T., 2016.

31. Cited in Horgan, J., 2014.

32. Newton, I. 1846, p. 384.

33. Swinburne, R., 1995, p. 68.

34. Collins, R., 2007, p. 461.

35. Carr, B., 2013, p. 168.

36. Cited in Lennox, J., 2010, p. 64.

37. Cited in Martin, S., 2016.

38. Polkinghorne, J., 2007, p.95.

39. Tipler, F., 1994, preface p. i.

Chapter Eight: Abiogenesis: The Search for the Origin of Life

1. In Lim, R., 2017, p. 58.

2. Davies, P., 2003, p. xxiv.

3. Trevors, J. and Abel, D., 2004, p. 736

4. Wald, G., 1954, p.48.

5. Wald, G., 1984, p.1.

6. De Duve, cited in Andrews 2017, p. 248.

7. Kenyon, D., 2002, p. 35.

8. Rands, C., Meader, S., Ponting, C., and Lunter, G., 2014.

9. Bryson, B., 2003.

10. Gitt, W., 2006, p.181.

11. Meyer, S., 2003.

12. Ward, P. and Brownlee, D., 2000, p. 62.

13. Alberts, B. et al, 2015, p. 109.

14. Lane, N., Allen, J., and Martin, W. 2010, p. 272.

15. Ibid p.272.

16. Pross, A., 2012, p. 27.

17. Plaxco, K., and Gross, M. 2006, p. 114.

18. Ibid, p. 129.

19. wie y ski, A. 2016.

20. Bernhardt, H., 2012, p. 7

21. Ibid, p. 7.

22. Kurland, C., 2010, p. 870.

23. McNichol, J., 2008, p. 257.

24. Robertson, M., and Joyce, G., 2012. p. 7

25. Lane, N., Allen, J., and Martin W., 2010, p.273.

26. Orgel, L., (2008, p. 00012.

27. Vasas, V., Szathmáry, E., and Santos, M., 2010, p. 1470.

28. Busby, C., and Howard, C., 2017, p. 172.

29. de Castro Fonseca, M., et al, 2016.

30. Gitt, W., 2006, p.99.

31. Ibid, p.106.

32. Ibid, p. 144.

33. Koonin, E., 2007, mp.19.

34. Hoyle as cited in Johnson, D., 2009, p. 89.

35. Hoyle, F., & Wickramasinghe, C., 1981, pp.19-21.

36. University of Tennessee, Knoxville, 2010.

37. Korthof, G., 2006.

38. Hoyle, 1982, p. 16.

39. Schroeder, G., 1997, p. 27.

40. Chain, as cited in Ronald W. Clark, 1985, pp. 147-148.

Chapter Nine: Cracks in Neo-Darwinism: Micro is not Macro

1. Cited in Whitfield, 2008, p. 282.

2. Hoyle, F. 1999, p. 3.

3. Ibid, p. 139.

4. Laughlin, R., 2005, pp. 168-169.

5. Lewontin, R., 1972, p.18.

6. Dobzhansky, T., 1973, p. 125.

7. Lewontin, R., 1972, p.181.

8. Colin Reeves' comment made with signature to the *Dissent from Darwinism Statement.*

9. Darwin, C., 1892, p. 61.

10. Darwin, C., 1879.

11. Freeland, S., 2008, p. 290.

12. Darwin, C., 1982, p. 458.

13. Dawkins, R., 2006, p. 9.

14. Darwin, C., 1982, p.459.

15. Lennox, J., 2010, pp. 101-102.

16. O'Leary, M., et al, 2013.

17. Beleza, S., et al, 2012.

18. Müller, G, 2017, p. 3.

19. Gauger, A., and Axe, D., 2011, p.13.

20. Sanford, J., Brewer, W., Smith, F., and Baumgardner, J., 2015, p. 27.

21. Lennox, J., 2010, p. 110.

22. Reeves, M., Gauger, A., & Axe, D., 2014. pp. 10-11.

23. In Meyer, S., 2009, p.17.

24. Bauchau, V., 2006, p. 36.

25. Yockey, H., 2005, p. 2.

26. Ayala, F., et al, 1999, p. 10.

27. McKay, B. and Zink, R., 2015, p. 689.

28. Johnson, P., 1999.

29. In Nitardy, C., 2012, p. 60.

30. Gould, S, 1977, p. 14.

31. ABCScience, 1998.

32. Peterson, K., Dietrich, M., and McPeek, M., 2009. p. 736.

33. Ibid, p. 737.

34. Darwin, C., 1982, p. 309.

35. Johnson, P. 1999.

36. Nagel, T., 2012.

37. Todd, S., 1999, p. 423; my emphasis.

38. Dembski, W., 2008.

39. Kuhn, J., 2012, p. 46.

40. Bechly, G., no date: Fossils vs Darwin.

41. Miller, K., 1999, p. 26.

42. Russell, R., 2008, p. 590.

43. Goswami, A., 2014, p.22.

44. In Walsh, J., 2013, p. 338.

Chapter 10: Answering the Tough Questions: God of the Gaps, Free Will, and the Problem Evil

1.   Drummond, H., 1894, p. 333.

2.   Gaither, C. and Cavazos-Gaither, A., 2001, p. 128.

3.   Bonhoeffer, D., 1972, p.311.

4.   Meyer, S., 2009, p. 429.

5.   Ibid, p. 429.

6.   Ibid, p. 160.

7.   Ewart, P., 2009, p. 123.

8.   Ibid, 125.

9.   In Durant, W., 1944, pp. 150-151.

10. In Eliaeson, 2002, p. 35.

11. In Lane, A., 1981, p.74.

12. Ibid, p. 74.

13. Einstein, A, and Infeld, L., 1938, p. 262-263.

14. In Geisler, N. & Corduan, W., 2002, p. 322.

15. Hick, J., 2007, p 256.

16. Frankl, V., 1985, p. 88.

17. Swinburne, R., 2010, p. 95.

18. In Grant, 2004, p. 222.

References

ABC Science (1998). Molecular basis for evolution. *Elsevier Science Channel*, November 27th. http://www.abc.net.au/science/articles/1998/11/27/17476.htm.

Aikman, D. (2012). *Jesus in Beijing: How Christianity is transforming China and changing the global balance of power*. New York: Regnery.

Alberts, B., Johnson, A., Lewis, J., Walter, P., Morgan, D., Raff, M., Roberts, K., & Walter, P. (2015). *Molecular Biology of the Cell*, 6th Edition. New York: Garland.

Andrews, E. (2017). *Is the Bible really the word of God? Is Christianity the One True Faith?* Cambridge, OH: Christian Publishing House.

Appolloni, S. (2011). " Repugnant"," Not repugnant at all": How the respective epistemic attitudes of Georges Lemaitre and Sir Arthur Eddington influenced how each approached the idea of a beginning of the universe. *Scientific Journal of International Black Sea University, 5:* 19-44.

Astronomy Essentials (2015). How long to orbit Milky Way's center? November 28th. http://earthsky.org/astronomy-essentials/milky-way-rotation.

Ayala, F., Cicerone, R., Clegg, M., Dalrymple, G., Dickerson, R., Gould, S., Herschbach, D., Kennedy, D., McInerney, J. & Moore, J. (1999). Science and creationism: A view from the National Academy of Sciences. Washington, DC: National Academy of Sciences.

Bahr, H. & Chadwick, B. (1985). Religion and family in Middletown, USA. *Journal of Marriage and the Family*, 47:407-414.

Barrow, J. & Tipler, F. (1986). *The Anthropic Cosmological Principle*, New York:Oxford University Press.

Batygin, K., & Laughlin, G. (2015). Jupiter's decisive role in the inner Solar System's early evolution. *Proceedings of the National Academy of Sciences*, 112: 4214-4217.

Bauchau, V. (2006). Emergence and reductionism: From the game of life to science of life. In Feltz, B., Crommelinck, M., & Goujon, P., pp. 29-40, *Self-organization and emergence in life sciences*. Dordrecht, The Netherlands: Springer.

Beaulieu, J., Bennett, D., Fouqué, P., Williams, A., Dominik, M., Jørgensen, U., Kubas, D., Cassan, A., Coutures, C., Greenhill, J. and Hill, K. (2006). Discovery of a cool planet of 5.5 Earth masses through gravitational microlensing. *Nature, 439:*437-440.

Bechley, G. (nd). Gunter Bechley: Fossils vs Darwin. https://gbechly.jimdo.com/

Beleza, S., Santos, A., McEvoy, B., Alves, I., Martinho, C., Cameron, E., Shriver, M., Parra, E. & Rocha, J. (2012). The timing of pigmentation lightening in Europeans. *Molecular biology and evolution, 30*(1), pp.24-35.

Bennetts, M. (2014). Who's 'godless' now? Russia says it's U.S. Washington Times, January 28.

http://www.washingtontimes.com/news/2014/jan/28/whos-godless-now-russia-says-its-us/?page=all.

Benzmüller, C., & Paleo, B. (2014). Automating Gödel's ontological proof of God's existence with higher-order automated theorem provers. In *Proceedings of the Twenty-first European Conference on Artificial Intelligence* (pp. 93-98). IOS Press.

Bernhardt, H. (2012). The RNA world hypothesis: the worst theory of the early evolution of life (except for all the others). *Biology Direct, 7: 1-10.*

Bingham, J. (2016). Religion can make you happier, official figures suggest. *Daily Telegraph*, February 2nd.

Blackburn, R. (2000). *The overthrow of colonial slavery: 1776-1848.* London: Verso.

Bonhoeffer, D. (1972). *Letters and papers from prison.* New York: Macmillan, 1972), 311.

Bromm, V., & Larson, R. (2004). The first stars. *Annual. Review of Astronomy and Astrophysics, 42*:79-118.

Brooks, A. (2003). Religious faith and charitable giving. Policy Review, October & November, 1-5.

Brooks, A. (2004). Faith, secularism, and charity. Faith and economics, 43: 1-8.

Bryson, B. (2003). *A short history of nearly everything.* New York: Broadway Books.

Buber, M. (2002). *The Martin Buber reader.* Asher Biemann (Ed.). New York: Macmillan.

Busby, C., & Howard, C. (2017). Re-thinking biology—I. Maxwell's Demon and the spontaneous origin of life. *Advances in Biological Chemistry, 7*:170-181.

Bussey, P. (2016). *Signposts to God: How modern physics and astronomy point the way to belief.* Downers Grove: IL: Intervarsity Press.

Call, V. & Heaton, T. (1997). Religious influence on marital stability. *Journal for the Scientific Study of Religion*, 36:382-392.

Cammaerts, E, (1937). *The laughing prophet: The seven virtues and G. K. Chesterton,* Methuen, York: England.

Carr, B. (2013). Lemaître's prescience: the beginning and end of the cosmos. In R. Holder and S. Mitton (eds.), *Georges Lemaître: Life, Science and Legacy* (pp. 145-172). Berlin, Heidelberg: Springer.

Centre for Research on the Epidemiology of Disasters (2015). The human cost of natural disasters: A global perspective. New York: United Nations.

Chesterton, G. (2001). The Collected Works of G.K. Chesterton, Vol. 20. San Francisco: Ignatius Press.

Christian, J. L. (2011). *Philosophy: An introduction to the art of wondering.* Boston, Wadsworth.

Clark, R. (1985). *The life of Ernst Chain: Penicillin and beyond,* London: Weidenfeld & Nicolson.

Cockell, C., Bush, T., Bryce, C., Direito, S., Fox-Powell, M., Harrison, J., Lammer, H., Landenmark, H., Martin-Torres, J., Nicholson, N. and Noack, L., 2016. Habitability: A review. *Astrobiology, 16*(1), pp.89-117.

Collins, R. (2007). Collins: Why this scientist believes in God. *CNN News.* http://www.cnn.com/2007/US/04/03/collins.commentary/index.html

Collins, R. (2007). The multiverse hypothesis: A theistic perspective. In Carr, B. (ed), *Universe or multiverse?, pp. 459-480.* Cambridge: Cambridge University Press.

Coyne, G. V., & Heller, M. (2008). *A comprehensible universe: The interplay of science and theology.* New York: Springer-Verlag.

Craig, W. (2008). *Reasonable Faith: Christian Truth and Apologetics.* Wheaton, IL: Crossway.

Craig, W. L. (2010). *On guard: Defending your faith with reason and precision.* Colorado Spring, CO: David C Cook.

Craig, W.., & Meister, C. (2010). *God is great, God is good: why believing in God is reasonable and responsible.* Downers Grove, IL: InterVarsity Press.

Crick, F. (1994). The astonishing hypothesis. New York: Scribner's.

Darwin, C. (1982). The origin of species. London: Penguin.

Darwin, C. (1879). To John Fordyce, 7 May 1879. Cambridge University Darwin Correspondence Project. ghttps://www.darwinproject.ac.uk/letter/DCP-LETT-12041.xml

Darwin, C. (1892). *Charles Darwin: his life told in an autobiographical chapter, and in a selected series of his published letters* (Vol. 5, edited by F. Darwin. London: John Murray.

Darwin, C., Burkhardt, F., & Smith, S. (1991). *The Correspondence of Charles Darwin: 1858-1859* (Vol. 7). Cambridge: Cambridge University Press.

Davies, P. (1982). *The accidental universe.* Cambridge: Cambridge University Press.

Davies, P. (1984). Superforce: The search for a grand unified theory of nature. New York: Simon & Schuster.

Davies, P. (2003). *The Origin of Life.* London: Penguin Books.

Davies, P. (2007). Taking science on faith. *New York Times,* November 24th. http://www.nytimes.com/2007/11/24/opinion/24davies.html?pagewanted=all

Dawkins, R. (2006). *The God delusion.* New York: Houghton Mifflin.

Dawkins, R. (nd). Debate with Dr. John Lennox ww.dawkinslennoxdebate.com.

Day, R., & Acock, A. (2013). Marital well-being and religiousness as mediated by relational virtue and equality. *Journal of Marriage and Family, 75:* 164-177.

de Castro Fonseca, M., Aguiar, C., da Rocha Franco, J., Gingold, R., & Leite, M. (2016). GPR91: expanding the frontiers of Krebs cycle intermediates. *Cell Communication and Signaling, 14:* 3.

Dembski, W. (2008). In defense of intelligent design. *The Oxford Handbook of Religion and Science, Oxford Handbooks in Religion and Theology, pp. 715-731.* Oxford: Oxford University Press.

Dervic, K., Oquendo, M., Grunebaum, M., Ellis, S., Burke, A., & Mann, J. (2004). Religious affiliation and suicide attempt. *American Journal of Psychiatry, 161:* 2303-2308.

de Tocqueville, A. (1994). *Democracy in America*, Bradley, P. (ed.). New York: Alfred A. Knopf.

Dimitrov, T. (2010). 50 Nobel Laureates who believe in GOD. *Scientific GOD Journal*, 1:166-182.

Dingle, H. (1972) *Science at the crossroads*, London: Martin Brian & O'Keefe,

Dobzhansky, T. (1973). Nothing in biology makes sense except in light of evolution. *The American Biology Teacher*, 35:125-129.

Dollahite, D. & Thatcher, J. (2005). How family religious involvement benefits adults, youth, and children and strengthens families. Salt Lake City: *The Sutherland Institute*.

Drescher, S. & Engerman, S. eds. (1998). *A Historical Guide to World Slavery*. New York: Oxford University Press.

Drummond, H. (1894). *Ascent of man*. New York: Pott & Co.

Duck, M., & Duck, E. (2014). *Waters of creativity: Navigating the straits between science and theology to find the source of one's beginning*. Lake Mary, FL: Charisma Media.

Durant, W. (1935). *Our Oriental Heritage*. New York: Simon & Schuster.

Durant, W. (1944). *Caesar and Christ*. New York: Simon and Schuster.

Durant, W. & Durrant, A. (1968). *The Lessons of History*, New York: Simon and Schuster.

Dyson, L., Kleban, M., & Susskind, L. (2002). Disturbing implications of a cosmological constant. *Journal of High Energy Physics*, 10: 1-26.

Easton, J. (2005). Survey on physicians' religious beliefs shows majority faithful. Medical Center Public Affairs, University of Chicago Chronicle. July 14.

Ecklund, E. & Park, J. (2009). Conflict between religion and science among academic scientists? *Journal for the Scientific Study of Religion*, 48: 276-292.

Einstein, A. (1923). *Sidelights on Relativity (Geometry and Experience)*. New York: P. Dutton.

Einstein, A. (1941). Science, philosophy and religion, a symposium. In *Conference on Science, Philosophy and Religion Their Relation to The Democratic Way of Life. New York*.
http://www.sacred-texts.com/aor/einstein/einsci.htm.

Einstein, A & L. Infeld (1938). *The evolution of physics*. Cambridge: Cambridge University Press.

Ellis, G. (2011). The untestable multiverse. *Nature*, 469:294-295.

Ellis, G., & Silk, J. (2014). Scientific method: Defend the integrity of physics. *Nature, 516:* 321-323.

Ellis, L. & Walsh, A. (2000). *Criminology: A global perspective*. Boston: Allyn & Bacon.

Ellis, M., Vinson, D., & Ewigman, B. (1999). Addressing spiritual concerns of patients. *Journal of Family Practice, 48:* 105-106.

Esch, T. & G. Stefano (2005). Love promotes health. *Neuroendocrinology Letters*, 3:264-267.

Ewart, P. (2009). The necessity of chance: Randomness, purpose and the sovereignty of God. *Science & Christian Belief, 21: 111-131*.

Forbes, K., & Zampelli, E. (2013). The impacts of religion, political ideology, and social capital on religious and secular giving: evidence from the 2006 Social Capital Community Survey. *Applied Economics, 45*: 2481-2490.

Forget, F. (2013). On the probability of habitable planets. *International Journal of Astrobiology, 12:* 177-185.

Flew, A., & Varghese, R. A. (2009). *There is a God.* New York: HarperCollins.

Folger, T. (2008). Science's Alternative to an Intelligent Creator: The Multi-verse Theory. *Discover Magazine,* December 10th. http://discovermagazine.com/2008/dec/10-sciences-alternative-to-an-intelligent-creator

Freedom House (2015). *Freedom in the World Index.* https://freedomhouse.org/report/freedom-world/freedom-world-2014

Fragile Families Research Brief (2005). Religion and marriage in urban America. Bendheim-Thoman Center for Research on Child Wellbeing, Princeton University Social Indicators Survey Center, Columbia University.

Frankl, V. (1985). *Man's Search for Meaning.* New York: Pocket Books.

Freeland, S. (2008). Could an intelligent alien predict earth's biochemistry? In Barrow et al, (eds.), *Fitness of the cosmos for life: Biochemistry and fine-tuning.* Pp. 280-315. Cambridge: Cambridge University Press.

Gaither, C. & Cavazos-Gaither, A., (2001). *Naturally speaking: a dictionary of quotations on biology, botany, nature and zoology.* London: Institute of Physics Publishing.

Gauger, A., & Axe, D. (2011). The evolutionary accessibility of new enzymes functions: A case study from the biotin pathway. *Bio-Complexity, 2011: 1-17.*

Geisler, N. & Corduan, W. (2002). *Philosophy of religion* (2nd ed.). Eugene, OR: Wipf & Stock.

Gitt, W. (2006). *In the beginning was information: A scientist explains the incredible design in nature.* Portland, OR: New Leaf Publishing Group.

Gonzalez, G., Brownlee, D. & Ward, P. (2001). Refugees for life in a hostile universe. *Scientific American,* 285: 60-67.

Gonzalez, G., & Richards, J. (2004). *The privileged planet: how our place in the cosmos is designed for discovery.* New York: Regnery Publishing.

Goswami, A. (2014). *Creative evolution: A physicist's resolution between darwinism and intelligent design.* Wheaton, IL: Quest Books

Gould, S., (1977). Evolution's erratic pace. *Natural History, 86:* 12-16.

Graebner, N. (1976). Christianity and democracy: Tocqueville's views of religion in America. *The Journal of Religion, 56:* 263-273.

Grant, E. (2004). *Science and religion, 400 BC to AD 1550: From Aristotle to Copernicus.* Westport, CT: Greenwood.

Grelle, B. (2016). *Antonio Gramsci and the Question of Religion: Ideology, Ethics, and Hegemony.* New York: Taylor & Francis.

Grim, B., & Grim, M. (2016). The socio-economic contribution of religion to American society: An empirical analysis. *Interdisciplinary Journal of Research on Religion,* 12:2-31.

Grossman, L. (2012). Death of the eternal cosmos, *New Scientist,* 213:6–7.

Gross, N., & Simmons, S. (2009). The religiosity of American college and university professors. *Sociology of Religion, 70*(2), 101-129.

Guiso, L., Sapienza, P., & Zingales, L. (2003). People's opium? Religion and economic attitudes. *Journal of monetary economics, 50*: 225-282.

Hall. D. (2006). Religious attendance: More cost effective than lipitor? *Journal of the American Board of Family Practice*, 19:431-433.

Harris, S. (2005). *The end of faith: Religion, terror, and the future of reason.* New York: WW Norton & Company.

Harrison, P. (2012). Christianity and the rise of western science. *ABC Religion and Ethics.*
http://www.abc.net.au/religion/articles/2012/05/08/3498202.htm

Hartsfield, T. (2016). String theory has failed as a scientific theory, Real Clear Science, January 8th.
http://www.realclearscience.com/blog/2016/01/string_theory_has_failed_as_a_scientific_theory.html

Haught, J. (2008). Is fine-tuning remarkable? In J Barrow et al, *Fitness of the cosmos for life: Biochemistry and fine-tuning.* pp. 31-48, Cambridge: Cambridge University Press.

Hawking, S. & Mlodinow, L. (2010). The *Grand Design.* New York: Bantam Books.

Hazard, J., Butler, W. & Maggs, P. (1977). *The Soviet legal system.* Dobbs Ferry, NY: Oceana.

Heile, F. (2016). Is it theoretically possible to build a collider that can test the predictions of string theory? https://www.quora.com/Is-it-theoretically-possible-to-build-a-collider-that-can-test-the-predictions-of-string-theory

Hewitt, D. (2016). Senior Chinese religious advisor calls for promotion of atheism in society. International Business Review, August 27th.
http://www.ibtimes.com/senior-chinese-religious-advisor-calls-promotion-atheism-society-2363850

Hewlett, M. (2008). Molecular biology and religion. In P. Clayton & Z. Simpson (eds.), *The Oxford handbook on religion and science*, pp.172-186. Oxford: Oxford University Press.

Heyer, W. (2011). Public school LGBT programs don't just trample parental rights. They also put kids at risk. The Witherspoon Institute.
http://www.thepublicdiscourse.com/2015/06/15118/

Hick, J., (2007) *Evil and the God of Love*, 2d. ed. New York: Palgrave Macmillan.

Hitchens, C. (2003). Mommie dearest: The pope beatifies Mother Teresa, a fanatic, a fundamentalist, and a fraud. *Slate*, October 20th.

Hitchens, P. (2010). *The rage against God.* London: Bloomsbury Publishing.

Hitchens, P. (2012). What's socialist about state ownership? Beats me. *Daily Mail*, October 11th.

Hoffman, N. (2001). The Moon and plate tectonics: Why we are alone. Space Daily. http://www.spacedaily.com/news/life-01x1.html

Holt, J. (1997). Science resurrects God. *Wall Street Journal*, December 24.

Horgan, J. (2014). The philosophy of guessing has harmed physics, expert says. *Scientific American*, August 21

Horgan, J. (2017). Why string theory is still not even wrong. *Scientific American*, April 27th.
https://blogs.scientificamerican.com/cross-check/why-string-theory-is-still-not-even-wrong/

Hosking, G. (1985). The first socialist society: A history of the Soviet Union from within. Cambridge: Harvard University Press.

Hoyle, F. (1982). The universe: Past and present reflections. *Annual Review of Astronomy and Astrophysics, 20:* 1-36.

Hoyle, F. (1999). *Mathematics of evolution.* Memphis, TN: Acorn Enterprises.

Hoyle, F., & Wickramasinghe, C. (1981). *Evolution from space.* London: JM Dent.

Hulme, C., & Salter, M. (2001). The Nazi's persecution of religion as a war crime: The Oss's response within the Nuremberg Trials process. *Rutgers Journal of Law & Religion, 3:*1-27.

Hummer, R., Rogers, R. Nam, C. & Ellison, C. (1999). Religious Involvement and U.S. Adult Mortality. *Demography* 36:273–285.

International Christian Concern (2017). *2016 hall of shame.* Washington, DC: ICC.

Isaacson, W. (2007). Einstein: His life and universe. New York: Simon and Schuster.

Jal. M. (2010), Interpretation as phantasmagria: Variations on a theme on Marx's Theses on Feuerbach. *Critique, 38:* 117-142.

Jastrow, R. (1978). *God and the astronomers (1978), W. W. Norton*

Jastrow, R. (1981). *The enchanted loom: Mind in the universe.* New York: Simon & Schuster.

Jastrow, R. (1992). *God and the Astronomers.* New York: WW Norton.

Jeans, J. (1930). *The mysterious universe.* Cambridge: Cambridge University Press.

Jennings, B. (2015). *In defense of scientism: An insider's view of science.* Vancouver, BC: Byron K. Jennings

Johnson, D. (2009). *Probability's Nature and Nature's Probability-Lite: A Sequel for Non-Scientists and a Clarion Call to Scientific Integrity.* Kingston, TN: Big Mac Publishers.

Johnson, P. (1999). The Church of Darwin. *Wall Street Journal,* August 16th.
https://www.wsj.com/articles/SB934759227734378961

Kainz, H. P. (2010). *The Existence of God and the Faith-instinct.* Selinsgove, PA: Susquehanna University Press.

Kennedy, D. (1907). St. Albertus Magnus. In *The Catholic Encyclopedia.* New York: Robert Appleton Company. Retrieved January 4, 2009 from New Advent: http://www.newadvent.org/cathen/01264a.htm. p. 265.

Kenny, M. (2008). Atheists, enjoy life? *The Guardian,* October 24th.

Kenyon, D. (2002). *Unlocking the mystery of life:* Script draft of video.
http://www.divinerevelations.info/documents/intelligent_design/unlockingthemysteryoflifescript.pdf.

Keyser, C. (1915). *The New Infinite and the Old Theology.* Yale University Press.

King, V., Ledwell, M., & Pearce-Morris, J. (2013). Religion and ties between adult children and their parents. *The Journals of Gerontology Series B: Psychological Sciences and Social Sciences*, 68: 825–836.

Kolakowski, L. (1981). *Main currents of Marxism: Volume III, the breakdown.* Oxford: Oxford University Press.

Koonin, E. (2007). The cosmological model of eternal inflation and the transition from chance to biological evolution in the history of life. *Biology Direct*, 2: 1-21.

Kopparapu, R., Ramirez, R., SchottelKotte, J., Kasting, J., Domagal-Goldman, S., & Eymet, V. (2014). Habitable zones around main-sequence stars: dependence on planetary mass. *The Astrophysical Journal Letters*, *787*(2), L29.

Korthof, G. (2006). Fred Hoyle's The Intelligent Universe: A summary & review.
http://wasdarwinwrong.com/kortho47.htm.

Krebs, R. (2006). *The history and use of our earth's chemical elements: a reference guide.* Westport: CT: Greenwood.

Kristeva, J. (1989). *Black sun: Depression and melancholia.* Columbia University Press.

Kuhn, J. (2012). Dissecting Darwinism. *Proceedings Baylor University Medical Center*, *25:* 41-47.

Kruk, E. (2012). Arguments for an equal parental responsibility presumption in contested child custody. *The American Journal of Family Therapy*, 40:33-55.

Kurland, C. (2010). The RNA dreamtime. *Bioessays*, *32:*866-871.

Lemley, B. (2000). Why is there life?. *Discover*, *21:* 64-69.

Lampert, L. (2001). *Nietzsche's task: an interpretation of beyond good and evil.* New Haven, CT: Yale University Press.

Lane, A. (1981). Did Calvin believe in free-will? *Vox Evangelica*, *12*, 72-90.

Lane, N., Allen, J., & Martin, W. (2010). How did LUCA make a living? Chemiosmosis in the origin of life. *BioEssays*, *32*: 271-280.

Laughlin, R., (2005). *A different universe: Reinventing physics from the bottom down.* New York: Basic Books.

Leiter, B. (2014). *Why tolerate religion?* Princeton, NJ: Princeton University Press.

Lennox, J. (2009). *God's Undertaker: Has Science Buried God?* Oxford: Lion.

Lennox, J. (2011). *God and Stephen Hawking: Whose Design is it Anyway?* Oxford: Lion Books.

Lewis, C. (2001). *Mere Christianity.* New York: Harper Collins.

Lewontin, R. (1972). Testing the theory of natural selection. *Nature*, *236:*181-182.

Lewontin, R. (1997). Billions and billions of demons. *New York Review of Books*, January 9th

Lightman, A. (2011). The accidental universe: Science's crisis of faith. *Harper's Magazine*, December.

Lim, R. (2017). *Self and the Phenomenon of Life: A Biologist Examines Life from Molecules to Humanity.* Hackensack, NJ: World Scientific.

Lipka, M. (2016). 10 facts about atheists. Washington, DC.: Pew Research Center.

Lipton, P. (2000). Inference to the best explanation. In W. Newton-Smith (ed.), *A companion to the philosophy of science.* pp. 184.193. Hoboken, NJ: Blackwell.

Loeb, A. (2010). *How did the first stars and galaxies form?* Princeton, NJ: Princeton University Press.

McKay, B., & Zink, R. (2015). Sisyphean evolution in Darwin's finches. *Biological Reviews, 90:* 689-698.

Malachi, M. (2008). *Keys of This Blood: Pope John Paul II Versus Russia and the West for Control of the New World Order.* New York: Simon and Schuster.

Marcuse, H. (1969). *An essay on liberation.* Boston: Beacon Press.

Marcuse, H. (2002). *One dimensional man.* New York: Routledge.

Margenau, H. & Varghese, R. (1997). *Cosmos, Bios, Theos: Scientists Reflect on Science, God, and the Origins of the Universe, Life, and Homo sapiens.* 4th ed. Chicago and La Salle, Illinois: Open Court Publishing Company.

Markham, I. (2010). *Against atheism: Why Dawkins, Hitchens, and Harris are fundamentally wrong.* New York: Wiley and Sons.

Marsh, J. (2012). *The Liberal Delusion: The Roots of Our Current Moral Crisis.* Bury St. Edmunds, England: Arena books.

Martin, S. (2016). Renowned physicist finds PROOF of God: Universe was created by DESIGN in huge 'matrix.' *Daily Express,* Dec. 12th. http://www.express.co.uk/news/science/742567/PROOF-of-God-real-Michio-Kaku

Maurin, A. (2013). Infinite regress arguments. *In Johanssonian investigations,* Svennerlind, C. Almäng, J. & Ingthorsson R. (eds.) pp.421-438. Heusenstamm, Germany: Ontos Verlag.

McGrath, A. (2010*). Mere Theology.* London: SPCK Publishers

McLeish, T., Bower, R.., Tanner, B., Smithson, H., Panti, C., Lewis, N., & Gasper, G. (2014). *A* medieval multiverse. *Nature,* 507: 161-163.

McNichol, J. (2008). Primordial soup, fool's gold, and spontaneous generation. *Biochemistry and Molecular Biology Education, 36*(4), 255-261.

Meyer, S. (1999). The return of the God hypothesis. *Journal of Interdisciplinary Studies,* 11:1-31.

Meyer, S. (2003). DNA and the origin of life: Information, specification, and explanation. In J. Campbrell & S. Meyer, *Darwinism, Design and Public Education,* pp. 223-285. East Lansing, MI: Michigan State University Press.

Meyer, S. (2009). *Signature in the Cell: DNA and the Evidence for Intelligent Design.* Grand Rapids, MI: Zondervan.

Miller, K. (1999). *Finding Darwin's God.* New York: Harper-Collins.

Minnicino, M. (1992). The Frankfurt School and 'Political Correctness.' *Fidelio,* I: 4-27.

Mithani, A., & Vilenkin, A. (2012). Did the universe have a beginning? *arXiv:1204.4658.*

Mua, K. (2016). Religion as a Tool for Economic/Political Transformation. *Political Transformation, Working Paper, 1-22.*

Müller, G. (2017). Why an extended evolutionary synthesis is necessary. *Interface focus, 7,* 20170015.

Nagel, T. (1997). *The last word.* New York: Oxford University Press.

Nagel, T. (2012). *Mind and cosmos: why the materialist neo-Darwinian conception of nature is almost certainly false.* New York: Oxford University Press.

National Aeronautics and Space Administration (nd). *Tests of Big Bang: The CMB.* https://wmap.gsfc.nasa.gov/universe/bb_tests_cmb.html.

National Aeronautics and Space Administration (nd). Tests of Big Bang: The light elements. https://map.gsfc.nasa.gov/

National Aeronautics and Space Administration (2016). The Magnetosphere: Our shield in space. NASA History Office. https://history.nasa.gov/EP-177/ch3-4.html

National Aeronautics and Space Administration (2017). The Sun, August 3rd https://www.nasa.gov/sun

Neill, A. (2012) Summerhill School: A new view (1960) of childhood. In de Freitas, S., & Jameson, J. (Eds.). *The e-learning reader.* Pp. 83-88. London: Continuum Publishing Group.

Newport, F. (2010). Americans' church attendance inches up in 2010. Pew Report, http://www.gallup.com/poll/141044/americans-church-attendance-inches-2010.aspx

Newton, I. (1846). *Newton's Principia: the Mathematical Principles of Natural Philosophy/by Sir Isaac Newton.* (N. Chittenden, Ed.). New York: Daniel Adee.

Nietzsche, F. (1997) *Daybreak: Thoughts on the Prejudices of Morality,* R.J. Hollingdale (trans.), Cambridge: Cambridge University Press.

Nietzsche, F. & Hollingdale, R. (1990). Expeditions of an untimely man. In *Twilight of the Idols; and, The Anti-Christ* (Penguin Classics, London: Penguin Books.

Nitardy, C. (2012). *Stumbling blocks of evolutions.* Maitland, FL: Xulaon.

O'leary, M., Bloch, J., Flynn, J., Gaudin, T., Giallombardo, A., Giannini, N., Goldberg, S., Kraatz, B., Luo, Z., Meng, J. and Ni, X. (2013). The placental mammal ancestor and the post–K-Pg radiation of placentals. *Science, 339:* 662-667.

Olsen, B. (2013). *Future Esoteric: The Unseen Realms.* San Francisco: CCC Publishing.

Orgel, L. (2008). The implausibility of metabolic cycles on the prebiotic Earth. *PLoS biology, 6*(1), e18.

Overy, R. (2004). The dictators: Hitler's Germany and Stalin's Russia. New York: W. W. Norton.

Pascal, B. (1958) Pascal's Pensees. (Introduction by T. S. Elliot). New York: E. P. Dutton.

Penrose, R. (2010). Scientist debunks Hawking's 'no God needed' theory. *Independent Catholic* September 29. http://www.indcatholicnews.com/news.php?viewStory=16815

Penrose, R. (2016). *The emperor's new mind: Concerning computers, minds, and the laws of physics.* New York Oxford University Pres.

Peterson, K., Dietrich, M., & McPeek, M. (2009). MicroRNAs and metazoan macroevolution: insights into canalization, complexity, and the Cambrian explosion. *Bioessays, 31*:736-747.

Pew Forum on Religion & Public Life (2009). Eastern, New Age beliefs widespread: Many Americans mix multiple faiths. Washington, DC: Pew Research Center.

Pew Research Center (2016). Religious landscape study. http://www.pewforum.org/religious-landscape-study.

Phillips, T. (2014). China on course to become 'world's most Christian nation' within 15 years. *The Telegraph*, April 19th.

Plank, M. (1949). *Scientific Autobiography and Other Papers* (trans. F. Gaynor). New York: Philosophical Library

Plaxo, K., & Gross, M. (2006). *Astrobiology: a brief introduction.* Baltimore, MD: Johns Hopkins University Press.

Polkinghorne, J. (2007). *One World: The interaction of science and theology.* West Conshohocken, PA: Templeton Press.

Pross, A. (2012). What is Life?: How chemistry becomes biology. Oxford: Oxford University Press.

Radford, T. (2010). The Grand Design: New answers to the ultimate questions of life by Stephen Hawking and Leonard Mlodinow, September 17th. https://www.theguardian.com/books/2010/sep/18/questions-life-cosmology-stephen-hawking

Rands, C., Meader, S., Ponting, C., & Lunter, G. (2014). 8.2% of the human genome is constrained: variation in rates of turnover across functional element classes in the human lineage. *PLoS Genetics, 10*:e1004525.

Raehn, R. V. (2004). The Historical Roots of Political Correctness. In *Political Correctness: A short history of an ideology. Alexandria, VA: Free Congress Foundation.*

Rasic, D., Belik, S., Elias, B., Katz, L., Enns, M., Sareen, J., & Team, Swampy Cree Suicide Prevention (2009). Spirituality, religion and suicidal behavior in a nationally representative sample. *Journal of Affective Disorders, 114*: 32-40.

Reeves, C. Comment made with signature to the *Dissent from Darwinism Statement.* https://dissentfromdarwin.org/2008/09/22/professor_colin_reeves_coventr/

Reeves, M., Gauger, A., & Axe, D. (2014). Enzyme families--shared evolutionary history or shared design? A study of the GABA-Aminotransferase family. *BIO-Complexity*, 2014:1- 16.

Richerson, P. & R. Boyd (2010). *Evolution since Darwin: The first 150 years.* In M. Bell, D. Futuyma, W. Eanes & J. Levinton, (eds.) Sunderland, MA: Sinauer, pp. 561-588.

Robertson, M., & Joyce, G. (2012). The origins of the RNA world. *Cold Spring Harbor perspectives in biology, 4*(5), a003608.

Rorty, R. (2000). Universality and truth. In R. Brandom (ed.), *Rorty and his Critics*, pp. 1-30. Oxford, Blackwell.

Ross, H. (1993). The Creator and the Cosmos: How the greatest scientific discoveries of the century reveal God. *Colorado Springs, CO: NavPress.*

Ross, H. (1994). Astronomical evidences for a personal, transcendent God. *In J. Moreland (ed.) The Creation Hypothesis: Scientific Evidence for an Intelligent Designer*, pp. 141-172. Downers Grove, IL: InterVarsity Press.

Ross, H. (2016). *Improbable planet: How Earth became humanity's home.* Grand rapids, MI: Baker Books.

Russell, R. (2008). Quantum physics and the theology of non-interventionist objective divine action. In P. Clayton & Z. Simpson (eds.), *The Oxford handbook of religion and science*, pp. 579-595. Oxford: Oxford University Press.

Sanford, J., Brewer, W., Smith, F., & Baumgardner, J. (2015). The waiting time problem in a model hominin population. *Theoretical Biology and Medical Modelling, 12: 1-28.*

Schaefer, H. (2003). *Science and Christianity: Conflict or coherence?* Watkinsville, GA: The Apollos Trust.

Schafer, L. (2006). Quantum reality and the consciousness of the universe. *Zygon*, 41:505-532.

Schroeder, G. (1997). *The science of God.* New York: Broadway Books.

Scharf, C. (2014). *The Copernicus Complex: Our Cosmic Significance in a Universe of Planets and Probabilities.* New York: Scientific American/Farrar, Straus and Giroux.

Schmacher, R. (2012). The myth that religion is the #1 cause of war. The Christian Apologetics & Research Ministry. https://carm.org/religion-cause-war

Schmidt, A. (2004). H*ow Christianity changed the world.* Grand Rapids, MI: Zondervan.

Schulzke, M. (2013). The politics of new atheism. *Politics and Religion, 6*:778-799.

Shackelford, K. (2016). Undeniable: The Survey of Hostility to Religion in America. First Liberty Institute, Plano: TX.

Shalev, B. (2003). *Religion of Nobel Prize winners. 100 years of Nobel prizes.* New Delhi: Atlantic Publishers & Distributors.

Sheen, F. (1948). *Communism and the Conscience of the West.* Indianapolis and NY: Bobbs- Merrill.

Sherwood, M. (2007). *After Abolition: Britain and the Slave Trade Since 1807.* London: I.B. Tauris & Co.

Simon, S. (2004). Big Bang: The most important scientific discovery of all time and why you need to know about it. New York: Harper-Perennial.

Smith, G. (2017). Does faith make you healthy and happy? The case of evangelicals in the UK. *Journal of Religion and Society,* 19:1-15.

Singh, S. (2004). *Big Bang: The Origin of the Universe.* New York: Harper Perennial, 2004.

Solzhenitsyn, A. (2006). Templeton Lecture, May 10, 1983," in *The Solzhenitsyn reader: New and essential writings, 1947-2005,* eds. E. Ericson, Jr. and D. Mahoney. Wilmington, DE: Intercollegiate Studies Institute p.

Sørensen, T., Danbolt, L., Lien, L., Koenig, H., & Holmen, J. (2011). The relationship between religious attendance and blood pressure: the HUNT study, Norway. *The International Journal of Psychiatry in Medicine, 42:* 13-28.

Spradley, J. (2010). Ten lunar legacies: Importance of the Moon for life on Earth. *Perspectives on Science & Christian Faith, 62:*267-275.

Sprig, P. (2006). *Homosexuality in your child's school.* Washington, DC: Family Research Council

Stark, R (2003). *For the Glory of God.* Princeton, NJ: Princeton University Press.

Stark, R. (2005). *The Victory of Reason: How Christianity Led to Freedom, Capitalism, and Western Success.* New York: Random House.

Stark, R. (2012). *America's Blessings: How Religion Benefits Everyone, Including Atheists.* West Conshohocken, PA: Templeton Foundation Press.

Stephan, A. (2000). Religion, democracy, and the "Twin Tolerations." *Journal of Democracy,* 11:35-57.

Stormer, J. (1964). *None Dare Call It Treason.* New York: Buccaneer Books

Straumann, B. (2008). The peace of Westphalia as a secular constitution. *Constellations, 15:* 173-188.

Strawbridge, W., Cohen, R., Shema, S., & Kaplan, G. (1997). Frequent attendance at religious services and mortality over 28 years. *American Journal of Public Health, 87:* 957-961.

Świeżyński, A. (2016). Where/when/how did life begin? A philosophical key for systematizing theories on the origin of life. *International Journal of Astrobiology, 15:* 291-299.

Swinburne, R. (1995). *Is there a God?* (First edition). Oxford: Oxford University Press.

Swinburne, R. (2010). *Is there a God?* (Revised edition). Oxford: Oxford University Press.

Tarter, J., Backus, P., Mancinelli, R., Aurnou, J., Backman, D.., Basri, G., Boss, A., Clarke, A., Deming, D., Doyle, L., & Feigelson, E. (2007). A reappraisal of the habitability of planets around M dwarf stars. *Astrobiology, 7:* pp.30-65

Tatara, C. (2013). Hitler, Himmler, and Christianity in the Early Third Reich. *Constructing the Past, 14:* 39-44.

Tegmark, M. (2009). The multiverse hierarchy. *arXiv preprint arXiv:0905.1283.*

Tegmark, M. (2014). Is the Universe made of math? Scientific American, December. https://www.scientificamerican.com/article/is-the-universe-made-of-math-excerpt/

Tipler, F. (1994). *The physics of immortality: Modern cosmology, God, and the resurrection of the dead.* New York: Anchor.

Todd, S. (1999). A view from Kansas on that evolution debate. *Nature, 401:* 423-423.

Tertullian, Q. (1842). *Tertullian: V. 1. Apologetic and Practical Treatises.* London: John Henry Parker. p. 349

Trefil, J., & Hazen, R. (2007). *The sciences: An integrated approach.* New York, Wiley.

Trevors, J. & Abel, D. (2004). Chance and necessity do not explain the origin of life. *Cell Biology International, 28:* 729-739.

United Nations Office on Drugs and Crime. (2014). Some 437,000 people murdered worldwide in 2012, according to new UNODC study. http://www.unodc.org/unodc/en/press/releases/2014/April/some-437000-people-murdered-

University of Tennessee at Knoxville. (2010, January 19). Bacteria are more capable of complex decision-making than thought. *ScienceDaily*.

U.S. Department of Health and Human Services (2011). *Births: Preliminary data for 2010*. Washington, DC: U.S. Government Printing Office.

Valencia, D., O'Connell, R., & Sasselov, D. (2007). Inevitability of plate tectonics on super-Earths. *The Astrophysical Journal Letters, 670*:45-48.

Vasas, V., Szathmáry, E., & Santos, M. (2010). Lack of evolvability in self-sustaining autocatalytic networks constraints metabolism-first scenarios for the origin of life. *Proceedings of the National Academy of Sciences, 107:* 1470-1475.

Wald, G. (1954). The origin of life," *Scientific American*, 191: 45–53.

Wald, G. (1984). Life and Mind in the Universe. *International Journal of Quantum Chemistry, 26*: 1-15.

Ward, P. & Brownlee, D. (2000). *Rare Earth*. New York: Copernicus Books.

Washington, G. (1796). Washington's farewell address, 1796. The Avalon Project, http://avalon.law.yale.edu/18th_century/washing.asp.

Walsh, A. (1998). Religion and hypertension: Testing alternative explanations among immigrants. *Behavioral Medicine*, 24:122-130.

Walsh, A. (2017). *Taboo issues in social science: Questioning conventional wisdom*. Wilmington, DE: Vernon Press.

Walsh, A. (2018). *The Gavel and Sickle: The Supreme Court, Cultural Marxism, and the Assault on Christianity*. Wilmington, DE: Vernon Press.

Walsh, J. (2013). *Old time makers of medicine*. New York: Simon and Schuster.

Walsh, M. (2015). *The Devil's pleasure palace: The cult of critical theory and the subversion of the west*. New York: Encounter Books.

Ward, P. & Brownlee, D. (2000). *Rare Earth*. New York: Copernicus.

Weber, M. (1930). *The Protestant ethic and the spirit of capitalism*. T. Parsons (trans.) New York: Charles Scribner.

Weitnauer, C. (2013). The irony of atheism. In T. Gilson & C. Weitnauer (eds.) *True reason*, pp. 25-36. Grand Rapids, MI: Kregel.

Weitoft, G., Hjern, A., Haglund, B. & Rosén, M. (2003). Mortality, severe morbidity, and injury in children living with single parents in Sweden: a population-based study. *The Lancet, 361:* 289-295.

Whitfield, J. (2008). Biological theory: Postmodern evolution? *Nature News, 455:* 281-284.

Wiker, B. (2005). How the world's most notorious atheist changed his mind. *Strange Notions*. http://www.strangenotions.com/flew/

Wilcox, B. (2004). *Soft patriarchs, new men: How Christianity shapes fathers and husbands*. Chicago: University of Chicago Press.

Wilson, E. (1993). *The moral sense*. New York: Free Press.

Winthrop, R. (1852). Addresses and Speeches on Various Occasions, Boston: Little, Brown.

Woit, P. (2006). *Not even wrong: The failure of string theory and the search for unity in physical law.* New York: Basic Books.

Wood, R., Goesling, B., & Avellar, S. (2007). The effects of marriage on health: a synthesis of recent research evidence. *Washington DC: Mathematical Policy Research.*

Xu, Q. (2014). *The evolutionary feminism of Zhang Kangkang and the developing dialogue between Darwinism and gender studies.* PhD dissertation, University of Helsinki, Finland.

Yahya, H. (1999). *The Creation of the Universe.* Istanbul: Global Yayincilik.

Yockey, H. (2005). *Information theory, evolution, and the origin of life.* Cambridge: Cambridge University Press.

Ziegler Hemingway, M. (2008). Look who's irrational now. *Wall Street Journal,* Sept. 19th.

Index

A

abduction 10-12
abiogenesis 108, 115-116
acetate 118
adenine (A) 119
adenosine triphosphate (ATP) 110
Advances in Biological Chemistry 118
agency 2, 61, 97, 147
Aikman, David 21
Alberts, Bruce 114
allele 130
Alliance Defending Religious Freedom 16
Alpha 126
America's Blessings: How Religion Benefits Everyone, Including Atheists 40
American Atheist 18
American Family Association 16
American Journal of Psychiatry 36
American Nazi Party 16
amino acids 88, 109, 111-116
ammonia 113
Anfinsen, Christian 23
Annual Review of Astronomy and Astrophysics 121
anticodon 111
Appolloni, Simon 60
Aristotle 4, 59, 73, 99
arrival of the fittest 125
astronomical unit (AU) 78
atheism
        and Christianity 31
        and Craig 62
        and Darwin 127-128
        and Dawkins 28
        and Flew 25-26, 111
        and free will 144
        and Germany 34
        and Harris 30
        and Lewis 29
        and liberalism 42
        and Marx 55
        and multiverse concept 91
        and Xu 33
        creation of 14
        creeping of 15-16
        Marxist 33, 35
        militant 18-19, 42
        morality 31-32
        new 17-18
        of materialism 9
        rock of 141, 149
        versus Christianity 35-36
atomic theory 6, 99, 127, 144
authority 151-152, 155

B

Bacon, Francis 27
Bacon, Roger 6
Batygin, Konstantin 82
Bauchau, Vincent 134
Bechly, Gunter 139
Behe, Michael 133
Beinart, Peter 65
Benzmuller, Christoph 99
Berkley 51
Bernhardt, Harold 116-117

beryllium 122
beta decay 81
Bible
    and Collins 7
    and Luther 45
    and O'Hair 9
    and the universe 73-74
    and Thomson 3
Big Bang Theory 61, 65
big whack 80, 85
Biochemical Predestination 108
Biochemistry and Molecular Biology Education 117
BIO-Complexity 133
Bioessays 137
Biological Reviews 135
Bishop of Lincoln 61
Bishop Samuel Wilberforce 5
Bohr, Niels 143, 149
Bonaparte, Napoleon 1
Bonhoeffer, Dietrich 142
Book of Isaiah 73
Book of Job 73
Born Atheist 18
Boscovich, Roger 6
bourgeoisie 52
Brights 18
Bruno, Giordano 104
Bruteau, Beatrice 21
Buber, Martin 20

C

C.S. Lewis 29-30
Calvin, John 147
Calvin, Melvin 6
Calvinism 46
Calvinist theology 147
Cambrian explosion 135, 137
Canadian Community Health Survey 36
carbon 79, 88, 113, 122

carbonates 113
Carr, Bernard 91
Catholics 36, 45
Cell Biology International 108
Chance and necessity 108, 113, 132-134
Chesterton, G.K. 28, 47, 55
Chinese Academy of Social Science 21
chirality problem 114-115
chlorophyll 88
chloroplasts 88
Christ, Jesus 151
Christianity
    and a moral society 29-35
    and charity 41
    and conservatism 42
    and cultural Marxism 49-52
    and democracy 43-44, 47, 55
    and economic benefits 40
    and free will 144
    and happiness 141
    and loving families 36
    and reason 6
    and science 3, 5, 22
    benefits of 2, 12, 17, 21-22, 28
    inspired science 10
    irrationality of 18
    versus atheism 35
Circumstellar Habitable Zone (CBZ) 78
Clemenceau, Georges 26
Clinton, Hillary 16
codons 110-111
Collins, Francis 7, 111
Collins, Robin 78, 104
Columbia University 50
common sense evolution 129
communism 35, 49, 55, 151
compartmentalization 118
compatibilism 148-149
conscience 30-31, 47, 66, 147, 151

consciousness 108
conservatism 33
conservative Marxist 18
conservatives 27-28, 42, 54
Constantine 44
Copernican Principle 89
Copernicus, Nicolaus 4, 89
co-rotation radius 78
cosmic microwave background
  (CMB) radiation 65
cosmological constant 6, 60, 68,
  72, 99
cosmological dark ages 67
cosmology 14, 91, 105, 108
coup d'etat 55
Craig, William 13, 23, 62
Craig, William Lane 23, 34, 62
creatio ex nihilo 59, 64
Creator's aim 72, 92, 96
Cremonini, Cesare 4
Crick, Francis 8, 107
critical theory 50
critical thinking 50
cuius region, eius religio 45
cultural hegemony 52
cultural Marxism 49, 55
cultural terrorism 49
cytoplasm 110
cytosine (C) 109

D

Daily Express 105
Daily Mail 56
dark energy 60, 69
Darwin, Charles 44, 127, 143
Darwinism 4, 125-132 139, 143
Davies, Paul 7, 61, 70-71, 108
Dawkins, Richard and atheism 28,
  30, 35, 42, 127, 129
    and the Four Horsemen 17
    and *The God Delusion* 46, 143

on God and multiverse 105
de Duve, Christian 108
De Genesi ad Literam 128
De Luce 61
de Tocqueville, Alexis 48
deduction 10-11
democracy 21, 24, 43-45, 47
Democracy in America 48
Democratic National Convention
  54
Democratic Party 53-54
Democrats 27-28, 54
Democritus 144
Dennett, Daniel 17
Department of Health and Human
  Services 38
determinism 143-149
deuterium 66, 71
deuteron 66
dextro (D) 115
Dicke, Robert 65
Dike 150
Dingle, Herbert 98
DNA 109, 111, 135
    and Crick 107
    and nitrogen 88
    and protein 116
    and RNA 115-116, 121
    as language of God 111
    complexity of 25-26,108, 112,
      139
    helicase 110
    replication 130
Dobzhansky, Theodosious 126
Donovan, William 34
Doppler Effect 60
Dostoevsky, Fydor 151
double helix ladder 109
Drummond, Henry 141
dualities 95
Durant, Ariel 48
Durant, Will 48

Dyson, Freeman 75

E

E=MC2 9
Ecklund, Elaine 22
Eddington, Arthur 10, 64
Einstein, Albert 4-5, 24, 30, 98,
    112, 149
electromagnetic 66-71
electromagnetism 10, 65, 71, 134
elliptical galaxies 77
Ellis, George 98
Encyclopedia of Wars 46
endoplasmic reticulum 110
Enlightenment 141
entropy 63, 72-73, 76, 94
epicurean chaos 48-49
Epicurus 144
equality 43, 53
Eratosthenes 73
ergodic 93
Eros and Civilization 51
establishment clause 138
Evolution from Space 121
evolution of the gaps 126, 143
Ewart, Paul 143
ex cathedra 92

F

Fabian Society 52
falsifiability 101
family 32-55
Family Research Council 49
Father Brown 28
Final Cause 129
First Amendment 16, 47, 138
First Amendment Defense Act 16
First Cause 13, 62-63, 128
First Liberty Institute 15-16
fixation 130

Flew, Anthony 25, 111
Ford, Henry 2
Fordyce, John 128
Forget, Francois 84
Four Horsemen 17, 21, 30, 52, 55
Frankfurt School 50-51
Frankl, Viktor 153
free will 141, 144-154
Freedom in the World Index 22
Freeland, Stephen 128
freethinkers 18, 23
Frued, Sigmund 39
Fundamentalist atheism 18, 28

G

Galactic Habitable Zone (GHZ) 76-
    77
Gallop Poll 26-27
Gay, Lesbian, and Straight Educa-
    tion Network (GLSEN) 49
general theory of relativity 60, 95,
    98
genes 109, 144
Genesis 20, 59, 64, 69, 86, 92
genetic mutation 130
geocentric model 4-5
Gilbert, Scott 125
Gitt, Werner 112, 119
God
        and atheists 17-19, 25-28, 56
        and Gramsci 52
        and mathematic truths 97, 99,
            122
        and morals 29-31
        and Pascal 36
        and reason 7, 21, 43
        and the problem of evil 149-
            156
        and war with scientists 5
        as cause 63

as creator 20, 59-62, 69, 86, 128-129
belief in 42
hypothesis 1-4
of the gaps argument 1, 120, 141-144, 148
omniscient 147-148
questioning 13
replacing 125
science growing out of 6, 8, 10
scientists belief in 23, 140
versus multiverse 91-92, 94-95
God is not Great: Religion Poisons Everything 18
God's Philosophers: How the Mideval World Laid the Foundations of Modern Science 21
Godel, Kurt 99
Golgi 110
Good Without God 47
Goswani, Amit 140
Gould, Stephen J. 136-137
Graebner, Norman 44
Gramsci, Antonio 49, 52
Grand Unifying Theory 95
Gravity
    and electromagnetic force 70
    and moon 81
    and planets 83-84
    and plate tectonics 85
    and string theories 95
    and sun 79
    as fundamental force of nature 65, 67
    in Job 73
    law of 68, 97
    Newton on 61, 98
Gray, Asa 128
Greenstein, George 51
Grib, Andrei 35
Griffiths, Robert 23
Grim, Brian 40

Grim, Melissa 40
Grosseteste, Robert 61
guanine (G) 109
Guardian 97
Guevara, Che 18

H

Haldane, J.B.S. 83, 113
Hall of Shame Report 15
Hall, Daniel 39
Hannam, James 21
Hannibal 52
Harris, Sam 17, 30-31, 46
Harrison, Peter 22
Hartsfield, Tom 103
hate groups 16
Haught, John 63
Hawking, Stephen 67
Hayes, Carlton 41
heat death 63
Heile, Frank 102
heliocentric theory 15
helium
    and gravity 76, 79
    and life 122
    and the sun 79
    as a first atom 66
    bonding 70-71
Hemingway, Mollie Ziegler 26
Hera 75
Heracles 75
heterochirality 115
Hick, John 153
higher-order automated theorem provers 99
Hilbert, David 13
Hitchens, Christopher 17-18, 31-32
Hitchens, Peter 32, 56
Homosexuality in your child's school 49

Hoyle, Fred 64
    and a first cause 62
    and Big Bang 63, 100
    and complexity of life 120
    and Darwinism 125
Hsp90 (heat shock protein 90)
    136-137
Hubble volume 93
Hubble, Edwin 60
Human Genome Project 7, 111
Hummer, Robert 39
Huxley, Thomas Henry 5
Huxley-Wilberforce 4
hydrogen
    and atmosphere 113
    and Big Bang 107
    and gravity 76, 84
    and Mendeleev 100
    and the sun 79
    as a first atom 66-68
    fusion 71
    to humans 88
hydrologic cycle 87
hydrothermal vents 117
hypotheses 11-12, 100-102, 143

I

induction 10-11
Infeld, Leopold 149
information 118-120, 134-135,
    145-146
Institute of Social Research 50
intelligent design (ID)
    and DNA 135
    and God of the gaps 142
    and Hoyle 120
    and Jones 138
    and Kaku 105
    and Kenyon 109
    and Lightman 92
    and theistic evolution 139

    and Todd 138
internal space 96
International Christian Concern
    (ICC) 15
International Conference of the
    Origins of Life 119-120
*International Journal of Quantum
    Chemistry* 108
Irenaeus 153
irreducible complexity 110, 130
irregular galaxies 78
Islam 7-8, 44, 46

J

Jastrow, Robert 63-64, 73
Jefferson, Thomas 45
Jennings, Kevin 49
Jesuits 4
Johnson, Phillip E. 136
Jones, John 138
Journal of Family Practice 39
Journal of High Energy Physics 72
Jupiter 81-83, 87

K

Kaku, Michio 105
Kalam Cosmological Argument 62
Kansas Board of Education 138
Karamazov, Ivan 151
Kenny, Mary 35-36
Kenyon, Dean 108-109
Kepler, Johann 4
*Kitzmiller v. Dover Area School
    District* (2005) 138
KKK 16
Koonin, Eugene 120
Korthof, Gert 121
Krebs cycle 119
Krebs, Robert 68
Kristeva, Julia 36

Kuhn, Joseph 139
Kun, Bela 49-50

L

Lagrange, Joseph-Louis 1
Lamaitre, Georges 6
Laplace, Pierre-Simon 1, 142
Large Hadron Collider 101-102
Last Universal Common Ancestor
  (LUCA) 109
Laughlin, Greg 82
Laughlin, Robert B. 126
laws 7, 45, 93-98, 146, 155
Leibniz, Gottfried 1
Leiter, Brian 16
Lemaitre, Georges 60
Lenin 18, 48, 55
Lennox, John
  and Dawkins 28
  and fruit flies 132
  and laws 146
  and personal agency 2, 97
  as a defender of faith 20, 23
levo (L) 115
Lewontin, Richard 2, 19, 92, 126
liberals 27-28, 42, 54
light elements 65-66, 83
light year 76, 102, 113
Lightman, Alan 92
lightning 89, 113
Lipton, Peter 11
lithium 66
Loeb, Abraham 76
Logic of Scientific Inquiry 126
London School of Economics 52
Lucretius 145
Lukacs, Georg 49, 52, 63
luminosity 80
Luther, Martin 45
Lutheranism 46
Lutherans 45

lysosomes 110

M

macroevolution 125-131, 134-138
magnetic field 84-85, 102
Magnus, Albertus 7, 140
Man's Search for Meaning 153
Marcuse, Herbert 51
Markham, Ian 18
Mars 19, 78, 80, 82-84, 86
Marx, Karl 32, 39, 55
materialism 2-4, 8-10, 107
mathematical truths 97
Mathematics of Evolution 125
matter 8-10
  and anti-matter 66
  and atheism's creation 14
  and Big Bang 61, 68-69, 76
  and gravity 60
  and origin of life 107, 116, 119
  and Tegmark's level I 94
  atomic theory of 127
McGrath, Alister 26
McNichol, Jesse 117
Mendeleev, Dmitri 100
mental causation 145
mentalism 10
Mercury 78, 82
messenger RNA (mRNA) 110
metabolism 87, 116-118
metabolism-first hypothesis 116-
  117
metal-poor population II stars 77
methane 113
Meyer, Stephen 12, 23, 143
microevolution 125-126, 129, 131,
  139, 143
Milky Way 75-76, 78
Miller, Kenneth 140
Miller, Stanley 113

Miller-Urey experiment 113, 115, 122

mind 10, 52, 145-147

Mind and Cosmos: Why the Materialist Neo-Darwinian Conception of Nature is Almost Certainly False 138

miracle 107, 151-152, 155

Mithani, Audrey 94

mitochondria 110, 119

Mlodinow, Leonard 67

modal realism theory 95

Molecular Biology of the Cell 114

monomers 114-115

moon 78, 80-82

moral behavior 29

morality
    and Christianity 29-31, 44, 53, 56
    and economic prosperity 40
    and love 41
    and the nation 48
    atheist 31
    constraints of 51
    epicenters of 32, 49

Morrison, Philip 64

Mount Wilson Observatory 60

M-theory 95-97, 101-105

Mua, Kelly 40

Muller, Gerd 131

multiverse 13
    and God 91-92, 104-105
    and mathematics 98-99
    and M-theory 95, 101, 104
    and Penrose 102
    hypothesis 92-93
    of the gaps 93, 112

mutation 127-134, 137

mystery 107, 151-152, 155

N

Nagel, Thomas 20, 138

National Academy of Sciences (NAS) 135

National Aeronautics and Space Administration 65, 67

natural laws 7, 144, 154-155

natural selection 104, 121, 126-134, 143

naturalism 8-9, 89, 92, 138-139

nebular cloud 79

necessity 8, 99, 108, 134-135

Neill, Alexander 50

neo-Darwinism 126

Nernst, Walter 64

Neutrinos 71

neutrons 66-67, 70-71

new atheists 15, 17-18, 42, 52

New York Times 19, 64

Newton, Isaac 7, 59, 61, 81, 104, 142

Nicholas of Cusa 104

Nietzsche, Friedrich Wilhelm 30

Nilsson, Heribert N. 136

Ninety-Five Theses 45

NIODA (non-interventionist objective divine action) 140

nitrates 89

nitrogen 88-89, 122

nuclear force 10, 65, 70-71

nucleotides 109-110, 116, 132-133

nucleus 70-71, 100, 109-110

O

O'Hair, Madalyn Murray 9

Obama, Barack 16

Office of Safe and Drug-Free Schools 49

Omega 126

Oparin, Alexander 113

orbital resonance 82
O-regions 120
Orgel, Leslie 118
origin of life (OoL)
    and complexity of DNA 25,
    and intelligent control 121-
      122
    the search for 107-108, 134
    theories of 3, 118
Owen, Richard 5
oxidation 113
ozone layer 84, 113

P

Paleo, Bruno 99
panspermia 120-121
Park, Jerry 22
Pascal, Blaise 36
Patriarch Kirill I 33
Peace of Augsburg 45-46
Peace of Westphalia 46
Penrose, Roger 72, 76, 92, 97, 102
Pensees 36
Penzias, Arno 64-65
perfect accident 117
period of heavy bombardment 82
periodic table 99
Pew Research Center 15, 27, 35,
    54,
phase-space 71-72, 76, 96
phenotypes 130
photons 67, 69, 149-151
photosynthesis 79, 88
physics 107-109
Planck time 65
Planck, Max 8- 9
plate tectonics 85-87, 155
platonism 95
polar molecule 87
Politizer, Georges 63
Polkinghorne, John 105

polymerization 114
polymers 114
positron 66
predictive accuracy 101
predictive scope 101
primeval atom 60
primordial soup 113-114, 116
principle of complementarity 149
principle of uncertainty 145
problem of evil 141, 149-151, 156
proletariat 33, 49, 52
proteins 88, 109-116, 134
Protestant Reformation 45
Protestants 36, 46
protons 66-67, 70-71, 100
Putin, Vladimir 33
Pythagoras 73

Q

quantum mechanics 9, 94-95, 143
quantum theory 95, 149

R

racemic 115
Radford, Tim 97
radiation 65-70, 77-78, 113-114
Raehn, Raymond 49
Rainbow Boys 49
Rationalism 11, 28
reason 4, 6-7, 21, 23, 43
Reeves, Colin 127
relational virtues 37
religion
    and Dawkins 42, 46
    and Harris 31
    and health 39
    and morality 32
    and science 4-5, 8, 22-24, 62,
      107
    and the family 37, 54

and Voltaire 29
founders on 17
in America 48, 53
national 138
Religion and Natural Science 8
religious pluralism 46
Renaissance 45
replication 114, 116-117, 120, 130
reproductive capacity 116
Republicanism 42
Republicans 27-28, 42, 54
ribosomal RNA (rRNA) 111
ribosomes 110-111, 115-116
ribozyme replicase 116-117
RNA polymerase 110
RNA world hypothesis 116-118
rock of atheism 141, 149
Rorty, Richard 54
Ross, Hugh 78, 87-89
Rovelli, Carlo 103
Royal Astronomical Society 98
Russell, Colin 5
Russell, Robert 140

S

Sagan, Carl 19, 83
Sandage, Allan 64
Sanford, John 132
Saturn 82-83
schizophrenia 145
Schrodinger, Erwin 112
Schroeder, Gerald 122
Schulzke, Marcus 17-18
Schumacher, Robin 46
Scientific American 95
Scientific Dissent from Darwinism
    127
scientific method 3, 6, 103
secondary causes 128-129, 144
secularism 18
settled science 61, 125, 127

sexual freedom 53
Shalev, Baruch 23
Shaw, George Bernard 52
Signature in the Cell 143
simplicity 101
singularity 60
Sir James Jeans 10
Sir Martin Rees 71
Sir Roger Penrose 72, 102
Slate 18
slavery 44, 51, 149
Smith, Quentin 62
social justice 53
socialism 28, 51-55
Socialist Party 53-54
Soil 88-89
Solzhenitsyn, Aleksandr 32-33
Southern Poverty Law Center
    (SPLC) 16
Spanish Inquisition 151
speciation 135-136
species 125, 129, 135-137
Spradley, Joseph 81
St. Albertus Magnus 7
St. Anselm 99
St. Augustine 128, 150, 155
stagnant lid 85
Stark, Rodney 7, 21, 40
Steinman, Gary 108
stellar nucleosynthesis 66, 121
Stepan, Alfred 44
Stone v. Graham (1980) 53
string theory 95-98, 102-103
strings 96, 101
strong nuclear
sun 79-87
Sun Tzu 18
supernova 66, 71, 107
superposition 94
Supreme Court 53, 138
survival of the fittest 125
Swinburne, Richard 104, 154

T

Taylor, Joseph 24
Tegmark, Max 93
Tegmark's multiverse levels
  level I 93, 94
  level II 94
  level III 94
  level IV 95
teleologist 129
Ten Commandments 53
Tertullian, Quintus 7
The American College of Pediatricians 16
The American Humanist Association 47
The Astonishing Hypothesis 9
The Atlantic 55
The Brothers Karamazov 151
The Core 84
The Demon-Haunted World: Science as a Candle in the Dark 19
The End of Faith 46
The Gavel and Sickle: The Supremem Court, Cultural Marxism, and the Assault on Christianity 53, 138
The Grand Design 96, 102
The Grand Inquisitor 151, 155
The Intelligent Universe 121
The Origin of the Species 127-129, 137
The Racial and Religious Paranoia of Trump's Warsaw Speech 55
The Rage Against God 32
The Victory of Reason: How Christianity Led to Freedom, Capitalism, and Western Success 21
Theism
  and conservatism 42
  and naturalism 8
  and science 8, 10
and secularism 18
Karamazov on 151
  pros and cons of 19
theistic evolution (TE) 139-140
theodicy 150, 152-156
Theorem 28 120
Theoretical Biology and Medical Modelling 132
theories 11, 99-103
theos 150
There is a God 26
thermodynamic equilibrium 63, 72, 94, 114
thermodynamics
  1st law 14, 86
  2nd law 53, 72, 92, 114, 118
Thirty Years War 46
Thomas, Norman 53
Thomson, George P. 3
Thomson, Joseph J. 142
thymine (T) 109-110
tidal lock 78, 80
tides 81
Time Magazine 21
Tipler, Frank 105
Todd, Scott 138
toleration 51
top-down causation 9
Transfer RNA (tRNA) 111
translation 120
Treatise on Celestial Mechanics 1
triple alpha process 122

U

ubermensch 31, *34*
universal salvation 153
University of Bologna 7
universum 63
uracil 110

Urey, Harold 113
useful idiots 55

V

vacuum energy 68-69
Venus 78, 86
Vilenkin, Alexander 94
volcanoes 86
Voltaire 39
Voyager I 83

W

Wald, George 108
Wall Street Journal 26
Walsh, Michael 50
Ward, Keith 105
Washington, George 47-48
water 3, 78-81, 84-88, 113
weak nuclear 65, 70-71
Weber, Max 21, 145
Weiqun, Zhu 33
well-being 31, 35, 39
West Side Story 37
Western Civilization and the
    Common Law of the United
    States 53
What Americans Really Believe 26-
    27
Wickramasinghe, Chandra 121
Wiker, Benjamin 25
Wilcox, Bradford 37
Williams, George 134
Wilson, Robert 65
wind 79-81, 83
Winthrop, Robert 47
Woit, Peter 102

X

Xu, Qingbo 33

Y

Yang, Fenggang 33
yellow dwarf 80
Yockey, Hubert 135

Z

Zedong, Mao 33
Zeus 75